Towards Just and Equitable Development

Towards Just and Equitable Development

Durgabai Deshmukh Memorial Lectures

Edited by

Rajiv Balakrishnan

in association with
COUNCIL FOR SOCIAL DEVELOPMENT
New Delhi

KONARK PUBLISHERS PVT LTD
New Delhi • Seattle

KONARK PUBLISHERS PVT LTD
206, First Floor, Peacock Lane,
Shahpur Jat,
New Delhi-110 049
Phone: +91-11-41055065, 65254972
e-mail: india@konarkpublishers.com
Website: www.konarkpublishers.com

Konark Publishers International
1507 Western Avenue, #605,
Seattle, WA 98101
Phone: (415) 409-9988
e-mail: us@konarkpublishers.com

Cataloging in Publication Data—DK
Courtesy: D.K. Agencies (P) Ltd. <docinfo@dkagencies.com>

Towards just and equitable development : Durgabai Deshmukh memorial lectures / edited by Rajiv Balakrishnan.
p. cm.
Includes bibliographical references.
ISBN 9789322008116

1. Social planning—India. 2. India—Social conditions. 3. India—Politics and government. I. Balakrishnan, Rajiv.

DDC 361.610954 23

Editor: Sudipta Gupta and Jayashree Menon
Typeset by The Laser Printers, New Delhi, and printed at ASK Advertising Aids Pvt Ltd, New Delhi.

Contents

Foreword

Dr Durgabai Deshmukh, the founder Chairperson of the Council for Social Development, was among the outstanding personalities who played a stellar role in India's independence movement and for several decades after Independence. She was a parliamentarian, an institution builder and a pioneer in social development. She was the first Chairperson of the Central Social Welfare Board. As a member of the Planning Commission, she endeavoured to integrate consciously and systematically, the element of social development into the planning process. For this task, she set up the Council for Social Development as a platform for generating new ideas, and for research, advocacy and field experiments in social development.

Since 1992, the Council for Social Development has been organising annual lectures in Dr Durgabai Deshmukh's honour. We have now been able to put these lectures together in the shape of this book. These lectures cover practically every major domain of social development. They are on traditional areas of social development such as education, health, population and gender issues. Two of them are concerned with a major problem that has cropped up recently, that is, displacement of project-affected people. Others bring out the sufferings, injustice and exploitation of the marginalised sections of the Indian population, particularly the dalits, tribals, girl child and the *nautch* girls. Some of the lectures deal with current challenges of a global nature, such as harnessing science for social progress, resolving the contradictions and dealing with discontents of globalisation, reversing the process of the encirclement of the commons and the ubiquitous problem of governance in developing countries like India.

Those who have delivered these lectures have come from varied background and expertise. These include sociologists, social anthropologists, political scientists, educationists and jurists. Most of them are also renowned social activists. They combine the deep knowledge of the subjects dealt with in these lectures with their widely known contributions as social activists. They are not among those busybody intellectuals and public figures who hog the headlines of newspapers or are regularly seen on the small screen. But they are known for their commitment to the cause of the poor and the marginalized and are recognized as authorities in their areas of specialisation.

Two of these eminent personalities, Dr N.H.Antia and Professor Ram Dayal Munda are no longer among us. Dr Antia, a highly qualified doctor, devoted his life time in quest of and advocacy for, a holistic approach to health care based on indigenous knowledge and resources and geared essentially to meet the needs of the poor. Professor Munda was an eminent leader of tribal resurgence and one of the intellectual architects of the State of Jharkhand. He was a scholar, an educationist, a teacher, a law maker and an artist who both created and performed. He was long associated with the Council for Social Development. I take this opportunity to pay my humble and respectful tributes to both Dr N.H.Antia and Professor Ram Dayal Munda.

Since the lecture series started twenty years ago, there is no doubt that the facts and data in some of them need to be updated. But even without that, the message of these lectures remain valid. They constitute a valuable contribution to knowledge in the respective fields. They suggest different if not new, approaches to dealing with some of the social problems that bedevil the country. These lectures would intellectually equip civil society organisations and social activists, to resist wrong policies and campaign for people-centred policies and approaches to social development. These lectures would also enrich and broaden the vision of general readers.

Finally, I would like to place on record the Council's gratefulness to those who delivered the lectures and sincerely thank Dr Rajiv Balakrishnan for his meticulous and painstaking effort in editing and putting together these lectures in the form of this volume.

M. Dubey.

(Muchkund Dubey)
President
Council for Social Development

New Delhi
June 27, 2012

Acknowledgements

I thank the Council for Social Development (CSD) and Professor Muchkund Dubey, the President of the CSD, for having given me this opportunity of editing and putting together the Durgabai Deshmukh Memorial Lectures in the form of a book. Durgabai was a renowned social and political activist and a builder of institutions, and I am happy I was able to play a small role in the Council's objective of profiling the lectures that were given in her honour by eminent speakers.

Rajiv Balakrishnan
New Delhi
February 6, 2012

Introduction

Rajiv Balakrishnan

Durgabai Deshmukh, a source of inspiration to many, was a dedicated social and political activist. In her early life, she actively engaged with the national movement and was even jailed for participating in the salt satyagraha. In time, she went on to become a leading criminal lawyer in Madras. Towards the end of 1946, she was elected Member of the Constituent Assembly. She later was appointed a member of the Planning Commission, in charge of Social Services, and then, Chairperson of the Central Social Welfare Board (CSWB).

Precocious Beginnings

In 1921, when Durgbai Deshmukh was 12 years old, she resolved to fight what she describes in her autobiography, *Chintamani and I*, as the "reprehensible" devadasi system. A devadasi, Durgabai tells us, "...was a woman who was dedicated to the Lord of the temple and remained unmarried, but [was] discretely utilised by the well-to-do for sensual indulgence." It was a social practice that originated in an arrangement by which accomplished dancers who performed before a shrine were rewarded with land allotments so they could maintain themselves. They were required also, as devadasis—servants of God, to be unmarried. At the tender age of 12, Durgabai was moved by the life circumstances of the devadasis of Kakinada and resolved to do something about it. She saw an opportunity in Gandhiji's forthcoming visit to Kakinada on 2 April 1921; if she could get him to speak to the devadasis, perhaps they could be persuaded to defy convention and change their way of life. She wanted Gandhi to also influence Muslim women in Kakinada to give up wearing the *burqa* or veil. Durgabai rallied support for her cause from the devadasis themselves, to whom she spoke about Gandhiji and his struggle in South Africa to promote the dignity and the rights of Indians living there.[1]

She asked the organisers of Gandhi's visit for ten minutes of his time so that he could address an exclusive meet of devadasis and Muslim women. The organisers consented to her plea, but told her that they expected her to raise a sum of Rs 5,000 as a contribution towards Gandhi's struggle for the nation's freedom. Durgabai went back to the devadasis, who assured her they would collect the money—which they did, in less than a week. Meanwhile, she and her devadasi friends met every day to talk about Gandhi's struggle for the country's freedom and sing patriotic songs.[2]

The problem of the purse to be presented to Gandhi had been taken care of, but another one remained to be tackled. The devadasis and Muslim women whose cause Durgabai championed weren't willing to attend the public meeting in Town Hall, so a separate meeting had to be arranged for them, and a venue for this exclusive meet had to be found. This posed challenges of its own, for in the days of the Raj, if one was found to be associating with Gandhi, one was liable to be thrown into jail. Durgabai asked her school headmaster, Siviah Sastry Garu, for permission to hold the meeting in the school compound. She told him he may be arrested if he consented—but the headmaster was undeterred; he was ready to go to jail. Since the school was located *en route* from the railway station to the Town Hall venue, Gandhi was first brought to Durgabai's meeting. About a thousand women were waiting there for the savant, of whom one, an elderly lady nominated by Durgabai, handed over the sum of Rs 5,000 that had been collected. The women were so inspired by Gandhiji that they went on to make additional offerings of things they were carrying with them—jewels, bangles, gold chains, and necklaces, the total value of which was later estimated at the (in those days) princely sum of Rs 25,000.[3]

Gandhi spoke at length to the gathering—for over half an hour, well exceeding the five minutes Durgabai had managed to wrest from the organisers of the Town Hall meeting. He said the abolition of the devadasi system and improvement of the situation of Muslim women were among the most laudable of goals for women's emancipation. So great was the impact of Gandhi's visit that the devadasis of Kakinada started getting their daughters married to boys who had the courage to withstand the social censure. Some 15 years later, in 1937, speaking of these events to Dr Muthulakshmi Reddy, member of the Legislative Council that was formed in Madras under the dyarchical system of government, Durgabai suggested to Dr Reddy that she sponsor legislation for the abolition of the devadasi system. On the latter's initiative, that goal was achieved.[4]

Family Influences

This is of the many instances of Durgabai Deshmukh's tenacious commitment to social purpose at various stages of her life, from a very young age. Her father—B.V.N. Rama Rao of Kakinada who, in her words "...always responded to people in need..." seems to have been an early influence. In *Chintamani and I*, Durgabai records how Sri Rama Rao attended to hundreds afflicted with plague and cholera. He and three of his friends used to carry the bodies of victims to the cremation grounds—a service few dared to perform, for fear that they themselves would succumb to the killer diseases. Not only did the ideals of public service run deep in Sri Rama Rao, he was also "...a warm and loving father and far more freely demonstrative of his affection for his children than was customary for fathers those days." From her mother's side too, there were family members who could have been important influences in Durgabai's life. Her mother's father, Manohar Rao Pantalu—the first Superintendent of Police in British India, was "...a close friend and supporter of the famous crusader for women's rights, Veerashalingam Pantalu".[5]

Convictions and Character

When Durgabai's father passed away, the relatives who came to offer condolences wanted her mother, who was still very young, to follow tradition and shave off the hair on her head. Custom in those days required that widowed women, even young widows in their teens, had to shave their heads and give up the use of adornments like bangles, *mangalasutra* and *kumkum*. "The underlying idea," Durgabai says, "was to make them look ugly and unacceptable to men." Durgabai reports in her autobiography of how she reacted when her relatives insisted that her mother shave off her hair: "I protested against this and told them that if they persisted in their demand they had better get out of the house. My mother had lovely, long hair. She was good looking. I requested her to resist... and finally she did not yield to the pressure. Since then I found her example being emulated in several families in the neighbourhood."[6]

Yet another instance of the force of will Durgabai demonstrated was in her first ever encounter with Jawaharlal Nehru in Kakinada, when the annual session of the Indian National Congress (INC) was held there in 1923. The fourteen-year-old Durgabai, a volunteer at the Khadi Exhibition Grounds, firmly instructed to bar anyone from entering without a ticket, stopped Jawaharlal Nehru because he neither had a ticket on him that would entitle him to enter, nor the two annas with which he could have purchased one. The organisers twisted Durgabai's ears and scolded her, asking if she knew who she had stopped. She said she did—that it was Jawaharlal Nehru but he didn't have a ticket. Nehru intervened at this point, saying the girl had done no wrong, and that the courage and conviction she displayed were qualities the nation was in need of.[7]

Durgabai and Nehru

Years later, the grown-up Durgabai Deshmukh, now a member of the Planning Commission, would display the same spiritedness in public life, even to the extent of chiding the Prime Minister and his Finance Minister. She reports in her autobiography: "I represented to Prime Minister Nehru and Finance Minister Deshmukh that there was no use talking about the need for bringing up the weaker sections of society and giving better status to women unless we had a budgetary provision to help them and to save the institutions working for their welfare from being closed down." She goes on to add: "My plea was accepted by the Planning Commission."[8]

Indeed, both Jawaharlal Nehru and his Finance Minister C.D. Deshmukh held Durgabai in high regard. That Deshmukh did so is testified to by the fact that he proposed marriage to her. Jawaharlal Nehru, for his part, deeply respected her for her integrity and commitment. One time, he handed her a cheque for Rs 25,000 and asked her to organise relief work in the drought and famine affected regions of Rayalseema in Andhra Pradesh. On another occasion, he put her in charge of carrying out the work of the Relief and Rehabilitation Committee that was formed in the wake of Partition.[9] That Durgabai was held in high esteem is demonstrated also by the fact that she was elected member of the Constituent Assembly as a Congress candidate. In 1954, Nehru asked her to work as Chairman of the CSWB full time. (Since August 1943, she had served as Chairman of the Board in an honorary capacity). At one point, she was also member of the Planning Commission (Social Services). She had been a member of the National Development Council too, but demitted that office once she was no longer a part of the Planning Commission. Nehru, however, asked her to continue on the Council in her capacity as Chair of the CSWB. He even had the Education Minister, Maulana Azad, give her the status of Minister of State.[10]

Durgabai and Sardar Patel

Durgabai endeared herself to many by her integrity, her courage, her convictions, and her concern for the common man. Sardar Patel, who greatly admired her, used to invite her to his residence for weekly luncheons. Initially, Durgabai stayed away, for she felt she was not "...trained in table talk and drawing-room conversations". The Sardar, being the redoubtable man he was, wasn't willing to take no for an answer. After the fourth spurned luncheon invitation, Patel's personal assistant visited Durgabai's residence to ask if she would be attending the luncheon scheduled for that day. Durgabai tried to wriggle out of it, saying she had guests to take care of. The secretary said his boss had instructed him to return with her, and if she had guests, they could come along. Durgabai goes on to complete the story: "I had no escape. I went. I found my seat next to Sardar Patel's."[11]

Political Activism

We have seen how, at a very young age, Durgabai stood on principle and wouldn't let Nehru into the Exhibition Grounds at Kakinada without a ticket. Another notable instance of her stand on principle occurred subsequently when she was arrested and sent to jail for participating in Gandhiji's salt satyagraha. The salt satyagraha, a movement Gandhi led, was aimed at defying the tax on salt; participants in the movement were encouraged to manufacture salt for their consumption, which meant that, since they didn't have to buy salt from the market, they were, in effect, violating the colonial government's salt tax, an act of political defiance and civil disobedience. Salt was an item of consumption by the common man and the salt tax a symbol of the colonial government's repressiveness.

The colonial government divided political prisoners who defied the salt law into three privilege-based classes—Class A, Class B and Class C. Class A prisoners got the best facilities and Class C prisoners the worst. Durgabai rebelled against the Congress Party for being a party to this. She felt it would drive a wedge between the satyagrahis who willingly went to jail for a worthy cause. Durgabai, herself an A class prisoner, witnessed the sufferings of the old and sick prisoners in C class. She requested the jail superintendent for a transfer to the C category. The superintendent said he was unable to comply with her demand, and that she should have pleaded her case with the magistrate at the time of her trial.[12]

Subsequently, on her release from jail, Durgabai brought up the issue at a meeting of the All India Congress Committee at Guntur. She moved a resolution calling on political prisoners not to accept "A" class unless it was given to all who were convicted of the same charge. Failing this, they should all opt for C class, and plead with the magistrate for C class status at the time of their trial. The resolution was unanimously passed—but in practice, very few satyagrahis gave up their A class privileges. Durgabai, for her part, asked for "C" class status the next time she came up before a magistrate. The magistrate said he knew her family and she deserved better, but Durgabai was insistent that either all political workers should be put in Class "A", or they should all be put into Class "C". While in jail, she reprimanded the jail authorities for keeping as many as 70 prisoners (including political prisoners) in one small room, and not providing them with the kind of food the jail rules required them to be served.[13]

During one of her incarcerations, at Vellore jail, Durgabai sought and received permission from the authorities to mingle with women convicts, some under life sentence. She was deeply moved to discover that some of these women, who were illiterate and uneducated, had pleaded guilty even though they were innocent. Some, not wanting to disclose their love affairs, had concealed important facts at their trial. She felt that just as women would freely confide in a woman doctor, so also they would confide in a woman lawyer. Durgabai resolved to study law and provide free legal aid to such women.[14] She eventually did achieve her purpose.

In 1933, she was released from Madurai jail after a year of solitary confinement, which left her grappling with mental illness; she had bouts of hysteria, brought on by the cries of women on death row who were jailed in cells adjacent to hers. Physically also, she was ailing; black blood oozed from her arms, and it was suspected that she was poisoned while in jail. Her physician, Dr Rangachari, advised that she should not be allowed to enter politics again, and that she needed a diversion—an "occupational therapy."[15]

Education and Professional Qualification

Evidently, the occupational therapy that engaged Durgabai subsequently was the pursuit of her studies. At the time, she had only completed the fifth standard in the vernacular medium at the Girls School in Kakinada. A botany professor at Kakinada, Gopalaraju Ramachandra Rao, who taught her the basics of English, was impressed by the pupil's progress, and encouraged her to appear for the Banaras Hindu University's matriculation examinations as a private candidate. She did so and passed matriculation. Subsequently, she received a fellowship and also passed the intermediate examinations. Durgabai went on to earn a BA (Honours) degree in Political Science, equivalent to a Masters degree, from Andhra University in 1939. She secured a first class. She then won a Tata Scholarship to study at the London School of Economics, and also procured a seat in the Inner Temple in London to study law. World War 2 intervened, however, and those opportunities were lost to her. Eventually, Durgabai enrolled in the Law College in Madras and earned a Bachelor of Laws in 1941. She was called to the bar in December 1942. Four years later, she was a leading criminal lawyer in Madras. As a practitioner of law, she never lost sight of her purpose; whenever she represented women, she harkened back to her discussions with the women convicts of Vellore jail.[16]

The Balika Hindi Pathasala

We now journey back to 1923—to a time when preparations were under way to hold the annual session of the INC in Kakinada. Women, who were being recruited and trained to work for the Congress session, needed to be taught Hindi, the language of the national movement. Gandhiji had already established the *Dakshina Bharata Hindi Prachar Sabha*—the South India Council for the Propagation of Hindi, whose office was temporarily housed in Kakinada to prepare for the first session of the *Hindi Sahitya Sammelan* (the Hindi Literary Meet), which, too, was to be held in Kakinada alongside the Congress Session. There was a need to impart knowledge of Hindi to the literary meet volunteers as well. The then fourteen-year-old Durgabai started learning Hindi and national songs in Hindi from the Sabha office in Kakinada, which was run at the time by Pandit Hrishikesh Sharma and his wife, Sarada Devi. It was an opportunity for Durgabai to also serve the social purpose by teaching Hindi to others while she herself was learning it. Her father and mother helped by giving her the use of a couple of rooms in the house. This was the genesis of the *Balika Hindi Pathasala*—the Girls Hindi School that she founded. In the six months to go before the Congress session, Durgabai, with the help of her Hindi teacher, Dinavahi Satyanarayana, taught Hindi to some 400 women, most of whom went on to become volunteers in the Congress session. She and some of her friends were however not allowed to volunteer for Congress session on the grounds of being too young—Durgabai was fourteen at the time. However, they were accepted as volunteers for the Sammelan.[17]

The Balika Hindi Pathasala attracted so many students that it had to shift to bigger premises made available by a philanthropic family. A few handlooms were installed there, and spinning and weaving were taught in addition to Hindi and patriotic songs. The pathasala continued to function even after the Congress session, and got to be periodically housed in bigger premises. It also began courses to prepare its students for Hindi examinations that the *Dakshina Bharata Hindi Prachar Sabha* had begun to organise. Every year 40–50 women were groomed for the examinations. Some passed in the first and second divisions. In time, the pathasala expanded further, acquiring a building donated by a close relation of Durgabai's—Sri G.V. Subha Rao. A few hundred books were donated by visitors who had heard of the pathasala at the time of the Congress session in Kakinada. Between 1923 and 1930, the pathasala put some 300 women through their paces and prepared them for the Prachar Sabha examinations. It went through a rough patch when it, along with the nationalist institutions, was kept under police surveillance. At one point, Durgabai was arrested for taking part in the Salt Satyagraha, and her mother took over the work of the pathasala; later, Durgabai's mother too participated in the Salt Satyagraha and was herself arrested. Those who continued to attend classes at the pathasala were jailed and school property confiscated. However, many of the pathasala's students established their own institutions in different parts of the country, and carried forward the pathasala's work of teaching Hindi and spreading the message of the spinning wheel. In 1946, at the convocation of the Hindi Prachar Sabha in Madras, Gandhi honoured Durgabai with a gold medal in recognition of her efforts to promote Hindi.[18]

The Little Ladies of Brindavan

The Balika Hindi Pathasala was one of the many institutions Durgabai would found. In 1937, some 15 years after she founded the pathasala, a new opportunity presented itself. Durgabai was studying for her BA Honours at Andhra University, Waltair. She stayed in a girl's hostel in Waltair, but spent her holidays with her mother and brother in Madras. Her brother had obtained a masters in political science from the Banaras Hindu University (BHU) and had become a personal assistant to Bulusu Sambamurti, the then Speaker of the Madras Legislative Assembly. Consequently, the family had their residence to Madras, where they stayed at 14, Dwarka, Brindavan Gardens. On her visits there, Durgabai saw four- to ten-year olds playing near the house amidst sand, bricks and stones. She and her mother managed to get them into the house and Durgabai's mother started teaching them Hindi. This was the inception of the Little Ladies of Brindavan, which undertook a range of activities, from preparing children to participate in the children's programmes of All India Radio, to teaching Bharata Natyam and organising music classes. Though the group was called the Little Ladies of Brindavan, boys also took part in its activities. In the evenings, mothers of the children came to learn

Hindi. The group, which started with 50 women and 100 children, was housed partly in the family home in Brindavan Gardens and also in Speaker Bulusu Sambamurthi's residence next door. Everyone chipped in; Durgabai's mother, who had taken up a job as a Hindi teacher at the Seva Sadan school, taught Hindi to the group. Durgabai's sister-in-law—her brother's wife, helped organise indoor games like carom.[19]

Andhra Mahila Sabha

In time, the Little Ladies of Brindavan metamorphosed into the Andhra Mahila Sabha (AMS). Of the many objectives of the sabha, one was to give coaching to women, none of whom had studied beyond Class 5, so that they could pass an examination equivalent to Matriculation or Secondary School Leaving Certificate. Many of the women who joined were indigent, and had to look after children and put food on the table. So, they were given training in employment-related activities like sewing, tailoring, embroidery, spinning, weaving, bamboo and cane work, preparing handmade paper, and mat weaving. From the sales of the products, the women who joined the work classes were paid at least Rs 2. Additional resources had to be mobilised, and to that end, about 300 life members were enrolled within a year of inception. Maharaja Vikramadeva Varma of Jeypore, who was invited to visit the AMS and was impressed by what he saw, donated Rs 5000, which helped the institution stand on its feet. Eventually, a Mahila Vidyalaya (a woman's college) was established as a subsidiary of the AMS, with the goal of preparing students for the BHU entrance examination and the Intermediate Examination of Madras University.[20]

Durgabai's brother, suspected of being a political activist and expelled from government service, chipped in to contribute to the AMS with his brain child—the monthly magazine of the Sabha, the *Andhra Mahila*. Durgabai Deshmukh fondly reminisces:

> The picture of my brother bringing the bundles of printed copies from the press in Tyagarajanagar, the hostel girls folding and wrapping up the copies and pasting addresses and postage stamps, and Sugunamani taking them to the post office for dispatch can never leave my mind. Social service was one hundred per cent voluntary in those days.[21]

The Deshmukhs

Later in life, this spirit was displayed in ample measure by both Durgabai and her husband, Chintamani Deshmukh. The couple were infused with the ideals of selfless service to the point of even allocating their personal funds and assets to that purpose, as this story illustrates: When Chintamani Deshmukh was hospitalised with heart disease, Durgabai resolved to establish a cardiovascular unit in Hyderabad for the benefit of ordinary people who could not afford travel to and stay in Bombay and Vellore, where facilities for treatment were located. Visiting Chintamani in hospital, she informed him of her plan to mobilise funds and to donate Rs 25,000 from the couple's personal savings to the cause. Chintamani smilingly consented, saying: "You can go ahead with your plan. It is a very good thing". The cardio-vascular unit was established in the AMS Nursing Home at Hyderabad. By means of a registered will, the couple also had their residence donated for "...medical education, medical training and action-oriented medical research."[22]

The Deshmukhs decided also that only one of them would accept a salary, and the other would serve the nation without remuneration. Consequently, when Durgabai was Chairperson of the CSWB, Chintamani Deshumkh, as Chairman of the University Grants Commission (UGC), accepted only a token amount of Re 1 per month, in lieu of his official salary of around Rs 3000; and when C.D. Deshmukh drew a salary as Vice Chancellor of Delhi University, Durgabai, who had quit the Chair of the CSWB, worked free of charge for the social activities she undertook.[23]

Participatory Paradigm

In their capacities as Finance Minister and Chairman, CSWB respectively, Chintamani and Durgabai Deshmukh travelled extensively in the country to monitor development projects for education, health, agriculture, and industry. They visited ten districts in each State, and covered 285 of the then 330 districts of the country by plane, train, jeep, and bullock cart. One of the objectives of these tours was to identify bottlenecks in project implementation—for instance, non-availability of steel, cement, iron, tiles and the like, or lack of trained manpower, on account of professionals like engineers or contractors not wanting to work in rural areas or small towns. The second was to connect with the local people, and ascertain their views on the projects that were being implemented for their benefit. On one occasion, the Deshmukhs visited Samalkot, East Godavari district, Andhra Pradesh. A couple of rooms had been constructed for a school there, but the locals felt that the school could function from a public place such as the temple or in the shade of the tree, and that the need of the hour was for a maternity centre and a dai (midwife). Durgabai announced a public meeting and in consultation with the locals, it was decided that a maternity centre would be built—whereupon the local people pledged a "matching contribution" to the CSWB for meeting the cost of the project.[24]

In principle, the idea of getting the local people engaged in dialogue about a proposed project was to remind them that it was they who were to be the beneficiaries. Without such a thrust, it was felt, it would be difficult to involve them in the completion or maintenance of the project. This was what had led to the idea of the "matching contribution" for rural welfare programmes, Durgabai explains. However, there were disquieting aspects to this approach, she goes on to add, because only a few of the rich in the village could afford to make a matching contribution, either in cash or in the form of tiles, cement, steel, etc. Consequently, by some clandestine agreement, the projects ended up primarily serving the rich; if an approach road was built, it was the locality of the rich that benefited, or if a well was to be dug, it would be dug within 200 metres of the houses of the well off. Thus, though the objective was to elicit the local people's involvement so as to ensure that their concerns were met, in practice, the majority of the villagers didn't benefit, and disparities increased.[25] Nonetheless, the perspectives on development that these experiences have thrown up, and the importance accorded to people's involvement, were and continue to be salient concerns.

Social Reform and Social Work

A closely related issue that comes through from Durgabai's writing is that of the unleashing of human agency through, for instance, the emancipation of women or the erasing of caste disabilities. Durgabai makes an important distinction between "social reform" and "social work". The former "...aims at changing the pattern of life of the whole community, while social work aims at meeting the needs of individuals and groups within the existing pattern". She goes on to elaborate: "Fighting for the equality of rights of women, pleading for a better deal for harijans, and launching a movement for a change in the manner of handling juvenile delinquents are activities that can be placed under social reform. Running an institution for rescued women, organisation of community services in a harijan colony, provision of shelter and education for neglected and delinquent children are instances of social work."[26]

Social reform entails changes that may impinge on the basic values and institutions of a society, and, in the Indian context, harkens back to social reformers (including missionaries) of the nineteenth and early twentieth centuries, who espoused causes like education of girls, emancipation of women, famine relief, temperance, charity, caste reform, and widow remarriage, and fought against sati, child marriage, infanticide, polygamy, and caste inequity. Social reform requires passion of the type demonstrated by the voluntary workers, while social workers, at best, "...are persons with a sense of social purpose and pride in the profession to which they belong". Social work in the form of charity and philanthropy, too was a long standing practice in the country, though the training of professionals for social work was a relatively new development, marked by the establishment in 1936 of the Sir Dorabji Tata Graduate School of Social Work.[27]

Grassroots Capacity Building

Durgabai Deshmukh took special interest in the circumstances of rural women who work alongside their men folk in the fields, and participate in activities like preparing and sowing seeds, harvesting and storing crops, care and milking of cows and buffaloes, maintaining kitchen gardens and selling vegetables in urban areas to supplement family income. The CSWB under the Chairmanship of Durgabai, set up 30,000 welfare centres for the benefit of rural women, each catering to five villages and staffed with a Grama Sevika (women welfare worker), a Craft Teacher and an Auxiliary Nurse and Midwife (ANM). Women seeking employment were recruited to these posts in large numbers.[28]

Reading between the lines, one can see that there were elements of both social reform and social work in these activities of the CSWB. At the same time, there was an effort at *capacity building* at the grassroots through which development goals could be achieved. Thus, *training* was an important facet of the social welfare work that the Deshmukhs undertook. Notably, Durgabai saw training as an important aspect of her work. Towards the end of her autobiography, she says: "...in whatever capacity we worked, we made it the first point to select the right kind of workers and train them, and that, too, in large numbers. No tree, big or small, can flourish under a banyan that shuts out exposure to sunlight and therefore the possibility of growth."[29]

Social Welfare and the State

In the case of the AMS too, as we have seen, the empowerment of indigent women who had dropped out of school was taking place. However, we also see more universal elements of social welfare in the activities of the Sabha; its medical, public health, educational, and welfare services were made available to all sections of society—men, women and children, regardless of caste, community or language group. In fact, though the plight of women moved Durgbai to intervene on their behalf, the commitment to social purpose she displayed was by no means confined to them; it extended to various spheres of social welfare.[30] Indeed, Durgabai's writings suggest that it is social welfare that needs to be the overarching concern. In a lecture she delivered on February 26, 1964 at the Asian Institute for Economic Development and Planning, Bangkok, she says that if the State is to promote social welfare only if it contributes to economic development, "...then much of social welfare activities will lie outside the State's direct responsibility. This is a very limited view of the role of the State. Care of the old or of the handicapped may not contribute to economic growth, but the State can hardly deny its responsibility towards these people for this reason."[31] She goes on to add: "...economic development is not desired for its own sake; it is only for the human welfare that economic development generates. And for the same reason social welfare activities form part of the State's responsibility."[32] Economic development would, in time, raise the standards of living, but social needs cannot be neglected in the interim. Thus, the State needs to step in proactively, to pursue welfare goals, and in this context, it also needs to support the efforts of voluntary organisations.[33]

Given that the welfare ideals of the Constitution in the Preamble, and the Directive Principles of State Policy in Chapter IV of the Indian Constitution, are non-justicable, that is, their non-implementation cannot be challenged in a court of law, Durgabai, as a member of the Constituent Assembly, sought to ensure that the government of the day was held to account. Consequently, she sought a mandatory reporting on what was being done to implement the Directive Principles. The amendment she moved to this end was however not passed. In another initiative, a document on *The Need for a Social Policy Resolution* was prepared at the Council for Social Development (CSD)—the institute Durgabai founded in 1962 after she retired as Chairman of the CSWB.[34] Henning Fris, Director of the Danish National Institute of Social Research, Copenhagen, on deputation as Advisor to the Council for Social Development, used *The Need for a Social Policy Resolution* to prepare his report *Social Policy and Social Research in India and the Contribution of the Council for Social Development*.[35] Fris used, as a frame of reference, the "Definition of the content of social policy" contained in the CSD document. Quoting from that source, Fris reports on the elements constituting social policy as conceived by the CSD. These relate to "the satisfaction of material, cultural and emotional needs that could not conveniently be left to the governance of market forces". According to him, "Social policy envisages a network of inter-related preventive, protective, promotive, curative and rehabilitative services organised by voluntary and governmental organisations, for the citizens."[36]

Durgabai Deshmukh Memorial Lectures

From the inception of the CSD, Durgabai Deshmukh served as its Honorary Director and Executive Chairman until she passed away in May 1981.[37] Since 1992, the CSD has been organising lectures to honour Durgabai's memory—the Durgabai Deshmukh Memorial Lectures. These have been compiled here in the form of chapters in a book.

Failings of State Functionaries

In the first lecture in the series (Chapter 1), Suma Chitnis takes as her starting point Durgabai Deshmukh's lament in 1964, at around the time the CSD was set up, that despite two decades of planning, "...the results have not been commensurate with the effort". One answer to why the State's planned programmes for social and economic change have not delivered to the extent they were expected to, Chitnis argues, is because unlike Durgabai, a social activist fired by a mission of service to society, the State's actors were not driven by social purpose. Chitnis cites NGOs engaged in social work who have displayed commitment, creativity and dynamism, and pleads the case for creating the space for such approaches in the State's activities.

The author finds fault with the State also on account of the vested interests that direct it. Focusing particularly on her area of expertise—the sphere of higher education, Chitnis laments that the State had sought to massively expand this sector at the expense of quality in a bid to tide over the frustrations of the unemployed. In another indictment of the State, the author scathingly speaks of the use of political clout to bypass the merit criterion for admission. Finally, she critiques the reservation policy in higher education and argues for special coaching for those with social disabilities at the school going stage itself.

Grassroots Capacity Building

As noted, in Chapter 1, Suma Chitnis deals with a lack of commitment to the social purpose that prevents the State from adequately discharging its responsibilities. One of the author's conclusions is that ways need to be found to make the State's institutions function effectively. It is this issue that is addressed in Chapter 2, by N.H. Antia, who presents to the reader the nuts and bolts of a people's framework of health care delivery, which he believes can be put in place at a modest and affordable cost. While lauding Independent India's phenomenal public health interventions in bringing to heel four major health scourges: malaria, smallpox, the plague, and cholera, he bemoans the rise of the profit-oriented curative sector and makes out a case for a low-cost framework of people's medicine, in which prevention and early-detection would be key features and all available health systems, rather than allopathic medicine alone, would feature.

Based on his own field experience, the author feels that even semi-literate or illiterate women can easily be imparted the necessary training to make simple, yet safe and effective interventions, and that a woman so empowered becomes eager to take on other responsibilities like running micro-savings groups and managing crèches. In the system of people's medicine Antia envisages, the functionaries at the lowest level will have the benefit of guidance from more experienced functionaries at higher levels, and only the most serious cases would go to specialist hospitals, thus reducing the burden on the formal health care system. Notably, in giving importance to capacity building at the grassroots, Antia's vision echoes Durgabai Deshmukh's understanding of development as one of training of field functionaries who can be agents of social change.

Biotechnology and its Applications

In Chapter 3, Puspa M. Bhargava deals with biotechnology and its scope, for instance, in the sphere of genetic engineering. Every living organism has *capabilities* that are contained in its biological makeup, or, more specifically, in its genetic material or DNA, and in genetic engineering, genetic material that has a particular capability is scissored out from one organism and transferred to another. For instance, a piece of human DNA which contains the capability to manufacture insulin is inserted into the genome of a bacterium called *E. coli*, and then this capability is made to manifest so that insulin is manufactured. Earlier, cattle or pig insulin was given to diabetics, but many of them did not respond to it. Similarly, plants can be genetically engineered to produce vaccines. A few hundred acres under an appropriately gene-engineered banana plant can produce vaccines in sufficient quantity to give 120 million children immunity against four common diseases, Bhargava tells us. The author also discusses a range of biotechnologies such as tissue culture, Genetically Modified Organisms (GMOs), and Artificial Reproductive Technologies (ART). He dwells both the prospects and the perils.

Missionaries and Mercenaries

In Chapter 4, Swami Agnivesh sets forth a vision for a *new* social order in which there would be no private property and wherein it is the spirit of service, rather than the profit motive, that is the driving force. Disparity and exploitation in society, the Swami believes, calls for a new social order, one that is geared to the greater good rather than to individual selfishness; one that has the potential to transform the "mercenary" order of our times into a "missionary" one, one that will embody traditions of selfless service and spiritual living.

Governance and Accountability

In Chapter 5, Aruna Roy speaks of the State's lack of accountability in its treatment meted out to project displaced people, slum clearance in the metropolises, the failure to remove hunger and poverty, the perpetuation of atrocities against the vulnerable, including dalits, women, and children, and the violation of human rights. Yet, avenues exist for successful collective action, and the challenge is to use and expand these democratic spaces, Roy argues. In this context, the author acknowledges the role of people like Durgabai Deshmukh. "We owe a lot to leaders like Durgbai, who were the architects of the independence movement, and who, through their commitment to democratic values even after Independence helped create a political culture of plurality with space for dissent". The author covers topics like the National Rural Employment Guarantee Act (NREGA), Social Audits, and the Right to Information Act (RTI).

The Girl Child

In Chapter 6, Leila Seth argues for the emancipation of women from gender stereotyped roles and makes out a case for harnessing women's energies and capabilities in the development process. As we have seen, Durgabai Deshmukh actively worked for these sorts of concerns over the course of her lifetime. Seth approaches the issue from the vantage point of the girl child and her early marriage, and tells of how a girl is groomed so as to prepare her for a role of subservience and domestic responsibilities. The author calls for attitudinal change and a major role for education, and draws the reader's attention also to constitutional and policy formulations that are auspicious for new beginnings. These include the Supreme Court ruling that free education is a constitutional right, and the fact that the Constitution not only affirms women's equality, but also empowers the State to pursue that goal by means of affirmative discrimination. In the policy sphere, the emphasis vis-à-vis women has shifted from development to empowerment, which is a happy augury. Also giving cause for optimism is the reservation of seats for women in local bodies. To ensure that the empowerment framework that is emerging is effective, Seth argues, there is a need to ensure that patriarchal viewpoints crumble and support services are built up to enable women break free of patriarchal shackles.

Women's Movement

Vina Mazumdar, in Chapter 7, talks of how, breaking free of the constraints of tradition, Durgabai took on roles in the freedom struggle that were outside of a woman's customary obligations to home and hearth. At the same time, Durgabai, through participation in the political process, committed herself to the cause of "...all those oppressed by poverty, ignorance and oppressive social institutions". Indeed, the logic of the opposition to obstacles in the way of equality, justice and dignity is such, Mazumdar argues, that it has to apply to all, and not just to women alone. This has been acknowledged by the Committee for the Status of Women in India, the author observes.

Mazumdar points out also that the freedom struggle was a time when, through political participation, women's roles were expanding outside of the realm of traditional obligations. This was a force for women's emancipation, as Durgabai understood very well. Durgabai's efforts to mobilise women at the grassroots for nation-building tasks through the CSWB, from this point of view, amounted to nothing less than political action, Mazumdar contends. The author goes on to talk of women's voices and their potential for development, and the role of women's organisations in taking up issues like dowry and rape, and agitating for reservations for women in local bodies.

Nautch Girls

In Chapter 8, which also deals with gender issues, Maheswata Devi profiles the nachnis, or nautch (dance) girls of Purulia, an impoverished and neglected district of West Bengal. Most girls who become nachnis come from dalit and tribal families. When they are still very young, they are sold by their poverty stricken families to rasiks—the masters of nachnis. The rasiks marry and have children, and maintain themselves on what the nachnis earn from singing and dancing. When old age claims them, the nachnis are reduced to destitution and beggary.

Even after three decades of Left Front rule, Maheswata Devi laments, the nachnis do not have any rights, "social or human." The author tells the stories of a number of nachnis, and goes on to describe how the nachnis have begun to organise for their rights.She ends with a quote from a social worker who cites the traditional prejudice against—and contempt towards working women, and argues that in the twenty-first century, it is time to put an end to such stigma.

Caste Enumeration

Chapters 6, 7, and 8, as we have seen, cover gender gender issues and the empowerment of women, which we know were central to Durgabai's concerns. Chapter 9, by Gail Omvedt, deals with another type of social disability, namely that of caste. More particularly, the author makes out a case for a caste census, which would help document caste-based discrimination. She refutes the objections to a caste census and debunks the difficulties that have been cited in carrying one out.

Arguing the need for enumerating caste, the author contends that caste is far from extinct. Signs of it abound, for instance, in atrocities against dalits; children of *bhangis* being forced to clean toilets in schools; denial of equal educational rights; use of special cups in tea stalls for untouchables; untouchables being prohibited from walking about in certain high caste areas of the village, and so on. Also, salient is the *continuing* discrimination against low caste converts to Islam, Christianity, and Sikhism. Finally, indications that caste continues to flourish can be seen in the fact of the wide observance of proscriptions on marrying into another caste.

Omvedt underscores the need for studying the system of caste discrimination as a whole, rather than focusing only on oppressed castes. Thus, a caste census ought to cover, not just the SCs, STs, and OBCs, but also, the Brahmins and other "twice-born castes", she argues.

The Tribal Situation

In Chapter 10, Ram Dayal Munda profiles the circumstances of another of the marginalised groups of the country, namely the tribal people of India. Their habitats are destroyed, and they are dispossessed and displaced to make way for mining, hydro-electric projects and the like, with the result that they find themselves poor in their own resource-rich lands, or they end up in the country's urban slums, while outsiders become rich. Munda tells us that a fifth of the country's tribal population, comprising two crore people, have been displaced and forced to relocate in slums. Moreover, the destruction and pollution of the land, the waters and the forests in areas where mining activities take place makes these places unfit for human habitation. On a concluding note, Munda calls for well-thought out development blueprints forged in consultation with a wide range of stakeholders, a bottom-up approach, people's participation as envisaged by the PESA Act, political will, a minimum of displacement, and a re-greening the land ravaged by mining and mineral extraction

Deficit Childhoods

So far, the lectures we have reviewed cover three vulnerable categories—women, caste and tribe. In Chapter 11, Shanta Sinha draws the reader's attention to a fourth vulnerable group—children. She speaks of India's childhood deficits in terms of malnutrition, hunger, lack of health care, child trafficking, child abuse, children infected with HIV-AIDS, torture and exploitation of child labour, child marriage, discrimination against girls, and displacement due to national disasters or civil unrest. Deficit childhoods need to be seen as failures of the State that have dire consequences for the quality of citizenship, she goes on to argue.

Sinha makes out a case for legal instruments for setting standards of health, nutrition, care, and protection, including guaranteeing the protection of children of informal sector workers or migrant labourers and establishing early child care centres and standards for such centres. Sinha speaks also of the need for punitive sanctions against erring officials; thus, she says, there is a need for a law to penalise functionaries who do not fulfil their responsibilities of immunising children. She argues also for the need to work out the basic entitlements of children below 6 years of age, who are not covered by laws. In the case of existing laws, the author argues, there is a need to plug loopholes.

Globalisation and Ecology

In Chapter 12, Vandana Shiva sketches out the deleterious impacts of globalisation on ecology and the livelihoods of the poor. One example the author cites is the destruction of ground water supplies and fisheries by shrimp farming to cater to American, European and Japanese markets. In India, intensive shrimp farming in the fertile coastal districts of Nellore and Thanjavur have hit agriculture and fisheries to such an extent that women from fishing and farming communities have organised *satyagrahas* against prawn farming. Patenting of seeds by multi-national corporations is yet another issue the author addresses.

Politics of Globalisation

In Chapter 13, Randhir Singh portrays globalisation's underlying raison d'être as that of constantly expanding markets in response to capital's unending pursuit of more and more profits. Singh's analysis shows that globalisation stems from the imperatives of the world capitalist system, which is geared to the consumerism of the rich, and leads to a wasteful use of resources. The author's view is that linking up to this system, and becoming a part of it, is not in the nation's interest. The more a nation is linked to the global economy, the author argues, the less control it has over its own destiny; as it becomes more and more subjected to the vagaries of the international economy, it will have to more and more contend with fallouts in terms of the impact of global prices, market business cycles, etc. This forms the backdrop to the author's plea for "delinking" from globalisation. More importantly, saying "no" to globalisation is about having clarity about what *kind* of growth we should aim for. Singh asks: "Is growth to be pursued so as to get the maximum welfare of all the people, with priority for the needs of the poorest sections and the most backward regions and for the protection of the environment? Or is it to satisfy the market-induced, ecologically unsustainable consumerist hunger of the privileged part of the population seeking to maintain or attain the 'high' living standards of the west?" These are questions that need to inform a search for alternatives, the author believes.

Educational Policy

In Chapter 14, Anil Sadgopal takes us on a comprehensive tour of the kind of values the educational system has been mandated to instill and how inimical changes were effected in the country's educational policy, with critical pedagogy, aimed at critiquing reality and engaging with it in order to transform it, a casualty in the new educational policy thrust. The author also decries the policy of parallel, low quality streams of education for disadvantaged children, which is contrary to the principle of equality in the Constitution of India. In this context, he makes a plea for a Common School system. Finally, Sadgopal chastises the State for not ensuring that the recommended 6 per cent of the GDP goes to education.

Gross National Welfare

In the last chapter—Chapter 15, Leela Dube makes a plea for Gross National Welfare (GNW) in place of Gross National Product (GNP). To that end, development requires removal of social inequalities in areas such as access to food, housing, education, and health. It needs to address issues such as those of exploitation, environmental degradation, child labour, gender relations, land alienation, caste conflict, the situation of the aged, communal disharmony, and the displacement of project affected people. In planning, monitoring, evaluation, and the search for alternatives, the author also observes, it is necessary to factor in resistance—for instance, the resistance of project affected people, and to understand people's own perceptions and categories of thought.

While stressing the need for fieldwork-based knowledge in understanding people's perspectives, the author acknowledges many ways of knowing, including the findings of large scale surveys, but believes these need to be tempered with qualitative data and inter-disciplinary approaches.

Summing Up

The concern with GNW brings us full circle. We started out with examples of the kind of social welfare activities Durgabai Deshmukh was involved with, and went on to investigate how social welfare was understood by Durgabai in various policy statements, including the CSD's policy paper on Social Development and the ideals of the welfare state in the Constitution of India, which Durgabai helped draft.

In the CSD's policy paper, *The Need for a Social Policy Resolution,* social policy relates to "the satisfaction of material, cultural and emotional needs that could not conveniently be left to the governance of market forces". It extends to health, education, housing, rehabilitation of physically, mentally and socially handicapped, social security services to meet contingencies like illness, unemployment, emergency relief measures, needs of members of backward communities, etc. In the Directive Principles of State Policy also, we see a broad canvas subsumed under the rubric of "social policy" or social development. Thus, in these policy documents, social welfare is not just about providing a stimulus to economic activity, for instance, through investments in health or education. Rather, social welfare equates with GNW, and social policy and social development are the routes to that goal. The fact that this needs to be stressed suggest that the State is lagging behind and needs to be reminded of its responsibilities.

At the same time, we also see more focused meanings of "Social Development", in terms of understanding and responding to people's felt needs; "social reform" to remove the shackles that constrain disadvantaged groups; and the training of development workers through grassroots capacity building. These core concerns are addressed by the authors of the volume and contemporary developments tracked. The discussion, as we have seen, covers a wide ambit that includes: instilling of values of service, commitment, and dedication in the social activist; making the educational system foster more responsible citizenship; creating a grassroots system of people's medicine that banks on the spirit of service and the unleashing of women power; addressing the issue of deficit childhoods and the concerns of dalits and tribals; countering globalisation's deleterious impacts on social development; investing in science and technology to serve social welfare goals; and arm-twisting the State into yielding more participatory space.

In the process of exploring these issues, the volume holds up a mirror to the contemporary pattern of development, depicts its shortcomings and indeed its inhuman and ghastly failures, which is a far cry from what the Constitution envisaged. It focuses on new developments and initiatives such as NREGA and the RTI that give cause for hope, and suggests alternative development vistas. In sum, it draws attention to limitations and failings of the current development paradigm, recounts some success stories, and points to the roads that need to be tread.

NOTES

1. Durgabai Deshmukh. 1980. *Chintamani and I*. New Delhi: Allied Publishers Pvt. Limited, p. 3.
2. Ibid.
3. Ibid., pp. 1–2.
4. Ibid. pp. 4–5.
5. Suma Chitnis. 1992. *The Institutionalisation of Social Purpose*. Durgabai Deshmukh Memorial Lecture. DDML-1/92/1000. New Delhi: Council for Social Development, p. 3.
6. Durgabai Deshmukh, *op. cit.* pp. 1–2, 6.

7. Ibid. pp. 7–8.
8. Ibid. p. 62.
9. Ibid. pp. 35, 46–47.
10. Ibid. pp. 24-25, 36, 38–39, 47, 52–53
11. Ibid. p. 29.
12. Ibid. pp. 11–12.
13. Ibid.
14. Ibid. p. 11.
15. Ibid. pp. 11–12.
16. Ibid. pp. 11–14, 24.
17. Ibid. pp. 6–7.
18. Ibid. pp. 9–10.
19. Ibid. pp. 15–16.
20. Ibid. pp. 17–21.
21. Ibid. p. 22.
22. Ibid. pp. 103–108.
23. Ibid. p. 80.
24. Ibid. pp. 82–85.
25. Ibid. pp. 85–86.
26. Ibid. p. 53.
27. Ibid. pp. 53–60.
28. Ibid. pp. 61–63.
29. Ibid. pp. 116–117.
30. Ibid. pp. 101–108.
31. Durgabai Deshmukh. 1964. *Social Development and Economic Development, Lecture 1.* Lecture delivered on February 26, 1964. Bangkok: Asian Institute for Economic Development and Planning,
32. Ibid.
33. Ibid.
34. Durgabai Deshmukh. 1980. *Chintamani and I.* New Delhi: Allied Publishers Pvt Limited. pp. 90–91.
35. Henning Fris. 1968. *Social Policy and Social Research in India and the Contribution of the Council for Social Development.* New Delhi: India International Centre.
36. Ibid. p. 3.
37. *Social Change.* 1981. "Resolution adopted by the Executive Committee of the Council for Social Development at its meeting held on July 2, 1981". *Social Change* 11 (2):3.

1

The Institutionalisation of Social Purpose*

Suma Chitnis

In my memory, Durgabai Deshmukh is one of the most dynamic and courageous woman I've ever known—a freedom fighter and founder of independent India who I've deeply respected, and a close relative who I've cherished and admired. I was Durgabai Deshmukh's niece, even if only by marriage and my relationship with her was a very special one. Both of us entered the Deshmukh-Chitnis family the same year as brides—she a wise, mature, experienced, confident woman in her forties, already established as a dignitary on the national scene and I, freshly graduated, just turned 20, on the threshold of adulthood. Separating us was a massive gap in status, wisdom, and experience—but a shared eagerness to be accepted, appreciated and to belong bridged the gap and bound us in a unique closeness as new brides in the family. Though this common ground faded away over the next few years, the bond it created remained. In fact, it grew stronger over the years—probably because, as a sociologist, I was closer to Durgabai's work than anyone else in the family.

I have struggled hard to find a theme that would do justice to Durgabai's distinctive personhood, to the rich spectrum of her service to the social purpose, and to the very special relationship I had with her. The causes she served were so many and so varied that it should have been easy for me to choose one. The nationalist struggle for freedom; literacy; the education of women; the training of *balwadi* workers and of medical personnel; law; the Planning Commission; the Constitution; family planning; social welfare; social development; social research—every single one of these issues would make an interesting theme. Or, for that matter, I could put all these issues aside, and from the vantage point of my interest in women's studies, try to explore the identity of this remarkably strong and liberated woman and share some of my precious memories about her life with a husband who, in turn, was liberated enough to cope with her extraordinarily independent and powerful personhood with gentleness and admiration. Impressed all my life by her tremendous drive and competence, and fascinated by her capacity to succeed at whatever she touched,

* Edited transcript of the July 15, 1992, Durgabai Deshmukh Memorial Lecture.

I was looking for a theme that would help me understand and portray the strength and dynamism that marked her work.

Failure of Planned Development

As I perused her autobiography, some biographical material on her, and writings on the work she had done, I was struck by an anguished comment she made at the time of the establishment of the Council for Social Development (CSD) in 1964. Explaining the objectives for which the Council was being set up, she said: "Two decades of planning have shown that results have not been commensurate with the effort ... The why of this cries for an answer. Is it the over-emphasis on economic development? Is it the lack of correlation between ends and means? Is it that outmoded administrative techniques are inadequate to the new tasks? The true answer can be found only after prolonged search into several complex factors ..."

Durgabai's question is essentially a question about the failure of planned development; that is, the inability of the State to successfully implement programmes for social, economic, and political development. At a more generic level, it is a question about the failure of the State to ensure the successful functioning of the institutions set up to serve the social purpose. Disturbed by the realisation that we do not yet, more than a quarter century after Durgabai first posed her vital question, have a satisfactory answer, I found myself reflecting upon the contrast between, on the one hand, the firm drive and dynamic effectiveness with which Durgabai herself, throughout her life, served every cause she took up, and, on the other hand, the poor performance of the institutions she, as one of the planners for independent India, helped establish. Knowing it would be presumptuous for me to try to answer this complex question, I felt nevertheless that I might at least begin to tackle it by briefly looking back at Durgabai's own social and political work with a view to identifying some of the key elements of her success, and then trying to look at where these elements stand in the State's effort to achieve political and economic development after Independence.

Durgabai's Service to Society

Durgabai was born in a progressive family. Her maternal grandfather, Manohar Rao Pantalu—the first Indian to become Superintendent of Police in British India, was a close friend and supporter of the famous crusader for womens' rights, Veerashalingam Pantalu. Durgabai's father was a man of many parts and a deep sense of public service. From her accounts, he also seems to have been a warm and loving father and far more demonstrative of his affection for his children than was customary for fathers in those days.

Despite her enlightened background, Durgabai was married at the tender age of eight. Fortunately, her schooling did not terminate with her marriage. In 1920, at the age of eleven, she had the maturity to recognise that marriage was not for her, for she decided to join the Indian National Congress (INC) and plunge into public service. At about the same time, she ended her formal education because she felt she had to heed Gandhiji's call to boycott all schools where English was taught. However, she started a school of her own—the *Balika Hindi Pathashala*, to teach Hindi and prepare volunteers for the Congress Session at Kakinada the following year. In a touching reference to this initiative, one of her biographers mentions how, as a little girl of eleven, she described herself as the "principal, teacher, and servant" of the *Balika Hindi Pathasala*, where more than 400 women, many twice her age, were enrolled. Another interesting incident from her childhood occurred when, as a volunteer at the *khadi* exhibition at the Congress Session at Kakinada, she stopped no less a person than Jawaharlal Nehru from entering the exhibition because he had no ticket! Was this little girl an activist? Was it social action she was involved in? Definitions are a tricky business. But, in each of the instances listed so far, what stands out is the clarity of Durgabai's purpose—the courage, determination, and competence with which she pursued every cause she chose to serve, even as a little girl, and the mature, focused, and direct character of her action.

Later, in 1929, when she was barely 20 years old, Durgabai took on the leadership of the Salt Satyagraha in Madras, following the arrest of Sri Prakasam. She, too, was arrested after a month. At her trial, she declined the special privileges accorded to Class A prisoners and insisted that she be given the ordinary Class C entitlements, because she considered the practice of dividing political prisoners into different classes part of the British policy of divide and rule.

Durgabai's work for the Salt Satyagraha brings out her ability to handle a difficult organisational task with efficiency. Her insistence on Class C as a prisoner underlines not only her pluck but also her willingness to suffer in the interest of social justice.

The course of Durgabai's university education reveals some other remarkable facets of her personality and her way of handling challenges. As her school education was continuously interrupted by the nationalist movement, Durgabai took private tuition for one year and passed the matriculation examination of Banaras Hindu University (BHU). Impressed by her performance, Pandit Madan Mohan Malaviya, who headed the university, gave her a scholarship, and she completed her intermediate examination. She would have continued in BHU, but she wanted to graduate with political science—and Pandit Madan Mohan Malaviya, with a somewhat conservative attitude towards the education of girls, insisted that she do literature. Unwilling to compromise, she decided to return to her own province and seek admission in Andhra University.

The Vice-Chancellor of Andhra University refused her admission because she had no place to stay while pursuing her studies. So Durgabai requested the Vice Chancellor to start a hostel. He initially refused, but finally agreed, on condition that he had at least six women students. Determined to bring together the required six students, Durgabai had an advertisement inserted in the local newspaper inviting applications for admission to a university hostel for women. She received twelve applications, which she took to the Vice Chancellor. He had no alternative but to keep his promise.

In 1939, Durgabai passed her BA with Honours, standing first in Political Science and Constitutional History. In 1940, she received the MA degree. Two years later, she earned her BL degree and was enrolled as an advocate in the Madras High Court. With determination, perseverance, ingenuity, and relentless pursuit of purpose, she had won.

Perhaps the best illustration of Durgabai's character and commitment comes from her work for the Andhra Mahila Sabha (AMS). In 1937, Durgabai's family shifted from Waltair to Madras, where her brother, Narayanrao had found a job. Durgabai was still at the hostel at Waltair. The family took a house in the Brindawan Gardens, at Mylapore. Eager to do something for the children in the neighbourhood, Durgabai, who often visited Madras, joined hands with her mother to teach the children dance and music and tell them stories. Also, the mothers of the children were taught Hindi. Before long, Durgabai and her mother had 100 children and 50 women on their hands. Durgabai named this group the *Little Ladies of Brindawan*.

As this organisation grew, it became necessary to house it in proper quarters and to employ paid teachers. At about the time she sensed this need, Durgabai came in contact with the Chennapuri Andhra Maha Sabha, which was essentially a men's club. In 1939, in Madras after completing her BA degree, Durgabai had helped this club design and plan its silver jubilee celebrations. The connection she established with the club's organisers helped her establish the Little Ladies of Brindawan (now named the Andhra Mahila Sabha) as the Women's and Children's Wing of the club. By 1940, she was able to house this wing in separate premises. Bit by bit, she added to the AMS's programme of need-based activities, which ranged from lessons in tailoring, spinning, bamboo and cane work, weaving and paper making, to condensed courses in school education for adult women. As the organisation grew stronger, she added a women's hostel and a Mahila Vidyalaya—a school for women (1944–46), a printing press (1953), a Nursing and Maternity Home (1950–52), a children's ward to the nursing home (1954–55), a hostel for nurses working at the nursing home (1955), a Shishu Vihar Montessory School (1955–56), a Vanita Bala Vihar (1957), an out-patients' block (1956), a dental clinic (1957), a family planning clinic (1957–59), another *vidyalaya* (1958), an operation theatre and surgical block (1957–59), an orthopaedic centre (1958–60), and a tourist hostel (1962–64).

The growth of the AMS at Madras as well as later at Hyderabad indicates, *par excellence*, Durgabai's sharp sensitivity to societal needs, her ability to take growth in proper phases from one stage to the next, her ability to find resources, her watchful monitoring of work, and her gift for stimulating voluntary effort. Her conception of the Central Social Welfare Board (CSWB), and of the CSD, and her administration of both these bodies later in the course of her career, reveal these capacities on a larger canvas and in a national context.

Social Action

While commenting on the failure of planned development, Durgabai was obviously looking at two decades of planned effort from the vantage point of her own track record.

Often, over the course of the past few years, reflecting on the work of social activists—such as Durgabai, the nineteenth century social reformers, and our own contemporaries like Mother Teresa or Baba Amte, I have been impressed by how fundamentally different their approach and mode of functioning was from State-run programmes established to serve the same or similar purposes. I have similarly been impressed by the difference between development or welfare programmes handled by the State and the same kind of work organised by social activist groups such as Christian missionaries. Comparisons such as these lead to a very basic question about the character of social action. In Durgabai's work, we witness the achievements of a socially and politically committed individual engaged in a personal mission of service to society, whose social and political work was inspired by two related but distinctly different impulses—first, a spirit of altruism and social service and second, a spirit of nationalism.

From the beginning of the nineteenth century until the attainment of freedom from British rule in the middle of the twentieth, these two impulses had shaped the lives of many eminent Indians who dedicated themselves to social reform, or to the nationalist movement for freedom, or to both. The history of the period through the nineteenth century up to the achievement of freedom is replete with the achievements of a string of social reformers and freedom fighters who, moved by these two impulses, made outstanding contributions to the service of society. They include reformers like Raja Ram Mohan Roy, Pandit Ishwar Chandra Vidyasagar, and Jyotiba Phule; thinkers and social activists like Agarkar and Maharshi Karve; and freedom fighters like Lokmanya Tilak and Mahatma Gandhi, who addressed themselves to challenges ranging from the eradication of odious practices (like female infanticide, Sati, and child marriage) to the establishment of schools, and eventually, freedom from colonial rule.

Social Action by the State

In India's programme of planned development after freedom, most of the responsibility for social action of the kind earlier taken up by social reformers and political activists was, at least initially, left to the State. How much the State in any society will take on, or for that matter, how much the State will permit non-governmental bodies to do, depends on the character of the State. In India, Independence and self-rule brought about a sea-change from colonial times, in the extent of the responsibility the State was prepared to take on. In fact, as the instrument of a democratic welfare state, the Government of India has, in principle, not only been charged with responsibility for welfare, but taken upon itself a highly interventionist role in the matter of solving societal problems, meeting societal needs, and removing societal disabilities.

However, the complex implications of placing the State in the role of full authority for planned development were never really understood. It was somewhat naively believed that with the establishment of self-rule and the assignment of the responsibility for social welfare and social justice to the State, the dreams that nationalist freedom fighters and subsequently the planners of independent India had dreamt would somehow come true. No matter how committed or responsible a State is, the quality of its delivery of any programme is defined by the scale on which it has to operate, the several responsibilities it must balance, the competing demands for the resources at its command that it must accommodate, and above all, by the quality and commitment of the bureaucracies through which it must function. The results the State is able to produce are, therefore, very different from what can be secured by a committed individual social activist or by a group of committed social reformers; by missionaries imbued with religious fervour; or by political or ideological activists involved in social action as part of some radical or revolutionary programme, as in the case of the nationalist social reformers in pre-Independence India.

Lessons from History

It is pertinent and useful to place the issue in its historical context and look at how social reformers were treated by the British in India. As is well known, the Indian movement for social reform was basically inspired by European liberalism, by European humanist values of social justice, and by the Christian concepts of brotherhood, compassion, and love. These were the values that the British rulers professed to live and rule by. Yet, as may be seen with respect to Indian pleas for legislation against sati, child marriage, the ban on the remarriage of widows, etc., the British rulers repeatedly dismissed Indian requests for reform-oriented legislation. Historical records reveal that the British unabashedly admitted that they hesitated to legislate in favour of reform for the simple reason that they were reluctant to interfere with indigenous customs and religious practices for fear that such interference would jeopardise the stability of their rule in India. Indian social reformers, slow to recognise this, were initially confused by the British reluctance to support their cause. Their faith in the British commitment to liberal, Christian, and human values was so firm that they never doubted the British government would help them with their efforts at reform.

Later, towards the end of the seventh decade of the nineteenth century, more than 40 years after the movement for social reform had been launched, some Indian leaders started to doubt whether the British genuinely intended to honour, in their governance of India, the ideology, values, and principles by which they claimed to live and govern. As is only too well known, it was the sharp rift between those who continued to have faith in the British commitment to reform and those who had lost this faith that triggered the separation of the nationalist movement from the movement for social reform. This break, which occurred during the decades of the seventies and eighties of the nineteenth century (1870s and 1880s), is poignantly illustrated in the rift between Lokmanya Tilak and Agarkar in Maharashtra.

While the social reform movement, the nationalist movement for freedom, and other events of that era have now receded into history, the basic lesson that surfaces from the behaviour of the British *vis-a-vis* the reformers continues to be relevant with a freshness that makes it immensely valuable to understanding why planning for development has failed. The lesson is that governments may, without compunction, turn their backs upon the ideologies and values they profess if the operationalisation of these is threatening to their power, stability, or survival. As a freedom fighter and planner for independent India, Durgabai could not even imagine that a nationalist government would display the same weaknesses that the country was plagued by under colonial rule. However, if we cast our sentiments and emotions aside and face the facts, it is evident that, in balancing the objectives of developments with its own survival, the government, in post-Independence India, has often had to bypass or at best do notional service to the spirit of planning and to the ideals and principles by which planning was inspired.

Planned Development

It is not surprising that planners, at the dawn of independence, were unable to visualise the constraints to the government's management of development. Planned development is such a complex undertaking that it was only when the plans were launched that the character of the problems involved became evident. When we look back, we can see how both the feasibility of State-administered development and faith in the ability of the State to deliver on its promises have deteriorated over the four-and-a-half decades since Independence.

The decade of the 1950s, when policies and planned programmes were first launched, was a time of new beginnings. Many difficult challenges confronted the young government. Though inexperienced, the government was fortified with a sense of unity, conviction, confidence, determination, and hope. The difficult struggle for Independence and the wounds of Partition had brought the country together. The euphoria of its newly acquired freedom and nationhood gave people confidence. They were willing to suffer in order to build. Moreover, the planners and politicians who steered the government enjoyed widely-perceived legitimacy, partly because they had brought freedom and partly because, in the traditional value system, they were the kind of leaders who were acceptable. Regardless of the fact that they had come to power through unfamiliar democratic processes, theirs was, in the eyes of the masses, the traditional authority of education, caste, and social status, converted into the authority of the new government. As business, trade, and manufacture started to blossom, the traditionally powerful business class retained its political influence. And it was easy to co-opt and bring into the coalition the landed and the other caste elite because there were new jobs and business opportunities to offer.

Through the decade of the sixties, this changed visibly. One of the most critical elements of the change that occurred was that the homogeneity of the legislative and policy-making bodies was disturbed. Political democracy in action brought into these bodies members from middle and lower castes. It also brought persons with very little or no formal education. The legitimation of trade unions changed the parameters, not only of economic activity but also of the functioning of government offices, educational institutions, and even hospitals. The operationalisation of provisions for the backward classes, aimed at equality, created new tensions, angers, and uncertainties. All this has been recorded by political scientists. What matters to our understanding of the failure of planned development is that as the homogeneity of the government eroded, efficiency suffered and its legitimacy came to be seriously threatened. While all this was happening, the promises made earlier turned out to be too big to keep. Inevitably the State's delivery of social purpose became weak and shaky. I will try to substantiate my statements with some illustrations from higher education, the field that I am relatively more familiar with.

Higher Education

The government of independent India deserves full credit for its generous provisions for higher education, which could be briefly summed up in terms of three bold commitments. First, the commitment that the country would be provided with full facilities for education in every technical, technological, and professional field. Consequently, all the manpower needed for the country's economic, political, and social development would be met. Second, the facilities for higher education would be complete enough to ensure that the country becomes fully independent of foreign expertise as well as of dependence, for higher education, on universities in developed countries. Third, all those who aspire to higher education after high school will be provided with the opportunity to pursue their aspirations. All three commitments have been met. Today, the country is fully self-sufficient in indigenously trained technical, technological, and professional manpower. It does not need to depend either on foreign expertise or on foreign universities. Supported by the government, higher education has grown phenomenally and practically everyone who aspires for further education after completing high school is able to get it.

Problems

However, as a system primarily supported by and dependent on the State, the system suffers from many problems. One of the most conspicuous is the size of the expansion. The system of higher education in the country has grown to be so large that it cannot be operated efficiently. When the First Five Year Plan was launched in 1950–51, there were only 28 universities, 695 colleges, and 1,74,000 students. Today, we have 169 universities, 27 deemed universities, 7,400 colleges, and 3,948,000 students. Within a few years of launching the First Five Year Plan in 1951, it was feared that higher education was expanding too much and too rapidly. In fact, at the time of the establishment of the University Grants Commission (UGC) in 1956, Dr C.D. Deshmukh, its first chairman, had categorically advised that the growth must be curbed. That statement has been repeated from one Five Year Plan to another. But neither the central nor the state governments have really curbed the growth of higher education. As a consequence, the facilities have been stretched to breaking point and the standards have declined enormously. This deterioration is visible in the functioning of all universities. So far, institutions like the Indian Institute of Technology (IITs) and Indian Institute of Management (IIMs)—set up as centres of excellence—have been relatively protected from the deterioration. But, gradually they too have begun to suffer.

Vested Interests

Both the central and the state governments have allowed higher education to expand against the advice of plan experts and observers. They argue that the growth has to be accepted in order to honour the national commitment to equality of educational opportunity. I believe that the government's claim masks at least two vested interests which it may not be willing to face, much less admit. The first is its interest in using higher education as an instrument to contain the frustrations of unemployment. If there were jobs for those who finished high school, there would not have been such a heavy demand for admission to colleges. I believe that the government has been expanding facilities for higher education because it cannot provide employment in adequate measure. The government's second vested interest is to use the expansion of higher education for political patronage. Our politicians have discovered that one of the easiest ways to keep voters happy is to start a college in the constituency. The government, which according to established practice, holds the authority to permit or withhold permission for setting up colleges, has in turn discovered that it can use this authority to bestow political patronage—by granting the required permission to the politicians it wants to oblige or please.

Deterioration in Standards

In all fairness it must be conceded that while allowing higher education to expand, the government has taken increasingly greater responsibility for financing it. In fact, the government's share of the expenditure on higher education has increased from a mere 57 per cent in 1951 to more than 88 per cent by now. However, the distribution of what the government spends is far from even. Elite institutions, such as the IITs, receive an extraordinarily large share. So do the Central universities. State universities receive much less. Within every university, the distribution between departments is again highly uneven. I cannot go into the details of these disparities, but in the arithmetic of fund allocation, State-supported universities end up very frugally supported.

With the limited resources available to them, these universities have, nevertheless, to expand in response to public demand. They have tended to cope with the pressure for expansion by enlarging their Arts and Commerce faculties, less expensive to operate than the departments of science or technology or any of the professions. But they have not been able to halt the deterioration in standards in teaching and in examinations. While this is clearly evident, it is interesting to look at what the government does to improve standards, for instance, the standards of the university examinations that are plagued by malpractices ranging from copying to physical violence against invigilators.

Lukewarm Efforts at Reform

As early as 1977, a major committee was appointed on examination reforms. The committee was charged with the responsibility of finding ways and means of removing malpractices. It recommended the replacement of the single annual examination with continuous evaluation. Further it pointed out that it was wrong to depend exclusively on the lecture system, and firmly advised a more interactive system of communication between teachers and students. With funds barely enough to pay existing teachers for the lectures required, there was no real possibility of introducing either continuous evaluation or a more interactive system of teaching—but the authorities were satisfied that the gesture of appointing a committee which made well thought out recommendations had been made. Of course, none of the recommendations of this committee could be implemented with any seriousness. In 1988, ten years later, another committee was appointed, again, to look into examination reform. Whether we consider the report of this committee as more realistic or feel sad about what it was reduced to recommending depends on how we look at the efforts of the State. The report starts with a series of observations about the problems faced and concludes with the comment that "we must do something to make examinations less prone to manipulation and corruption, and more honoured and efficient". I feel this recommendation bears witness to the fact that the country had been getting used to the poor performance of universities.

Politicisation

Another consequence of the government taking on the major share of the responsibility for higher education is that administrative matters as well as academic issues tend to get highly politicised. Academic staff unions, non-academic staff unions, and student unions, as well as bodies like the University Senate, Academic Council or Senate and College Managements are occupied by politicians. They use the university and its various activities as an arena in which to fight their political battles. Government decisions on university matters are contested by parties in opposition to the party in power. Only recently, the Vice-Chancellors of all the non-agricultural universities in Maharashtra went through a nightmare, being *gheraoed* by Akhil Bharatiya Vidyarthi Parishad (ABVP) activists protesting a fee hike introduced by the government. As the Vice-Chancellor of SNDT University, I was *gheraoed* mercilessly for five hours—locked in my room with about hundred ABVP activists, who demanded that I reduce the fees at our university or resign. Barely four or five of these 100 odd activists were SNDT students.

I did not have the authority to reduce the fees, nor did the Executive Council of the university, unless it could provide funds to make up the difference between what it would want to charge and what the government would have the university charge. But the activists insisted that I bring pressure to bear on the government. Two months later, on the occasion of Guru Poornima, the same activists came to me with flowers, saying that they wished to touch my feet in order to pay me the traditional respect due to gurus. I told them that I could not understand their desire to thus honour me, only two months after their ugly behaviour over the issue of fees. I told them that I could not possibly accept their flowers. It was quite a strain to speak to them without being abrasive.

As a Vice-Chancellor, I should be looking after the administration of my university, and concentrating on taking responsibility for its academic advance and growth. Instead, I have to gear myself to handling one political confrontation after another. What makes this even more difficult is that almost invariably, these confrontations have their genesis in political differences or dissensions that are only marginally relevant to the university.

Mixing Objectives

Yet another major problem that arose with the government taking the responsibility for financing higher education is that it expected universities, in return, to help with several of the tasks of development. For instance, through schemes like the National Social Service (NSS), it expects to involve students and teachers in the accomplishment of targets for literacy, adult education, population education, and other programmes. On paper, the plans to involve students appear impressive. It seems as if they are truly designed for mutual benefit. While programmes targets are to be achieved with the voluntary help of students, the students, in turn, benefit through the experience they are meant to receive.

There is no doubt that this happens on a small scale. By and large, however, the outcome of these programmes is very different from what the glossy reports on their evaluation claim or suggest. To start with, only a fraction of the students are really able to participate. Moreover, only a few of those who participate are inspired by altruism or develop any real commitment to social service. Most students demand that their participation is rewarded with marks or some other credits that can be counted in the final assessment of their academic performance. Thus, the net result of such arrangements is questionable.

It is not that the programmes cannot be made more productive. Able managers of such programmes can not only meet programme targets, but also ensure that students gain experience and cultivate sensitivity to the country's needs and problems. However, administered as they normally are by highly centralised bureaucracies, these arrangements leave much to be desired. One suspects that universities and colleges reach out not because they are inspired to national service but because the grants that are assigned for these programmes provide the much needed funds for at least a modicum of extra-curricular activity. Moreover, the targets achieved in literacy, or adult education, or whatever, can be a way of currying favour with the government.

Incompatible Commitments

Yet another illustration of how the implementation of political obligations and objectives through the system of higher education can damage the quality of education is seen in the implementation of the policy of reservations. Under this policy, as is well known, a quota of admissions is reserved for students belonging to backward social groups. The consequences of such reservations differ significantly from one type of institution to another. I will make my point with specific reference to the IITs, which were set up as apex centres for higher education in science and technology. These institutes are very well funded and are allowed full autonomy. In all fairness, it must be granted that while higher education was otherwise stretched to accommodate all those who aspired to it, the government made a determined effort to keep these islands of excellence free from the pressures of expansion. They were always protected from having to dilute their standards.

At the outset, as part of the policy of making it practical to pursue standards, these institutions were not required to implement the policy of reservations. But about 15 or 20 years ago, they too were required to reserve a quota of admissions. As soon as they started to do so, they found that there was a massive gap in the capabilities of students who came to them through open admissions and those who were admitted to reserved seats. This problem was immediately and consciously tackled. In order to bridge the gap, they gave the students admitted to the reserved seats a year's bridge course. Students admitted to the reserved quota could not go on to regular work without finishing this course. Unfortunately, the students resented having to spend an extra year.

Before long, this issue became politically explosive. The course was criticised for being discriminatory and had to be withdrawn. As a result, the IITs are now required to accommodate the students who occupy the reserved seats without any extra preparation. This causes an unhealthy strain on the teachers as well as on the students who come through open competition.

I am not opposed to reservations. It is a national commitment I respect. However, in the context of our concern for the failure of development, it is important to recognise that the government's approach in the matter of the implementation of the policy of reservations is defined by the immediate political pressures it faces rather than by basic or long term development concerns. Organisations like the Homi Bhabha Science and Mathematics Education Centre at Bombay have carefully researched the issue of preparedness and performance of socially and otherwise disadvantaged students, and have come to the conclusion that to overcome the disadvantages which affect their performance, such students must get special help from Standard III onwards. If this is not possible, they should get help at least from Standard VIII onwards. The Centre has developed scientifically designed teaching materials and strategies for the purpose. If the government is serious about equality, it must provide students who are eligible for reserved admissions at institutions like the IIT this extra help and support. It does not do so. On the contrary, in response to the suggestion that students admitted to reserved quota are given a year's coaching, questions are being asked in Parliament as to why courses at the IITs are allowed to be so "elitist" as to cause serious problems to Backward Class students!

Pressures

Several other features of higher education illustrate the problems linked with State control over the delivery of development. It is not possible to discuss all of them but I will briefly dwell on the issue of admissions. In principle, admissions are to be given strictly on merit. In practice, influential persons are able to make room for students, regardless of whether they do or do not qualify by merit. One of the first decisions I made as Vice-Chancellor was that all the institutions owned and conducted by the university will admit students only by merit. On hindsight, I feel that the courage to take this decision and to stand by it came from my lack of experience of the system! The first step was to give up the seats to be filled by me at my discretion in my capacity as a representative of the 'management'. At admission time, as expected, I experienced an onslaught of requests for admissions. I received telephone calls and requests for appointments from every quarter—from eminent citizens, from social workers, from politicians, and not the least, from the highest quarters in the Sachivalaya (the Secretariat), including at the ministerial level.

The requests from the Sachivalaya were usually made over the telephone. Each time I received a call from the Sachivalaya or any other government office, I would tell the calling party that I could never be sure that the call was not spurious or bogus and would be grateful to have the request written on the letter heads of the office from which it was being made. These letters did not arrive, but the telephone calls continued. Occasionally, the minister's or secretary's secretary would come with a note claiming that he was representing his boss. In such cases, I would draft a polite letter to the Minister or official concerned with a reference to the telephone calls and/or visit and requesting the Minister or Secretary to confirm that he/she had asked for admission. When VIPs came to meet me in person, I would try to explain why admission could only be given on merit. This was difficult. I had to face threats and anger, though I must confess, on rare occasions, callers have appreciated the stand I took.

Over the course of the three years I served the university, the requests for admission have practically ceased. In becoming so strict, the university may have lost some of its clout and influence in official and political circles. On the other hand, our college principals say that they have gained enormously in strength, self-respect, and confidence. It has not been easy to sustain this course of action. For instance, just two weeks ago, the president of the Pradesh Congress Committee of one of the small towns adjacent to Bombay came to admit his daughter. He forced his way past my secretary, who was instructed to refuse appointments for those who wished to see me on admission matters. When I told him that admissions were made strictly on merit, that his daughter did not qualify, he pointed out that he could help the university get all its grants quickly and that he could help clear all kinds of administrative matters through the State Education Department. While answering back to say that the university did not make any such transactions, it did cross my mind that he could very well wreak vengeance by delaying our grants. All I could do was hope that his political activities would not leave him time to pursue vindictive action against me or my university. My experience has been frustrating enough, but principals and the managements of some universities said they were threatened with severe physical violence and held to ransom over admissions.

NGOs

While State-run programmes for development have come up against serious trouble, Non-Governmental Organisations (NGOs) are the new hope on our horizon. NGOs as they are now called, were only beginning to appear on the scene in Durgabai's time. Today they are active in full measure. NGOs are organised in a variety of different ways. Some NGOs are run by individual activists and are autonomous in every way. There are NGOs who function as groups or teams voluntarily organised for a cause, and there are NGOs who work on behalf of larger organisations. The latter are often paid employees like any other bureaucracy. Overall, as compared with programmes operated by the State, one can observe several of the distinctive qualities of Durgabai's work in the functioning of NGOs. I will try to place before you two examples of NGO work which may help validate this claim.

Society for the Promotion of Area Resources Centre (SPARC)

The first is the work of the organisation Society for the Promotion of Area Resources Centre (SPARC). This organisation works for slum dwellers. It was started by an imaginative professional social worker, Sheela Patel. She started her career with one of the oldest and most respected social work agencies in the city of Bombay, and, in the course of administering routine welfare programmes in health, education, provision of gainful employment, recreation etc., she felt the women beneficiaries of the programmes were not as enthusiastic as she expected, or would have liked them to be. Disturbed by what she saw as a lukewarm response to the efforts she and her agency put into their work, she decided to openly ask the women why they were so unenthusiastic about the programmes that were being provided for them. The answer she received was incredibly firm and clear. The women said they appreciated the efforts on their behalf and were grateful for what was done for them, but could not be fully involved in activities like the literacy programmes that were organised when they had more immediate basic and urgent needs to worry about. Startled by this reply and recognising that it was necessary to probe into the women's needs if she really intended to help them, Ms. Patel set up a unique process of dialogue wherein she was able to make a sharp assessment of their real needs. Based on this, she designed a plan of action. The agency she worked for was old, established, and set in its ways and was reluctant to support her action plan. So, with the help of a couple of her class mates, she decided to launch out on her own. They founded SPARC. One of SPARC's basic decisions was to reorganise the marginalised communities for development and to make women central to this reorganisation. SPARC identified pavement dwellers as the most marginalised community in Bombay, because apart from being marginalised by poverty and migration, they were victims of authority, particularly of municipal demolition squads. Every few days, these demolition squads would descend on them and wipe out their habitation.

Following up on its decision to work with and through the women in the community, SPARC made a very sharp and subtle distinction between the "condition" and the "position" of women. According to this distinction, the term "condition" refers to where the women stand in terms of day-to-day material needs such as education, food, shelter, clothing, etc., whereas the term "position" indicates where they stand in the structure of society. SPARC contended that all State-level programmes work only against the *condition* of women, but do not really change their *position*. Its declared policy, therefore, was to work through the position of the women to change their condition. With their framework for action thus defined, the members of the organisation once again initiated a dialogue—this time *with and between* the women of the community they had chosen to work with. This time, the women's complaints were monitored more systematically in discussions. As a result, SPARC workers were able to identify a pattern of deprivation in the sufferings the women described and the complaints they made. The next step was to get the women themselves to see these patterns. Then SPARC did something really remarkable. It decided that while its clients gained in strength in terms of being able to handle their problems, they ran the risk of dislocating their relationship with their husbands, or with the other men in the family, if these men—excluded from the programme—grew to be jealous or suspicious of the women's new capacity to assert and be effective. So they decided to co-opt the men in the programme by involving them in community sessions.

The first community sessions centred on how to handle demolition squads and what to do when demolition finally happened. It so happened that the municipal squads came when the men were out at work. So, before long, the men in the community sessions were saying to the women *"ye to apko khud dekhna chahiya, hum log tho hothey nahin ghar me"* (This is something you women must handle yourselves, for we are hardly at home). Upon this, in the presence of the women, the social workers coaxed and cajoled the men into taking up the responsibility, asking them how they expected their womenfolk to handle the demolition squads on their own. The men invariably answered that if they were to tackle the demolition squads, it would mean foregoing the daily wage. The men were then gently led on to accepting the women in their families as principal functionaries and leaders in the matter of handling eviction.

The women were next informed about their rights vis-a-vis the demolition squads. They were made aware of the distinction between demolition and eviction, and guided to recognise that the right to one did not necessarily give demolition squads the right to the other. Using available plans for the Bombay city and metropolitan area, the social workers taught the women how to identify vacant land. They were also taken by buses to these spots. Thus, when government and municipal authorities told them there was no land to rehabilitate them, they were able to show these patches. Finally, with all these facts in hand, they were guided to work out proposals as to where they could be shifted. After this, they were encouraged to make little models of the houses they wanted. Engineers and architects were brought in to listen to them.

Looking back upon their own experience, the social workers who launched SPARC say: "We had no message to start with; we had no plans. We only knew we wanted to operate through the needs of the women, speak to them in their own language and advance them towards the fulfillment of their needs". Today, the strategy used by SPARC is considered one of the most successful. SPARC workers, for their part, deny that they have any strategy! Reflecting upon their own experience, they say the trouble with government programmes is that they aim at a product, whereas the secret of working successfully with the poor is to master the process of getting them to recognise their own needs

and themselves initiating action. SPARC social workers speak in terms of "outcome" rather than of "products", and explain that instead of aiming at any specific target, they work with the broad idea of helping the women help themselves. "We work together," they say, "and what we accomplish at the end of the day is something that evolves, even when what is needed is not seen clearly at the beginning. It is seen as we go along."

Kashtakari Sanghatana

The second example I would like to cite of social action by an NGO is equally impressive. It relates to the work of a Peter Prabhu who works near Dahanu, in the coastal district of Maharashtra. This man, an ex-Jesuit, left the order to fight against bonded labour. Convinced that it was impossible to understand the suffering of people unless one lived with them, he set up headquarters in the midst of the tribal villages he served. He learnt the languages of the Katkari and Warli tribes, which was a very difficult thing to do. He also familiarised himself with the religious practices, legends, beliefs, and folklore of these tribals. This was important, because the level at which these tribes functioned was so primitive that in their conception fact merged imperceptibly into fable, and it was practically impossible to determine the line dividing the two. Prabhu and his team struggled through and managed to establish clear communication and rapport with the tribals.

Prabhu's work in connection with the release of bonded labour and the restoration of tribal land really illustrates how committed activists function. Without going into details, let us briefly look at Prabhu's programme of literacy. One of the two tribes Prabhu and his group worked with—the Warlis, paint on their floors and walls beautiful paintings with rice-flour paste, on surfaces prepared with wet application of rich red mud. These paintings have ritual meanings and are specifically designed for different occasions like births, deaths, weddings, harvest time, sowing time, etc. Prabhu and his team developed for their literacy and awareness programmes a set of 60 paintings which basically depicted Katkari and Warli legend and folklore in the Warli style of paintings. Messages relevant to the integrated development of these tribes were carefully woven into these depictions. The paintings were then used as the core visual materials for the programme of non-formal education conducted by this group (the Kashtakari Sanghatana).

Literacy was one aspect of this programme of non-formal education. Making the villagers, both men and women, aware of the political and economic exploitation that they were vulnerable to, and of the gender exploitation they themselves practiced, and to indicate solutions, was the other. The lessons were conducted with tremendous sensitivity and a rich sense of humour. The pictures and discussions that were used to discuss problems and solutions doubled as material for the literacy programme as the tribals, learning to write, identified items from the pictures. One of the picture-episodes that linger in my mind is about the harvesting ritual. This picture conveys a message of how the landlords the tribals work for recover the money they pay as wages through the liquor shops they run.

Commercialisation of NGOs

I have painted a positive and approving picture of NGOs. That is because so many of them are full of vitality and highly effective in their functioning. It would, however, be misleading to paint a uniformly rosy picture. Some get co-opted into the lethargic public delivery system. Others fall easy prey to funding agencies looking for "good" programmes to boost their own status. More often than not, funding by such agencies is governed by very specific and inflexible project requirements. Some of the best projects in the country are known to have clipped their wings in order to fit into these requirements and qualify for funds. The possibility of acquiring massive funds has generated yet another malaise, that is, the writing of impressive project proposals for programmes that have neither substance nor soul. Again and again, one comes across instances of hollow proposals gaining grants merely because they were well written or, worse yet, merely because the proposers had good contacts. At the same time, there are a host of dedicated and successful activists who know very little about funding, are unable to write project proposals of the kind that fetch funds, or who are just too busy with their work to be able to do the workshop and seminar rounds where funding transactions are initiated. NGOs must be protected from such vested interests.

Institutionalising Social Purpose

In my brief review of Durgabai's work, I have tried to identify her distinctive qualities. Picking up from that review, I list the following: clarity of purpose; courage and determination in action; competence; the ability to resist pressure and to measure up to an emergency; the capacity to handle difficult organisational tasks with efficiency; a willingness to suffer in the cause of social justice; ingenuity; perseverance; a relentless pursuit of purpose; an ability to raise resources to stimulate voluntary effort and cooperation; and above all, an ability to advance a cause in proper phases from one stage of growth to the next, and a watchful monitoring of each stage. Surprisingly, very few or hardly any from this long list of qualities is visible in State sponsored social action. Occasionally, one may come across a devoted bureaucrat serving with a sense of mission. But, for the major part, the movement for change that planners had expected to launch by employing the State to deliver development has turned out to be as limp as a revolution fought by mercenaries.

To an extent this is inevitable. After all, government servants are neither social activists nor revolutionaries. In fact, conceptually, the term "bureaucrat" could well be seen as the antonym of the term "social activist". Moreover, it is significant that even the work of social activists is known to take on a bureaucratic character as soon as it is established into an organised system, either to replicate work done, or give a successful programme conducted by a single activist or a small team of workers stability, a measure of permanence, and a more widely usable frame. Sociologists define social institutions as widely accepted and firmly established practices and procedures aimed at meeting societal needs. Established practices and procedures are vital to the functioning of society, but so is spontaneous action. The truth is that the fulfilment of social purpose requires both the dynamism of an activist approach and the stability of institutionalised functioning. The challenge is to keep the two in a balanced and socially productive interaction. This perhaps is the need of the decade of the nineties—to sustain and promote the alertness, purposiveness, pertinence, and efficiency of NGO activity and to support it with relevant facilities and provisions available with government and other established agencies, and at the same time, to bring to the functioning of the latter some of the dynamism with which the work of successful NGO is infused.

Administrators as Activists

Planned development administered through the State is one of the most powerful ways of institutionalising social purpose. Legislation in support of the cause to be served or the need to be met is one of the most important arms of the State in this task. From the nineteenth century onwards, we have put great faith in legislation. After Independence, we have in the same spirit made legal and constitutional provisions in support of objectives such as equality or secularism. Therefore, in order to understand the course of planned development administered by the State, it would be useful to look at how legislation works.

Much hope was placed in legislation in pre-Independence dreams for an independent India. After Independence, we have continued to function with the same faith and produced some impressive legislation. For instance, since the decade of the 1970s, there has been a considerable amount of legislation on rape, dowry, family violence, etc., all geared to improving and advancing the status of women. However, at the end of two decades, we find that the achievements of the objectives of this legislation are thwarted because of the hair-splitting demands for definition in the legal process—the definition of dowry, for instance, or the definition of rape. To be exactly and unquestionably applicable, definitions of what constitutes the criminal act are made to be narrow and precise. As a result, there are instances where behaviour that is visibly criminal may not fit into the narrow legal description covering that particular act. The efficacy of legislation can be further affected by the legal requirements of proof. Such requirements, made with the explicit objective of protecting the innocent from being wrongly accused, are absolutely essential. But imposed or implemented by a judge or jury who are not committed to the cause that the legislation is designed to serve, they can be reduced to harsh brakes on social justice. The point I am trying to make is very well illustrated in the matter of legal action against rape. The public upheaval caused by the Mathura case pertaining to the rape of a tribal girl in police custody, and the publicity given by the media to the issue, resulted in considerable reform of the existing legislation on rape. For the first time, the sentence for rape was clearly specified—ten years for the rape of a pregnant woman, for gangrape, and for the rape of a little child, and seven years or less for others. But the kind of proof that was required to establish a charge made it well nigh impossible to punish a culprit unless the judge was prepared to read between the lines of the evidence presented.

Records on some of the cases brought to court are revealing, for instance, the case of a 21-year-old boy alleged to have raped a 7-year-old girl. The argument was that the injuries on the boy's body did not show adequate resistance from the girl. The law requires that for the physical contact to count as rape, the penis of the accused should show physical injury. This requirement is based on the assumption that the physical struggle, at the time of the rupturing of the hymen, must cause an injury to the penis. One wonders whether a frightened 7-year-old could ever put up enough physical resistance to injure someone three times her age. In the absence of the required proof, the boy was acquitted. Or again, as late as 1989, we have a case where a girl of five was raped, and the rapist was let off because the child could not give "proper evidence".

On the other hand, records reveal that even prior to the revised legislation, as early as 1958, both the High Court and the Supreme Court have taken the position that in cases of rape, the demand for the establishment of proof beyond doubt was ridiculous. Further, commenting on the fact that the accused often took shelter under the provision which required proof that the victim had not "consented" to the act, they categorically pointed out that the demand for establishment beyond proof that "there was no consent from the girl" was ridiculous, because compliance obtained under fear and pressure was not consent.

Thus, experience indicates that legislation is only as strong as its implementation. Progressive legislation cannot really serve its purpose unless its implementation is presided over by a committed and progressive judge—in fact, by a judge who is a social activist of a special kind. Legislation is only as strong or effective as its implementation.

Helmsmen Matter

Whether it is the implementation of reform-oriented legislation, programmes aimed at economic growth or social justice, or whether it is the democratic process in general, people at the helm of affairs matter. One of our major problems is that most of our progressive, development-oriented institutions are run by people who continue to believe in and function with feudal values.

Nowhere is this more pathetically visible than in the functioning of political processes in the country—all the way from the top to the grassroots. In fact, regardless of inadequacies in State-administered development, one is sometimes grateful that the functioning of the State is not quite as feudal as that of some of the politicians who exercise control over it.

Chintamani Deshmukh, Durgabai's husband, was once ill and Durgabai courageously decided that he must be operated upon. Chintamani Deshmukh was in Bombay for medical treatment at the time, and Durgabai was still in Hyderabad. When we told him about her opinion and asked him what his decision was, he said: "In this matter, the decision lies with my wife because my life is hers". His answer sums up the quality of their extraordinary relationship with each other. What we need to remember is that both of them, and each in a distinctive fashion, had the same relationship with their work. Their lives belonged to the social purpose they served.

2

Community Healthcare: A Delivery Framework*

N.H. Antia

The increasing cost of healthcare when sold as a marketable commodity in a field where consumer resistance is at its lowest has meant that the rich, who can afford to pay, are dangerously over-investigated, overmedicated, and over-surgicalised. The middle class, on the other hand, has to contend with severe financial strain when illness strikes. As for the poor, expenditure on illness care is second only to dowry as a cause of indebtedness. Ironically, this is so notwithstanding the fact that low cost healthcare is an attainable goal; some 850 million of our people who live in some 700,000 villages and urban slums suffer from the diseases of poverty, which chiefly affect the young and are relatively easy to prevent as well as cure at low cost.

Colonial Impact

The colonisation of the subcontinent by the British is a significant determinant of this dismal health scenario. The colonisers imposed their own system of medicine as being "scientific" and hence superior. They also denigrated our age old health culture and lifestyle, as well as our highly evolved holistic systems of health and medical care like Ayurveda and Yoga, which deal as much with the mind as with the physical body. Ruthless economic exploitation led to repeated famines, severe malnutrition, and widespread prevalence of the diseases of poverty. Those like me, who have personal experience of the effects of three centuries of plunder prior to Independence, have vivid memories of barefoot, ill-clad walking skeletons who were decimated by smallpox, plague, malaria, and cholera, apart from tuberculosis and a host of other endemic diseases. These harbingers of misery and death were contained *within* the British cantonments by means of the then available knowledge and technology, but not *without*. Not surprisingly, therefore, the life span of our people at the time

*Edited transcript of the July 16, 2001, Durgabai Deshmukh Memorial Lecture by Dr N.H. Antia.

of Independence was 27 years—which is equivalent to that of the UK three centuries earlier.

Our medical texts in Sanskrit were burnt on the orders of Lord Macaulay in order to replace our indigenous systems of health with the formalised medical one of the colonial masters, based on hospitals, doctors, and nurses. This system was further promoted by the opening of western style medical schools and colleges for training the children of our elite in what was considered the superior system of the rulers. Even in this, the emphasis was on the curative aspects of medicine, while the most relevant and useful aspects for public health, based on the knowledge of microbes and their vectors, was relegated to the low profile Preventive and Social Medicine Departments of medical colleges. This despite the fact that they were most effectively used by the colonisers in their cantonments. Medicine was hence used as a subtle means for inculcating Western dominance in the local elite, who willingly accepted the "superiority of science and culture", especially of its lucrative curative component. Medicine was based on the predominantly western curative model and became the monopoly of the urbanised MBBS doctor and now, increasingly, of specialists who fail to serve the basic health needs of the rural population at the Primary Health Centres, even after being trained at public expense. Unfortunately, this persists even half a century after the departure of the colonial rulers. A new elite has replaced the old.

Public Health Interventions

Ironically, these developments occurred despite the remarkable experience in the first two decades following Independence, when malaria, which affected 100 million people and resulted in two million deaths each year, was reduced to 65,000 cases with no deaths by 1965. This was the most dramatic example of public health intervention ever achieved in the world—an achievement by a newly liberated and enthused people, supported by a few equally enthused public health professionals trained under the British, and with an equally supportive political leadership. Smallpox was also eradicated in the same period, and cholera and plague brought under control. These three diseases, along with malaria, were the four major health problems of the pre-Independence era. And yet, this unique and unsurpassed achievement in healthcare has failed to receive its due recognition and acknowledgement even to this day.

Alas, the decade of the 1990s witnessed a slowdown and even a setback in the improvements that were taking place in the health conditions of our people, along with the recurrence and/or resurgence of many diseases like tuberculosis, malaria, dengue; waterborne diseases like typhoid; *kala azar*, filariasis, and encephalitis. It was a period when we had reopened our doors to the West following the demise of the Soviet Union—a time when poverty increased and public sector financing for health was reduced by 20 per cent as a result of the Structural Adjustment Policy imposed by the International Monetary Fund

(IMF) on a sector that provided public health services to all our people, as well as curative services to those who could not afford to pay for private medical care.

TINA (There is no Alternative)

The decade of the nineties has also seen the promotion and proliferation of the curative, profit-oriented private health sector, many of whose professionals were trained at public expense. Both the public as well as the private sectors are now virtually dictated to by western agencies and institutions like the World Bank, USAID, WHO, and UNICEF, which promote programmes that have little relevance to our people's overall integrated health problems and needs, while increasing the country's foreign indebtedness in the process. It is a vicious cycle that perpetuates poverty and disease. Their demand for handing over public institutions like hospitals, together with their assets, to a profit-hungry private sector, which now accounts for three-fourths of our healthcare expenditure, has little regard to the universal experience of the private sector having converted health into a lucrative medical business, in collaboration with the pharmaceutical and instrumentation industry. Signing the WTO agreement will now deprive the poor even of basic health-care services as well as of cheap and essential life-saving drugs. Today, the drug industry is dominated by a purely profit-oriented and foreign-dominated pharmaceutical industry.

Data from three districts—one in Maharashtra and two in Madhya Pradesh, collected over the course of a study carried out by the Foundation for Research in Community Health, shows that even the poorest were forced to divert 20 per cent of their meagre household expenditure from food to the wrong kind of doctors and medicines. Since illness cannot be predicted, it leaves one with little choice but to seek the 'best' that is available for the care of a loved one. Relatives are distraught and have little time or choice in selecting the most rational and cost effective form of care and its provider. This state of affairs has unfortunately been promoted by the government itself, by creating an exaggerated impression of the inefficiency of the public sector, first by starving it of funds and then through by political interference, while simultaneously boosting the image of the private sector, which claims that it alone can provide the latest and best medical care, regardless of the cost or relevance. The public is made to believe that health is a subject so complex that it can only be delivered to the people in this mode and that *There is no Alternative* (TINA).

Health is too important a subject to be left entirely in the hands of medical practitioners and the powers that exist in the public or private sectors that are in league with the pharmaceutical and medical instruments industry and now also with the private medical insurance sector. All these can only serve as a supportive service but ought not to be allowed to appropriate people's health for their own benefit. There is ample evidence that effective and appropriate healthcare can be provided to all citizens at remarkably low cost without any need for private insurance. This has been demonstrated by China, Sri Lanka, Costa Rica, and India's Kerala State, as reported in the 1985 Rockefeller Foundation report *Good Health at Low Cost*. It is feasible only if the people themselves are involved and in control of a health system devised to suit their own requirements without unnecessary frills and without allowing an excessive profit motive to operate.

Community Healthcare System

To put in place a people-oriented culture of medicine, we need to return to the basics. We have to strengthen, not weaken, the age-old health culture and practices that have sustained the bodily and mental health of our people over the ages. These need to be used along with the most appropriate and relevant aspects of all available systems of health and medical care. Equally important is the use of traditional folk practices and home remedies, which are not only often effective, but can also serve as useful placebos, whose contribution to medical care is not adequately appreciated because of its low profile and insignificant cost. More often than not, the patient seeks medical advice to ascertain whether the condition is serious and requires urgent care or could become serious if neglected, or whether it is self healing, with simple medication, as in the case of the common cold. Such counseling, together with the use of our indigenous remedies and systems, can also serve an important role in reviving faith in our own traditions, culture, and practices, which are eroded by a heavily medicalised and marketised model of so-called healthcare.

The general practitioner has now replaced the family doctor with his ubiquitous injections, intravenous saline, and pills for real or imagined ills. There is also an increasing nexus between him, the pharmaceutical industry, the diagnostic clinics, and the specialists. Appropriate information and knowledge is important in avoiding such unnecessarily expensive and even dangerous practices of allopathic medicine, to which even practitioners of other systems are falling prey. Despite its useful and definite role for well-defined conditions in both health as well as medical care, the allopathic system of medicine carries with it the unfortunate western trait of converting all goods and services into commodities for sale in the market place at the highest price they can command. As a result, it fails to promote, leave aside utilise, its best and most cost-effective aspects for preventive, promotive, and curative functions. Yet, this should not prevent us from using it selectively in keeping with our needs and our culture.

Fortunately the 1981 ICSSR-ICMR report *Health for All: an Alternative Strategy* provides us with a remarkably appropriate model for tackling most of our problems of health as well as medical care, by utilising appropriate knowledge and technology from all available sources. The report starts by defining the existing problems and their underlying causes. It differentiates health from its failure, which is what concerns medical care. Even in the latter, it further differentiates important preventive and promotive aspects of medicine from the curative aspects which unfortunately dominate the present health scene. More important, it defines an alternative people-oriented and people-operated strategy. It defines the role of the people themselves, of their own health functionaries, of paramedics, and of medical and nursing profession at all levels, from the village to the services of the specialist hospital. It also describes the social, cultural, and the technical strengths and limitations of each of these functionaries as also the knowledge, skills, and facilities required at each level. Only this can help to ensure an acceptable as well as sustainable service in keeping with the available human and economic resources and local health requirements, while permitting latitude for variation in different regions, states, and even at the levels of the local self-governance bodies in rural and urban areas—the panchayats and *nagar palikas*.

Underneath the Mango Tree

The imparting of such information, knowledge, and skills to the people and their local health functionaries is most effectively achieved often under a tree or in a temple of the village rather than by didactic lectures in a distant formal "training centre". This ensures intimate interaction in our *guru-shishya* tradition between those who will subsequently work as a team under conditions relevant to local needs, local culture, and the local social and economic realities. Such training would chiefly encourage the use of existing local knowledge of health and medical practices and also relevant and cost effective available methods and systems for prevention as well as treatment. It is an approach that builds on intimate relationships and empathy, and constant availability. Notably also, the village worker, who is part of a community which she considers an extended family of 50 households, is always available and far more accountable than any external functionary can be. The public or private or even the voluntary sector could never provide these things.

Interestingly, we found that the receptivity to the readily available medical knowledge for many of the activities, even knowledge of allopathic medicine, was so high that information could be communicated in simple language, seated on a floor, to even semi-literate and even illiterate women. The knowledge, skills, and facilities required for most of such work, which can be carried out in the village setting, is remarkably simple, yet effective, safe, and cheap. The approach however requires that we discard our tendency to equate intelligence with education. There is no reason why semi-literate local women with inherent social skills cannot undertake these functions if they are provided with simple but effective medical knowledge and skills, and supported by a local functionary trained for two years and responsible for catering to a population of 2,500 to 5,000. This can ensure a graded referral service from the village to the people's health complex at the 100,000 population (*taluka* / block) level. A health training centre as well as a people's hospital providing broad-based medical and specialist services in surgery could be factored in as well. Except for the doctors and nurses, all staff of this community healthcare system would be locally recruited and trained to serve specific functions at each level, including certain clinical pathology, immunisation, and other paramedical and peri-medical functions.

Improving Hospital Services

It can be appreciated that there may be opposition in the early stages from the established professional and bureaucratic sectors. Yet, in actual practice, a decentralised system of the type I propose can help screen medical problems and relieve doctors and nurses of unnecessary overload, thus allowing them to devote more of their time to problems requiring the higher professional knowledge, skills, and facilities for which they were trained. This would also help re-establish the doctor–patient relationship. As a specialist, I am convinced and have demonstrated that the majority of specialist care can be undertaken effectively at a remarkably low cost at a people's hospital with basic surgical and medical facilities. This could also apply to the large urban public and private hospitals if the profit and kudos motives are eliminated.

Village Health Functionaries

It is evident that the majority of the functionaries at almost all levels must be women, since 70 per cent of the population consists of women and children and 90 per cent of all health and medical problems concern this group. It is also this gender that has the natural caring and nurturing instincts so essential for healthcare. Notably, in the erstwhile USSR, 80 per cent of all health workers from the *feldsher*[1] to the super specialist were females. The majority of the functions that such workers have to perform require no hard manual labour. The village health functionary should be a married woman of her own community, willing to provide part-time services to her extended family of about 200 people, more as a social service than as a health provider. She would be trained only in those aspects of healthcare that are prescribed by WHO for use by non-professionals.

Our experience shows that a woman, once empowered as a health functionary, will also take upon herself other responsibilities such as providing public information and running local micro-saving groups and other activities for her community, apart from performing functions related to veterinary medicine and running *khelwadis* for children. By taking on these kinds of responsibilities, women become empowered, while simultaneously engaging in gainful employment within their own community and home, be it a village or an urban neighbourhood. The danger of medical malpractice, which is often raised, can be readily overcome by informing the community of her training and its limitations.

A major problem of the existing public sector is its over-professionalised, over-centralised, and consequently over-bureaucratised and impersonal nature. Faced with transfers and target pressures to cater to a population of 5,000, the far more highly paid Auxiliary Nurse and Midwife (ANM) cannot establish the social rapport and commitment to the community she is paid to serve. Her functions are not decided by the requirements of her local community—they are decided in distant Delhi or in State capitals and dictated to her as 'targets' to be achieved in a formal top-down bureaucratic manner. The agenda of her work is dictated by international organisations, agencies and donors rather than by the actual local needs of the people, which vary not only from region to region but from village to village and even within each village.

Panchayati Raj and Healthcare

The Bhore Committee's[2] and WHO's Alma Ata Declaration for achieving "Health for All" will continue to remain an idle cliché until the people are provided the necessary authority and support to implement what is rightfully within their domain. It remained for the aforementioned ICSSR–ICMR report *Health for All: An Alternative Strategy* of 1981 to define a healthcare framework operating under the Panchayati Raj system of local self-governance that has been ushered in by the 73rd and 74th Constitutional amendments. Panchayati Raj Institutions (PRIs) provide the Constitutional authority for self-governance right up to the village Gram Sabha and the urban ward. Notably, health is one of the 29 subjects within the domain of the local bodies. Universal adult franchise, provided by the vision of the founder fathers of our nation, now enables the people to establish their right to for self-governance in a truly participatory manner. Though it would be a slower process than was implemented in China by the use of force, it will be in keeping with our unique culture of non-violence. Our proposed framework of people's medicine will provide extensive employment to grassroots level functionaries, and will also help to correct the dehumanising urban industrial malaise of jobless growth. This new form of health and illness care may also provide a unique contribution to the world at large, which is drifting towards a mindless materialism based on ruthless exploitation, even in a field like health.

People's Medicine in Action

The following are a few examples of how even some of the major diseases and health problems can be tackled in a comprehensive community healthcare system of the type I've discussed above. Two researchers—Dr Abhay and Dr Rani Bang, have demonstrated that tribal mothers have been able to markedly reduce deaths from acute pneumonia—the commonest cause of mortality in children, by simple monitoring of respiratory signs and giving a simple sulphonamide antibiotic. To cite another case in point, it is possible to take simple and effective measures to contain water-borne diseases, which account for 80 per cent of illnesses in rural areas. Once the presence of microbes in water are demonstrated through the school microscope and people are taught how to clean and chlorinate their water sources, the Village Health Functionary (VHF) can mobilise the community for this purpose. She can also ensure rehydration therapy in the early stages and refer a few advanced cases to her own *sahayogini* at the group Gram Panchayat level for intravenous or intra-peritoneal rehydration (see Chart).

Since the Village Functionary knows the index case of tuberculosis in her community, she can readily track new cases in the locality utilising the five cardinal symptoms taught to her. This enables early detection and reference to the people's hospital for confirmation of diagnosis. Continuity of treatment as well as prevention of spread can be ensured by her by personal communication, example and support. The system can be far superior to a separate vertical programme of DOTS operated by a highly paid external functionary—all at virtually no cost. Any complication of the diseases or the drugs can be referred to the next level/s of reference (see Chart). Again, in the intensely personal area of family planning, there can be no better functionary than the local village health functionary who is a friend, and who will guide a woman with contraceptive practices suitable for her specific needs. She will also take care of the mother as well as of her children without "target" pressures. This can help her achieve results better than a far more highly paid ANM serving a population of 5,000.

Organisational Aspects

The organisational chart demonstrates that about 70 per cent of all health and medical care can be undertaken by part-time VHFs responsible for a population of 200 living in 50 households in her neighborhood, when she is supported by trained personal operating at the 2,500–5,000 population level. The latter, after undergoing a two-year period of training, would have greater knowledge, clinical skills, and facilities and be supported with simple telemedicine and communications. It is estimated that about 85 per cent of all problems can be tackled at this first referral level. Ninety-five per cent can be taken care of within the block/taluka, with recourse to the people's health and hospital complex at that level (see Chart). All staff from the village level to the people's health complex must be under the administrative and financial control of *panchayats*, if the system is to function efficiently. Only a few problems would remain to be addressed by super specialist care at the district or city hospital. A Reverse Referral System (RRS) would ensure weekly contact for health and medical purposes between all functionaries, the community and patients (see Chart). It also would provide for continuous monitoring and support of all activities, ensure education of all functionaries within this system, and maintain a traditional *guru-shishya* relationship between all functionaries.

That such a system can be technically, socially and economically self-sustaining has been demonstrated in our project at Parinche, near Pune. Of the 17 originally trained by us, six trained another 50 who have in turn trained 1,400 in other districts of Maharashtra, in addition to those who have come to learn from other States. Armed with the self confidence their training has given them, they have proved to be highly effective communicators on health and many other subjects concerning rural development.

Chart: Organisational Structure, Community Health Care System (CHCS)

<table>
<tr><th>Population (approximately)</th><th>Functionary</th><th>Responsibility to</th><th>Proportion of total services covered</th></tr>
<tr><td>200</td><td>Community Health Functionary</td><td>Neighbourhood Group</td><td>70%</td></tr>
<tr><td>1,000</td><td>Village Health Functionary</td><td>Gram Panchayat</td><td></td></tr>
<tr><td>5,000</td><td>Sahyogini (referral centre functionary)</td><td>Group Gram Panchayat</td><td>85%</td></tr>
<tr><td colspan="4">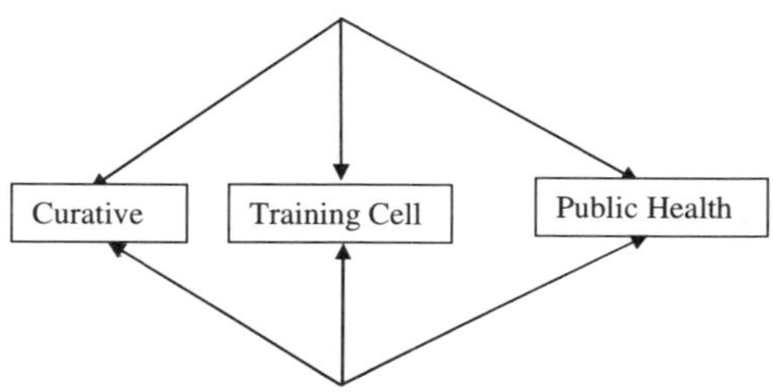
</td></tr>
<tr><td>1,00,000</td><td>People's Health Complex</td><td>Panchayati Samiti</td><td>95%</td></tr>
</table>

Cost Effectiveness

A cost effective community healthcare system of the type I have described can be provided at about Rs 200 per capita per annum to cover 95 per cent of all health problems at the block/*taluka* level and enable effective healthcare for all citizens at less than half the government's expenditure of Rs 678 per capita (1999–2000) (Table 1). It will do so in a more personalised and humane manner. Such a system can also be adopted for the Nagar Palikas—the local self-governance bodies in urban areas. Even allowing for another Rs 100 per capita—for tertiary care as well as administrative costs, the proposed scheme would provide 'Health for All' citizens at less than half the expenditure of Rs 678 per capita (1999–2000), releasing about Rs 30,000 crores for expenditure on auxiliary health-giving activities like public information, education, empowerment of adolescent girls and women, and improvement of the Pubic Distribution System (PDS).

The following are some of the reasons for the cost-effectiveness of the community healthcare system:

- high visibility to all;
- low salaries for almost all staff at local scales, except for the few doctors and nurses recruited at the prevailing market rate;
- use of locally available buildings and building material and facilities such as *dharmashalas* and the like;
- use of limited number of generic drugs through bulk purchase;
- use of all systems, including folk medicine;
- improved prevention, early detection, and early treatment; and
- absence of the profit motive.

Demystifying Medicine

People's medicine through a Community Health Care System has the potential to provide useful employment to millions of women within the communities. It is also an effective means for women's empowerment, introduced by demystifying one of the most mystified of all subjects. This I believe is as important as the health and medical care that is provided. A well informed, self-confident woman who can sustain herself economically by undertaking a variety of tasks within her community and society, can also provide the basis for successful implementation of Panchayat Raj. It is a scenario that chimes in with the vision of Durgabai Deskmukh who as a social reformer, had infinite trust as well as confidence in the women of this land. I believe that with their quiet strength, they will help us achieve our goal.

Table 1: Integrated Community Health Care System for a Population of 100,000—Administrative Framework and per Capita Cost of Health Care per Annum

Level	Number of Units	Number of Staff	Per Capita Salaries	Cost per Annum (Rupees)	
				Drugs & Supplies	Total per capita Cost
Village	100	500	28.80	19.20	48.00
5,000 Population	20	80	19.00	12.67	31.67
People's Hospital	1	44	29.00	19.33	48.33
People's Health Complex	1	18	15.00	22.50	37.50
Sub Total		642	91.80	73.70	165.50
Transport & Communications					20
Total Cost per Capita per Annum					185.50

NOTES

1. A medical or surgical practitioner without full professional qualifications or status in some east European countries and especially Russia (Merriam-Webster) http://www.merriam-webster.com/dictionary/feldsher
2. The Bhore committee was set up by the government of India in 1943 to investigate and recommend improvements to the Indian Public Health system. Under the chairmanship of Sir Joseph Bhore the committee made many landmark recommendations in its final report in 1946.

3

Promise and Problems of Biology and Biotechnology*

Pushpa M. Bhargava

An important prediction over the last 15 years or so made by scientists all over the world (and I have been just one of them) is that our lives—certainly for 200 years if not more—would be governed by advances in just about 10 areas. Let me list them: biotechnology and modern biology, information technology, space, energy, robotics and automation, microelectronics, computers, nanotechnology, new materials, and artificial intelligence. My objective here is to share my perception of one of these areas, that is, modern biology and biotechnology, with its various implications.

The history of science has repeatedly demonstrated that once we begin to understand the basic rules that govern any area in science, we automatically gravitate towards applying this knowledge for the benefit of or gain to mankind. This is what happened in chemistry: when we began to understand the laws of chemical combination and so on, we had the Industrial Revolution. This is what happened in physics around the beginning of the last century. It led to the physics-based revolutions, with radio, television, X-rays, lasers, optical fibres, and integrated circuits. And this is what happened around the 1970s in biology: enough came to be known about the fundamentals of life—the chemistry, the biochemistry, the structure, and the function of *living* systems—to make the emergence of modern biotechnology inevitable.

Scope of Biotechnology

When I finished my university education, which was more than five decades ago, only 5 per cent of the scientific literature was in biology including, medicine and agriculture. Today, over 80 per cent of the entire scientific and technological literature is represented by biological sciences.

* Edited transcript of July 15, 2003, Durgabai Deshmukh Memorial Lecture by Dr Pushpa M. Bhargava.

Today's biotechnology consists of at least 25 well-defined areas, some of which were predicted while others came about unexpectedly. I would now like to list the above-mentioned areas of biotechnology and say a few words about those which would not seem to be self-explanatory.

(i) Genetic engineering: I had the privilege of coining the term "genetic engineering" in 1973; I was, in fact, one of the two who did so independently that year. Today, the term is a part of common vocabulary. Genetics—that is, the DNA of the organism—determines its capabilities, while the environment determines the extent to which these capabilities would be converted into abilities. Let me explain with an analogy. I have no doubt that normally, anyone in India can, if required, learn Spanish or Chinese, but the chances are that there would be relatively few who would be proficient in either of these languages as of now, the reason being that they never had the need to learn the language. Similarly, there are a large number of people in the country, for example in our villages, who do not know how to drive a motor vehicle but given an opportunity, most of them would have no problem in doing so. On the other hand, the mighty elephant or the powerful tiger or lion cannot learn any of the languages we can, nor can we teach them how to drive a truck or a car, for the simple reason that they do not have the genetic capabilities for doing so.

In genetic engineering, all that we do is to identify a piece of the DNA, or the genetic material that is responsible for a particular capability of the parent organism, scissor this DNA out and transfer it to an organism which does not have the above capability, in such a way that the foreign DNA now becomes an integral part of the total complement of recipient DNA, that is, the foreign DNA is incorporated in the recipient genome. As a consequence, the genome now acquires a new capability. The second challenge in genetic engineering is to convert this newly acquired capability into ability by providing the right environment in the recipient organism.

The common bacterium, *E.Coli,* or yeast, does not have the capability of making human insulin, a widely used drug for treating diabetes. However, we can, today, isolate the gene—a piece of the human DNA, for human insulin, and transfer it into *E. Coli,* so that *E. Coli* now has the *capability* to make insulin. We can then make this gene express in *E.Coli* or yeast so that it now *actually produces* human insulin. This is how human insulin is being made today. Less than a decade earlier, the insulin used was cattle or pig insulin, to which a number of patients did not respond. Innumerable lives are now saved because human insulin produced by genetically engineered micro-organisms is now available commercially. In India, too, our own human insulin made through genetic engineering as above will be in the market later this year.

Genetically engineered microbes are today widely used in the above manner to produce and make available on a large scale and at a low cost, many drugs and vaccines of great importance besides human insulin, such as erythropoietin, interferon, and Hepatitis B vaccine. Indian companies are already marketing genetically engineered erythropoietin and Hepatitis B vaccine at costs which are a fraction of what the cost of the imported product was before we started manufacturing it.

Genetically engineered plants—for example, those that make their own pesticides or are resistant to weedicides—are already in the market. Thus, over 60 per cent of the acreage under soya bean in the United States has now genetically engineered soya bean that is resistant to a weedicide called Roundup. In fact, the total acreage under genetically engineered crops (for good or for bad) around the world exceeds 100 million acres today.

Genetically engineered plants are also poised to produce vaccines. A few hundred acres of genetically engineered banana plantation can provide enough vaccine to annually immunise120 million children who need to be protected against four common diseases. One of the future sources of cheap protein-drugs in the coming years would be genetically engineered animals who would secrete these drugs in abundance (1-15 mg/ml) in their milk, thus making them available at a cost which could be three or more orders of magnitude lower than the current cost.

(ii) *Gene therapy:* This refers, in a way, to genetic engineering of humans. It allows a person suffering from a disabling genetic disorder to lead a normal life. The first case of gene therapy occured two decades ago when a young girl suffering from adenosine deaminase deficiency (a genetic disorder that causes immunodeficiency) was treated in this manner. Her blood cells were taken out, genetically engineered to correct the deficiency, and then put back.

(iii) *Immuno-technologies for diagnosis and therapy:* Antibodies, a special set of proteins, are an important weapon in the armoury of higher animals such as humans. Antibodies in their blood enable them to fight incursion of their bodies by harmful chemicals or micro-organisms. *Monoclonal* Anti-Bodies (MABs) are a species of antibodies prepared in the laboratory by a special technique for which a Nobel Prize was awarded in the 1980s to Cesar Milstein and Georges Kohler. MABs can have different functions. For diagnosis of human diseases, one can use, say, mouse MABs; for therapy, however, one would require human MABs. As human MABs are difficult to produce in the

laboratory, genetically engineered plants are poised to find wide application in the production of human MABs. Technologies are also being developed to humanise animal MABs. The market for MABs for diagnosis alone, in just Hyderabad, may be about Rs 10 crores.

(iv) *Tissue culture:* Modern tissue culture technologies allow the multiplication in the laboratory of cells isolated from plants and animals. Tissue culture of both plant and animal cells has applications for micro-propagation of elite or exotic materials (such as orchids), production of useful compounds such as taxol (the widely used anti-cancer drug) and vanillin, and preparation in the laboratory of "natural" tissues such as arteries for arterial graft, or skin for burn victims. In the case of plant tissue cultures, one can grow in the lab a whole plant from a single cell. This technology was developed more than five decades ago by Stewart in the United Kingdom. The second largest foreign exchange earner for Thailand is export of orchids grown through tissue culture, which brings the country revenue of some 700 crores of rupees every year. It is unfortunate that we are not doing something of the sort, given the 600 and odd species of orchids found in Arunachal Pradesh—especially when techniques for growing them in tissue culture have already been standardised by Arunachal Pradesh's scientists.

(v) *Stem cell techniques*: Stem cells are cells that are either totipotent (as most plant cells are)—that is, they have the capability to produce any desired cell type or organ of the body under specific conditions—or they can be pluripotent, that is, they are able to develop into several, though not all, cell types or organs. As embryonic stem cells are more likely to have capabilities nearing totipotency than stem cells from adult tissues, the immediate emphasis in the area of stem cells is going to be first in the direction of establishing cell lines derived from early human embryos, from which stem cells could be isolated. The numerous infertility clinics of our country will be, perhaps, the best source of such embryos. Stem cell techniques involve purification and isolation of stem cells from various tissues, and their directed development into the desired tissue, which could then be used for transplantation. This can be of immense practical value. Remember, for example, that as of today we have only some 2,000 kidneys available annually as of today for transplantation, when over 90,000 patients require such transplantation every year.

(vi) *Enzyme engineering and technology:* Enzymes are biological catalysts (generally proteins) and are poised to replace the inorganic catalysts widely used in the chemical industry today. The use of enzymes in today's chemical industry offers many advantages: no by-products (so, lesser expenditure on purification of the primary product); no

pollution; and much less expenditure on energy—for enzyme-catalysed reactions take place at our ambient temperatures (30-37°C) and at ordinary pressure, unlike reactions catalysed by inorganic catalysts that require high temperature and pressure.

(vii) *Increasing photosynthetic efficiency:* to increase biomass production in the plant, using the same amount of light and other inputs.

(viii) *New DNA technologies:*

- DNA fingerprinting (which allows unequivocal identification of an individual even from a single hair-root). The DNA fingerprinting technology developed in the CCMB (Centre for Cellular and Molecular Biology) at Hyderabad by Lalji Singh has helped resolve innumerable paternity disputes and some hundreds of criminal cases such as the Rajiv Gandhi assassination case and the Tandoor murder case.
- Development of DNA-based probes for diagnosis of inherited disorders (some 5,000 such disorders are already known), is another DNA technology.[1] Production of DNA-based probes for diagnosis of genetic disorders is bound to become a major business.
- Sequencing of genomes (genomes, as we have earlier noted, refer to the total complement of DNA).
- Plant identification and characterisation by developing new molecular markers.
- Antisense technologies aimed at blockage of the function of a particular stretch of DNA (that is, a specific gene).
- Computing. DNA technologies can also be used for computing. As of today, DNA-based computing is slow but it is a matter of time for it to become competitive. Remember how slow the computers at the beginning of the last half-century were when compared to today's machines.

(ix) *Plant-based drugs:* Use of modern biological techniques for validation, standardisation, and manufacture of indigenous plant-based drug formulations (where necessary, appropriately modified). This area is of special interest to our country and has the potential of making us the world-leader in medical care. We have some 40,000 unique traditional plant-based drug formulations that have come to us through the documented Ayurveda, Unani, Siddha, and Tibetan systems of medicine, and the undocumented-tribal medicine systems. They are based on, perhaps, 10,000 medicinal plants out of which at least 7,000 have been documented already. There are infallible arguments supporting the view that while a proportion of these formulations is unlikely to work if tested impartially, using modern validation protocols, a fair number of them—in my estimate, at least 4,000—are extremely likely to work and be shown to be efficacious. Against this background, it is extremely sad that we have only one traditional formulation, Liv 52, marketed by Himalaya Drug Company, which is today a prescription drug in some parts of the world outside India. We ourselves have prepared a project according to which it should be possible to document these 40,000 formulations over a period of 10 years and to market at least 100 standardised and validated traditional plant-based drug formulations during this period, which would bring in a net profit (after deduction of tax) of above rupees 6,000 crores at the end of the tenth year at today's prices.

(x) Peptide synthesis: Proteins, the major constituents of living systems, include peptides, which are small proteins of, say, 2 to 50 aminoacids.[2] As it turns out, over the last three decades, a very large number of peptides have been shown to have useful pharmacological activity. For example, when we discovered in the CCMB (Centre for Cellular and Molecular Biology) the 47 aminoacid peptide, seminalplasmin, it was the second such peptide shown to have antimicrobial activity. Peptides are used to make new drugs or other materials of industrial and/or commercial importance, such as salmon GnRH analogue (Ovaprim) to induce ovulation in fish. Today, there are perhaps more than 1,000 such peptides known. Many peptides are already in the market to serve various purposes but that is clearly not even the tip of the iceberg. In fact, we can safely predict that by the end of the next four decades, plant-based drug formulations derived from traditional medicine around the world (such as India, China, and Latin America), will account for some 50 per cent of the drugs in the market; 20 per cent will be produced through genetic engineering, 5 per cent will be monoclonal antibodies, 5 per cent would come through rational drug design, and 20 per cent would be peptides.

(xi) Assisted Reproductive Technologies (ART): Assisted Reproductive Technologies refer to the use of biotechnology to facilitate reproduction. It includes artificial insemination (using husband's or donor semen); technologies called "In Vitro Fertilisation" and "Intracytoplasmic Sperm Injection"; and techniques involving egg donation, embryo transfer, and surrogate motherhood to help couples who are infertile or to help women who do not wish to go through a pregnancy to have their own biological child. Infertility is the most highly prevalent "disease" in the world, with some 15 per cent of couples being infertile. As of today, with the help of the assisted reproductive technologies I have mentioned above, it is possible to take care of 85 per cent of the infertility cases and make them conceive. In Vitro Fertilisation (IVF) was first used successfully by Robert Edwards and Patrick Steptoe to produce the first test-tube baby, Louise Brown, who was born in July 1978. Today, the technology has

advanced to a stage where one can just take a single sperm (say, from men that are infertile on account of low sperm count) and then inject it into an oocyte to effect In Vitro Fertilisation; this technique is called Introcytoplasmic Sperm Injection.

One can today freeze embryos and then bring them back to life at any given point later on and implant them into the uterus of a woman. Thus, a woman can give birth to a child from her husband even after he has passed away.

In surrogate motherhood, a couple who is otherwise normally fertile but the wife does not want to go through the nine-month pregnancy that would confine her for a substantial period, can have the egg of the wife fertilised by the sperm of her husband in the test tube and then have the fertilised egg implanted, not in the uterus of the wife but that of another woman who would then give birth to a child totally unrelated to her. The development of IVF technologies has made it possible for an infertile couple to have a child using the egg or the sperm of a donor if necessary.

(xii) *New cloning technologies:* As you would recall, Dolly was the first cloned animal produced in the laboratory. That is what we do when we grow another plant from a cutting. Similarly, when we grow an entire plant from a single cell in tissue culture, we are essentially cloning the plant from which the cell used for the tissue culture was derived. As it turns out, the cloning of animals has been much more difficult. These difficulties have now been largely overcome and cloning of animals is now commonplace. The Centre for Cellular and Molecular Biologyat Hyderabad has been trying to conserve endangered animal species through cloning.

(xiii) *Organ transplantation, especially xenotransplantation:* that is, transplantation into humans of organs from other animals. It appears that, for xenotransplantation, the pig may be the most suitable, biochemically, anatomically, and immunologically. The major problem in xenotransplantation is the hyper-acute immunological rejection of the "foreign organ", which occurs in a matter of minutes. By contrast, hyper-acute immunological rejection does not occur in homotransplantations, for example, in the case of a kidney transplant from one human donor to another human recipient. Hyper-acute immunological rejection has been recently overcome by identifying the molecular basis of the hyper-acute rejection and then genetically engineering a pig to avoid it.

(xiv) *New drug-delivery systems:* It has been found that different people have different circadian or biological rhythms. Thus, the level of drug-metabolising enzymes may be minimal at, let us say 12 p.m., midday, and 12 a.m. in one individual, while this may be so at 6 a.m. and 6

p.m. for another individual. If we give the drug to the patient at a time that it would be metabolised to a much lesser degree, one would need to give smaller amounts of the drug than otherwise. When we have ways and means of quickly assessing such circadian rhythms, we would be entering the age of individualised medicine which would be less expensive and less toxic for the individual.

Another notable development in drug delivery is the use of electrical patches to dispense medication at pre-determined intervals. Thus, a patch on your skin (if you are diabetic) could take care of your insulin requirements for, say, a month. All that you would need to do is to carry a small pocket computer (like a cell phone) which has been programmed to direct the electrical patch to release a measured amount of drug at pre-defined intervals; the drug would then get electrophoresed through the skin on account of the generation of a voltage gradient and then get into the blood stream. This would replace the cumbersome injections of insulin that so many around the world have to take, often twice a day.

(xv) *Nutraceuticals:* These are organisms that help recovery after surgery or after an episode of a major disease, or help protect one against certain medical and health problems. For example, a Swedish company, Probi, has isolated a strain of *Lactobacillus planetarum* which is apparently present in the digestive tract of Europeans and Americans. (Indians have not yet been tested for its presence). The presence of this organism has been correlated with the ability of the person to recover after major surgery or after chemotherapy of cancer; this organism also seems to protect people against a vast range of stomach disorders including stomach ulcers, irritable bowel syndrome, and constipation. If this organism is depleted from the digestive tract, one becomes far more susceptible to the after effects of surgery or cancer chemotherapy. Probi is, therefore, marketing this organism in various forms including a highly delicious soft drink!

(xvi) *Rational drug design:* Until a few decades ago, the only way to discover a new drug was to synthesise a very large number of compounds, mostly on an *ad hoc* basis, in the hope that one of them would turn out to be effective against a particular disease. This led to a situation where it cost something between half a billion to a billion dollars for bringing a new drug in the market. Consequently, over the last many years, we have not added more than, say, 10 new drugs per year to the repertoire of medicines already available. In rational drug design, we first identify the molecular target that we wish to attack. To do so, it becomes necessary to understand the mechanism of causation of the disease. Once we understand this mechanism and identify the molecular target, we have, today, highly effective computerised programmes to design a molecule which would hit the target. This is what rational drug design is about. It could cut the cost of discovery of a new drug by one order of magnitude and, in addition, reduce the time from concept to marketing (now 12–15 years) to 7–8 years.

(xvii) *Production of useful materials - existing or new- from so far unutilised or underutilised but widely available resources, such as marine organisms:* India is already producing high quality beta-carotene (which gets converted to vitamin A in the body). Beta-carotene, like polyunsaturated fats, is essential for normal vision. Beta-carotene is being manufactured from *Donaliela,* a marine alga, at a factory of *Shantha Marine* near Tiruchendur in Tamil Nadu. I have the pleasure of being the Chairman of Shanta Marine. We are able to produce beta-carotene at a very low cost, as the Tiruchendur coast has some 340 days of uninterrupted sunshine and the right temperatures all through the year. All that we need to do is to pump the sea water from the coast in open raceways, and seed them with the organism that we have isolated. The sun does the rest. We have, therefore, an enormous saving in energy cost. We have, in fact, offered to take care of the entire Vitamin A requirement of our children as prescribed by the WHO for Rs 8 per child per month if the government is willing to put it in the midday meal programme and we are assured that what we supply would be used for this purpose.

(xviii) *Production of new materials using new ideas, observations or research findings:* such as bacterial ropes or biodegradable polymers. For example, bacterial ropes that essentially consist of certain mutant bacteria which have the ability to grow into spaghetti like structures, when impregnated with certain metal ions, can be stronger than steel but much lighter and biodegradable.

(xix) *DNA vaccines:* which would be much cheaper than protein antigen-based vaccines that are generally used today.

(xx) *New medical diagnostic technologies:* Let us take the case of a person suffering from neurocystosarcosis—a disease caused by a parasitic infection of the brain. This infection can occur through uncooked pork or unwashed raw vegetables. The parasite can undergo three possible fates in the brain: remain active and alive, die, or remain dormant. If you look at the MRI of such a brain, you will be able to see the cysts caused by the parasite but not know which cyst is dead, alive or dormant. This becomes important as we have drugs which can be safely given only if the number of live cysts is small. PET-SCAN can distinguish between an active, a dormant, or a dead cyst. Thus, we are talking about the combination of the well known technique of MRI, which gives information about the structure of a system, with the new technique of PET-SCAN, which gives information on the system's functioning.

Unfortunately, we do not have any commercial full-fledged PET-SCAN machine in India as of today. The Department of Atomic Energy (DAE), at a meeting held in Mumbai on April 17, 2003, has apparently decided to locate two medical cyclotrons—one in Kolkata and the other in Hyderabad—to produce the short-lived radioisotopes needed for a PET-SCAN. If the DAE does that, a consortium of hospitals in Hyderabad is ready to buy the PET-SCAN machine and run the whole establishment.

(xxi) *Biosensors:* for example, optical sensors using special thin films for detection of bacteria.

(xxii) *Use of microbes (selected or genetically engineered) for effecting chemically difficult transformations:* for example in the field of steroids that are widely used as drugs.

(xxiii) *Bio-remediation:* for example of effluents or waste, using biological systems. A septic tank and an oxidation pond are simple examples of such bioremediation. Production of biogas is value-added bioremediation!

(xxiv) *Processing of low-grade ores using micro-organisms:* Commercially viable bio-processes are available today for processing such ores of over a dozen metals.

(xxv) *Bioinformatics:* including genomics and proteomics. It is amazing how quickly bioinformatics has, like biotechnology, become a part of the common vocabulary of man around the world. Bioinformatics involves analysis of data pertaining to biological systems and converting this analysis into commercially exploitable knowledge. This could be data on the sequence of the building blocks in DNA or in protein. For example, one could look at the sequence of the genome (DNA) of a pathogenic microorganism and discover new drug targets—an exercise in which, as of today, amongst others, the bioinformatics group of Sathyam Computers at Hyderabad is actively engaged. Remember, there are several million species known. The sequence of the building blocks of DNA of just one human being alone will fill nearly 700 books (typed single space) of 500 pages each. So there is an immense amount of information pertaining to biological systems that is waiting to be analysed!

(xxvi) *Nanobiotechnology:* in which the operating or useful unit is of the scale of, say, a nanometre (millionth of a millimetre). It is today possible to entrap molecules in nanostructures and carry out reactions in such structures, which offer many advantages. However, as of today, this is only an emerging and exciting field to pursue.

(xxvii) *Biological warfare:* Recall the anthrax attack in the US in 2001. Today, it is possible to design even ethnic weapons that would target only a particular group.

Advantages of Biotechnologies

Biotechnologies are always non-polluting and, often, labour intensive. They make use of replenishable natural resources and help their conservation. They help, directly or indirectly, in saving energy. The cost of products produced through a biotechnological process is almost always less than that of the same product produced, say, through a chemical synthetic route.

Biotechnologies are less accident-prone. In spite of their high level of intellectual sophistication, it is easier to train people to handle biotechnologies than other technologies. Above all, they are interesting and exciting for all those involved with them.

No other country in the world today has the unique set of advantages that India offers for large-scale practice of biotechnology. We have one of the largest bio-diversities—including human biodiversity—in the world. We also have one of the largest coastlines anywhere. We have at least seven distinct climatic zones, and one of the largest and most varied set of marine organisms anywhere. The ambient temperature in most parts of the country—often all the year round—is just what living organisms need for their activities that result in a biotechnological product; this curtails immensely the cost of cooling or heating which becomes obligatory for the practice of biotechnology in most parts of the Western world. There are places on the Indian coast (like Tiruchendur already mentioned), where there is uninterrupted sunshine for some 340 days in the year so that one can grow marine organisms in open raceways.

We have an enviable infrastructure and a large pool of trained manpower, with experience in most of the areas of biotechnology. Our labour and infrastructural costs are, perhaps, lower than anywhere else where biotechnology can be done and is being done, with the possible exception of China. We have large tracts of land where the plants required for agriculture-based biotechnologies can be grown. We have experience of building world-class institutions in virtually every sector of human endeavour—from outstanding basic research to efficient industrial production. We have, of course, many problems but we also know how to overcome them; in a nutshell, the advantages, far outweigh the disadvantages.

It is a pity that we started much later in biotechnology than we should and could have, but even now, the prospects for the future are bright, provided we have an appropriate biotechnology policy, adequate investment both in the private and the public sector, and adequate cooperation between research institutions and industry.

Implications of Modern Biotechnology

Never before in history have newly emerging areas of knowledge had so many diverse implications and import as modern biology and biotechnology. The primary reason for this is that biology touches our lives as no other science does.

The areas in biotechnology with significant socio-politico-economic, ethical, moral, and legal implications are genetic engineering, gene therapy, tissue culture, stem cell culture, DNA technologies (including DNA fingerprinting, DNA-based diagnosis, and sequencing of genomes), plant-based drugs, assisted reproductive technologies (ART), cloning technologies, organ transplantation, bioinformatics, and biological weapons. I will deal with the implications of ART and genetic engineering in some detail, but before I do that I would like to give a few examples from other areas.

DNA Fingerprinting

Not long ago, a case was referred to the CCMB (Centre for Cellular and Molecular Biology) at Hyderabad by the British immigration authorities. It involved an Indian couple living in England with two children, who had a third child in India while they were visiting the country. When they wished to take the third child back to England, the immigration authorities asked them to establish that they were the biological parents of the child, in order to rule out the possibility that they were bringing an abandoned child for sale in the UK. The case was referred to the CCMB for DNA fingerprinting. When Lalji Singh, the then Director of the CCMB, did the DNA fingerprinting of the entire family, he found that while the child born in India was the child of the husband and wife who were taking it to the UK, one of the two children living with them in England was not their child. The wife evidently had had a clandenstine extra maritial affair and the child in question was born of that liaison. The question Lalji Singh faced was: what was he to say to the immigration authorities? If the truth was told to them and later became known to the parents, the family may break up. On the other hand, would hiding the truth be ethical? What Lalji Singh finally decided was to answer only the question that he was asked by the immigration authorities, and keep to himself the other relevant information he had discovered. Did Lalji Singh do the right thing?

Genetic Disorders

Let us consider the ethical implications of another area of biotechnology—predicting the likelihood that an individual whose genetic makeup makes him susceptible to a disease will actually contract that disease at some point in the future. Genetic disorders can be classified broadly into two categories. In the case of one category, if you carry the particular defective gene(s), you are bound to suffer from the disorder sooner or later in your life. This is the case with sickle cell anaemia, thallasemia, cystic fibrosis, haemophilia, or albinism. There are, however, a much large number of genes, called susceptibility genes, the presence of which only makes one susceptible to the disease sometime in the person's life. As of today, we do not know what environmental or lifestyle factors are responsible for converting the susceptibility status in such cases to the diseased status later in the life of an individual. All we can say today in this regard is based entirely on statistical data; so we can only say what the chances are of a person having a particular susceptibility gene becoming diseased later in life. For example, if a woman carries a BrC 1 or BrC 2 gene, it makes her more likely to have breast cancer later in her life than those who do not have such a gene. Thus, the incidence of one of these genes amongst the Parsis is the highest in the country; so is the incidence of breast cancer in Parsi women. However, having these genes does not mean that one is bound to have breast cancer.

Now put yourself in the position of a doctor, say 20 years hence, when we should have cheap technologies available for screening a new-born child for the presence of a large number of such susceptibility genes. You take your child to the doctor and he finds out that the child is carrying a gene that puts him at a 20 per cent risk of suffering from a particular disease after he crosses 40. Should he or should he not share this information with you? If he does, and the child turns out to be amongst the 80 per cent who does not suffer from the disease after crossing 40, you could sue the doctor for keeping you and the child in suspense for 40 years for nothing. If, on the other hand, the doctor does not share the above information with you, and the child happens to be amongst the 20 per cent who suffers from the disease after crossing 40, you could again sue the doctor for withholding information which would have made you better prepared to meet the challenge of the disease.

Plant Based Formulations

Suppose you have obtained a traditional plant-based drug formulation from a tribe which the tribe has been using for a 1000 years. You then commercialise and make money out of it, without sharing it with the tribe. Would it be ethical? And even if you wished to share the profits, how much should go to the tribe?

There is a plant called *Phyllanthus amarus* which has been used widely in virtually all parts of the country in several indigenous medical systems of ours, as well as in many other parts of the world, to cure certain liver disorders. Since the use of our traditional drugs is based on symptoms, what is implied is that the above plant-based drug formulation could take care of certain symptoms, without the disease as we know of it today having been identified. What the Nobel prize-winning scientist, Barry Blumberg (who discovered the Hepatitis B virus) did was to show that extracts of *Phyllanthus amarus* inhibited two key enzymes of the Hepatitis B virus and eliminated the virus from the system in an animal model, thus indicating that the extract could be a cure for human Hepatitis B and might even clear off the Hepatitis B virus from its nearly 300 million carriers worldwide. He obtained two patents on this work,[3] giving due credit to ancient Indian tradition for use of the plant to treat diseases whose symptoms corresponded to those of, amongst other diseases, Hepatitis B. Legally, these patents could not be challenged, as none of the ancient medical systems in our country ever claimed to have cured Hepatitis B using extracts of *Phyllanthus amarus*. However, were these patents morally or ethically justified?

Consider also the case of vanillin. We are all familiar with its fragrance — who has not heard of vanilla ice cream? Till recently, virtually the entire vanillin of the world came from Malagasy Republic where 70,000 farmers have been involved in cultivation of vanillin. Now, vanillin is being produced more cheaply through tissue culture by American and Japanese companies. There is, therefore, no market for vanillin produced naturally, and the 70,000 farmers may be facing unemployment. Has all this been fair?

Another case in point pertains to a protein called thaumatin, found in a particular plant endemic to parts of Africa, such as Nigeria. Thaumatin is 5,000 times sweeter than sugar and is completely non-toxic. Being a protein, it is degraded in the digestive tract after ingestion and, therefore, does not get into the blood stream. It has been also produced through genetic engineering. I believe it may not be difficult to make it 50,000 times sweeter than sugar. Once we do that we can produce it at a cost which would be a fraction of the cost of the cheapest cane sugar or beet sugar around the world. If that happens, some seven million workers in the sugarcane industry in the third world alone may face unemployment. This would be a major socio-economic problem. How should we brace ourselves to face it?

Therapeutic Cloning

Is therapeutic cloning ethical? By therapeutic cloning, I mean cloning an individual and allowing the foetus to grow to a stage where organogenesis has begun, so that one could harvest organs, which could then be further grown in the laboratory, to be eventually transplanted in the cloned individual. In such cases, there will be no immunological rejection of any kind. No two individuals, except twins, who are like clones of each other, are immunologically identical— in all other cases, without an immune-suppressive drug, the transplanted organ will be rejected. Cloning for the harvesting and transplantation of organs offers a solution in that it obviates the need for expensive immune-suppressive agents like cyclosporine. But the question remains: Is the therapeutic cloning of humans ethical?

We have seen earlier, while discussing the various types of biotechnologies, how hyper-acute immunological rejection has been recently overcome by identifying the molecular basis of the hyper-acute rejection and then genetically engineering a pig to avoid it (item xiii of the list of biotechnologies). There can, however, be ethical concerns about xenotransplantation using pigs. There may be objections to it on religious grounds, amongst certain sections of the world population. If so, how should one deal with it? Will such transplantation be considered ethical by Muslims?

There was recently a case in the United States in which a child born to an American couple was found to be suffering from a rare blood disorder. A remedy was suggested to the couple: if they agreed to produce another child—which they wanted, in any case, the newborn could be the salvation of the sick offspring. A procedure was envisaged by which, after IVF (In Vitro Fertilisation), an embryo whose immunological makeup corresponds to that of the sick child is implanted in the mother. Eventually, transplantation of cells from the newborn could cure his ailing sibling, with no harmful effects to the former.[4] This was precisely what was done by the couple. The second child was a son; cells from the umbilical cord of the second child were transplanted into the diseased child, who was then cured. It was a win-win situation for everyone. Yet the question was raised: was it ethical to produce a pre-selected child? Notably, a similar procedure was recently approved for a British couple in the United Kingdom. [5]

In the latter part of the last half century, the Chinese had a female chimpanzee inseminated with human sperm. It is believed that the idea of the Chinese was to develop a race which would have the minimal intelligence of human beings and the strength of a chimpanzee—a kind of a slave race. In fact, the pregnancy was established. It was, however, terminated during the Cultural Revolution. Scientifically, the results of such an experiment would be extremely interesting, and such experiments are not difficult to do. Should we permit them or put a moratorium on them?

Biological Warfare

Biological warfare is upon us. I have discussed its history and various ramifications in a series of articles in the *The New Indian Express*.[6] As I have already mentioned, we can today design ethnic weapons that would affect only a particular segment of world's population. For example, Americans above 50 are known to have a depleted immune response. Therefore, certain pathogenic organisms released in the environment may affect only the elderly Americans but would leave us, the Indians, completely unaffected. The depleted immune response in the older Americans is likely to be a consequence of the fact that they have lived in a virtually semi-sterile environment so that their immune system has not been challenged enough and could have atrophied. On the other hand, we in India are being continuously challenged by low levels of infection in our environment and, therefore, our immune system is robust. We can thus exploit this advantage to produce an ethnic-specific weapon. Would that be ethical?

Recently, a group of Australian scientists inadvertently produced a virus which, like HIV (the virus which causes AIDS), affects the immune system. Imagine what would happen if such a virus is released in the environment. To cite another example, the Russians, not long ago, genetically engineered the legonnaire disease-causing organism, to make it more deadly.

The list of biological weapons on which considerable work has been done includes nearly 60 bacteria, viruses, other organisms, and toxins. (Examples would be: viruses that cause small pox, Ebola fever, Marburg fever, Lassa fever, and various haemorrhagic fevers; bacteria that cause anthrax, plague, glanders, and tularemia; and toxins such as botulin and ricin). How ethical is it to manufacture and store them, as is being done by many countries? Great Britain, the US, the erstwhile USSR (now Russia), Canada, Germany, South Africa, Japan, Iraq, Iran, Syria, and North Korea are known to have had extensive biological weapons development programmes. Botulin is the most deadly poison known to us, its LD50 (the amount required to kill 50 per cent of the exposed individuals) for human beings being 6 nanograms per kilogram weight, that is, approximately 400 nanograms per person. We may thus need less than one kilogram of botulin to kill the entire population of the world, and the delivery of it would be easy: just put it in the water supplies (botulin is an intestinal toxin). Then, there are pests that can be released to destroy our agriculture.

There is indeed no doubt that biological weapons are the most dreaded ones today—far more dangerous than nuclear, chemical or conventional weapons. It is, therefore, not surprising that the Fifth Review Conference on the Biological Weapons Convention held in December 2001 was a disaster. The United States refused to sign the proposed inspection and verification protocol for biological weapons. Has all this been ethical?

Before we conclude, let us examine in more detail, two controversial areas of biotechnology, namely, Assisted Reproductive Technologies (ART) and technologies pertaining to Genetically Modified Organisms (GMOs).

ART in India

With a population of over one billion, India should have at least 300 million individuals in the reproductive age group.This translates into 150 million couples. With the incidence of infertility in India being approximately 15 per cent—as, perhaps, elsewhere in the world—we would have approximately 22.5 million infertile couples in the country at any given time. If we assume that 10 per cent of these couples would provide a market for infertility treatment every year, this would mean approximately 2.25 million couples per year who, if their resources permit and if adequate facilities exist in the country, may like to visit an infertility clinic for advice and treatment.

On an average of, say 50,000 Indian rupees per couple, this would amount to 112.5 billion rupees per year as the potential market for infertility in the country. As of today, perhaps only 10 per cent of those who have an infertility problem have access to appropriate professional medical advice. This translates to 2,25,000 couples and a market of Rs. 11.25 billion.

We have no registry of, or a licensing system for, infertility clinics in the country so far, therefore, we have no way of knowing as to how many such clinics exist in India as of today. However, several estimates place the figure at somewhere between 200 and 300. Assuming the upper number to be close to reality, and an even distribution of patients across the clinics, it works out to

750 new cases of infertility reporting at each clinic every year, on an average. As everywhere else, some clinics would have a larger clientele, but the *average* gross income (turnover) of an infertility clinic in India, at present, could be approximately Rs 37.5 million.

Infertility Clinics

While India, no doubt, has several infertility clinics, the facilities and quality of which would match with similar clinics anywhere else in the world, the unfortunate element in the story is that there are many which have extremely inadequate facilities and staff. It is also widely known that many clinics, including some of those that have excellent facilities and staff, engage in a number of unethical practices. Let us look at some examples.

Many instances are known where a patient has only been given Intrauterine Insemination (IUI) but charged for In Vitro Fertilisation (IVF). Many other similar malpractices become possible in India because 70 per cent of the country is rural and about half the women of the country (a much larger proportion in the villages) are illiterate. The average per capita income in the country may be about the lowest in the world, if one takes away the upper creamy layer of the society which, say, pays tax and represents a very small proportion (less than 5 per cent) of the population. Therefore, paying for IVF when only IUI has been done on an infertile couple must cause an immense financial strain on the couple. As having a child in India is of paramount importance—both socially and economically—and a stigma is attached to a couple (specially the woman) if the couple does not have a child, the couple does everything possible to have one. Often, people in the villages sell their land and/or other assets to come to an infertility clinic. It would, therefore, be not only unethical but even criminal from the social point of view for such a couple to be charged for IVF if only IUI has been done.

There was a case in 2002 in the state of Andhra Pradesh in India where a woman was declared pregnant by an infertility clinic, following an ART procedure on her. Later, it was found that the woman was never pregnant. There is no law in the country which would allow appropriate and expedient action to be taken against the erring ART clinic.

There have been advertisements in Indian newspapers by ART clinics saying that their success rate in IVF has been over 60 per cent—that is, more than three times the average success rate around the world. Such clinics have been clearly misleading the people through such advertisements to gain advantage over other infertility clinics.

There have also been advertisements in the recent past in our newspapers by infertility clinics saying they can give a couple a child of the desired sex by pre-natal sex selection—that is separation of the X and Y spermatozoa—when the fact is that no established technique yet exists which would separate X and Y sperm with 100 per cent efficiency. Techniques for enriching a sperm faction with X or Y cells are, of course, known but in that case, the concerned doctor in the infertility clinic should state that all that he or she will be able to do is to merely increase the chances of the couple having a child of the desired sex, without guaranteeing the sex of the prospective child. Instead of doing this, such infertility clinics bank on the fact that 50 per cent of the time, they are going to be right. In instances where the procedure has failed, in view of the vast ignorance of an average infertile couple, the doctor of the infertility clinic can lay the blame on the couple for not strictly following the instructions given to them at the time of insemination, in the full knowledge that if the number of such instructions is large and if they are complex (irrespective of their relevance to the desired objective), they can always lay the blame on the couple for not following one or more of these instructions.

In many infertility clinics in the country today, there is no professional counselling available. There is no codified system to decide as to when the couple must be asked to give up the treatment on ethical grounds, and advised to adopt a child; instead, the treatments are prolonged unnecessarily over a large number of cycles in spite of the fact that the gynaecologist knows that the expense that the couple would be incurring would be infructuous. There is no check on such malpractices in the country, as of today. Some gynaecologists engage in artificial insemination by the husband's semen (AIH) or by donor semen (AID), when no adequate facilities exist with the gynaecologist for the processing of semen, or for doing appropriate checks if the semen that is being used is of the designated individual, or for documentation of what is being done.

In my estimate, unethical practices such as those mentioned above, today perhaps result in an infructuous expenditure of somewhere between three and four hundred million rupees by the people of the country, most of whom would have sacrificed a great deal to be able to pay the expenses of treatment at an infertility clinic.

Ethics of ART

In addition the above concerns at the way ART is practiced in India, I will discuss here some of the ethical dilemmas we are currently facing in the country. Some of these problems probably exist everywhere, but some are no doubt the consequence of the special social and economic conditions prevailing in India.

Artificial Insemination

An important issue in the practice of ART in India is: who should be the donor of semen for AID? In this respect, we ought to remember that a vast majority of the population in India today still live as a part of the larger joint family. Further, barring a small proportion of the emancipated, the mother-in-law still exercises substantial control over the daughter-in-law, especially in a joint family. Let us also remind ourselves of the widely prevalent deficiencies in the country in regard to the status of women. (I must add here that ours is a country full of diversities, even contradictions. In fact, the only statement that is true about India is that no statement about India is either true or false. Therefore, there are exceptions to everything that I have said or will say about the country in this article). Against this background, let me present a common Indian scenario.

Traditionally, if a couple is infertile in India, the family always lays the blame on the woman, even though, in about half the diagnosable cases, a male factor is the cause of infertility. The mother-in-law would never acknowledge in public that her son, and not the daughter-in-law, is at fault. Therefore, even if she is convinced of the biological fact that the daughter-in-law is fine but her son has a problem, she would want to make sure that her son's infertile status is kept as close a secret as possible. Therefore, she takes the daughter-in-law to an infertility clinic and, following the advice of the clinic that the daughter-in-law needs to be inseminated by donor semen, the mother-in-law asks the clinic to inseminate the daughter-in-law by the semen of the husband's brother or of a close family friend. The daughter-in-law would normally have no say in this regard, no matter how opposed she might be to the idea of being inseminated by the semen of someone whom she has been seeing and would continue to see all the time. The psychological stress that the daughter-in-law will go through for the rest of her life, including during pregnancy, on account of the knowledge that the biological father of the child she is carrying is someone whom she knows and has social intercourse with all the time, would not be a matter of concern to the rest of the family. We have to remember that in the current social milieu in the country, lack of concern for the daughter-in-law, and exploitation of her by the rest of the family in almost every conceivable way, is extremely common. It is for this reason that there are hundreds of what are called dowry deaths in the country every year, where a woman either kills herself or is killed by close relatives (such as the husband or his parents) because she has not brought enough dowry at the time of the wedding, or because she is unable to get more money from her parents after the wedding, to satisfy the greed of those who control her new home after marriage.

Consequently, quarrels between a mother-in-law and her daughter-in-law are not yet a thing of the past in India. Against this background, imagine the following scenario. At the instance of the mother-in-law, a woman is inseminated with the semen of her husband's brother or friend. A few years later, the mother-in-law and the daughter-in-law quarrel. The mother-in-law then says publicly that her daughter-in-law has committed adultery and names the person with whom the adultery has been committed. DNA fingerprinting—a technology which has been widely used in India since 1986 and in the development of which in the country I had a small role—will establish that the basis of mother-in-law's allegation that the child is not the daughter-in-law's husband's child but the child of another man, is correct. As the infertility clinics are, as of today not required to keep appropriate records, there will be no way that the daughter-in-law can establish that she never slept with the man who is the biological father of the child, and that she was artificially inseminated with that man's semen with the express approval—even suggestion—of the mother-in-law.

When we asked the National Commission for Women, a statutory organisation set up by the Government of India, for their opinion in regard to the anonymity or otherwise of donors of semen in cases such as the one mentioned above, the Commission was strongly of the opinion that all sperm and egg donation must be anonymous. The situation I have outlined above would clearly support this view. I hope the following incident that actually happened in Hyderabad, would clear any doubts anyone may still have on this score. A woman—more courageous and self-reliant than usual (as what I am going to say now, would establish)—was taken by her mother-in-law to an infertility clinic to be inseminated at an appropriate time later by the semen of a close friend of the husband, whom the woman knew well. An advance was paid to the clinic for the procedure of AID to be performed on the woman later on. A while later, the woman went back to the clinic, this time, all by herself, and asked that the money paid to the clinic as advance on her behalf be returned to her. When the clinic asked why this request was being made, the woman said that this was so because she was now pregnant. The doctors at the clinic were naturally puzzled and asked her how she became pregnant. She then answered that since she was going to be inseminated by the semen of her husband's friend, whom she knew very well, she saw no harm in sleeping with him at an appropriate time just once. The pregnancy was a natural consequence of this act which she did not consider as unethical, for she had promised herself that she would never sleep with that man again. She clearly did not perceive any difference between being inseminated by the semen of a person whom she knew very well and sleeping with him just once for achieving the objective of AID, without having the family spend any money. I leave it to the reader to judge whether, given the circumstances I have mentioned, what she did was ethical or unethical.

Oocyte Donation

The second major question that the ART clinics in India are facing today pertains to donation of the oocyte. Who should be an oocyte donor? As of today, in India, it is almost always a close relative from the side of the man or the woman. The idea of having a close relative or friend of the family as donor of the sperm or the egg is that the entire story is kept within the family-friend boundary. The other implications—including the genetic and the social implications—of such donation are not understood. For reasons mentioned in the preceding section in respect of sperm donation, I strongly believe that donation of sperm or eggs by a close relative or a close friend is unethical and that we should have a law requiring that both sperm and egg donation be anonymous. We need to have sperm banks that would also keep track (for example, through appropriate advertisement) of possible oocyte donors against monetary compensation. We also need to encourage the system of egg sharing in which an indigent infertile couple that needs financial resources for ART agrees to donate oocytes to an affluent infertile couple wherein the wife can carry the pregnancy through but cannot produce her own oocyte, in return for IVF with the sperm of the male partner of the affluent couple, and for a monetary compensation that would take care of the expenses of an ART procedure on the indigent couple.

Surrogacy

The third question being raised in our country in regard to the practice of ART pertains to surrogacy. Who may act as the surrogate mother? As of now it, again, is a close relative—for example, the mother of the male partner or the sister of the female partner. Thus, in many cases in the country, a woman has given birth to her own grandchild without incest. On the other hand, there are also regular advertisements, for example in the magazine *Woman's Era*, for surrogate motherhood. I believe it is unethical to have a close relative act as a surrogate mother, especially in the Indian environment where family ties are very close. In a closely-knit family, the fact that the child was delivered by so-and-so will always be known to the members of the family and, eventually, to the child. Carrying a child in one's own womb is, in the Indian society, the epitome of a close relationship. Therefore, such a relationship could come in the way of the child establishing the expected relationship with the biological mother, without confusion in the child's mind, especially if the child and the surrogate mother see each other frequently. Perhaps, the ideal solution would be what is already being practiced by some in the country, that is, to advertise for a surrogate, and strike an appropriate financial arrangement that will adequately compensate the woman who agrees to act as a surrogate mother.

In one instance, surrogacy led to a curious incongruity. In 2001, a woman came to one of the best-known maternity hospitals in Hyderabad, to be admitted for delivery. She wanted to be registered in the name of her sister as she was acting as a surrogate mother for her sister's and brother-in-law's child. Not having handled such a case earlier, the doctor-in-charge of the hospital—an eminent and highly ethical person—agreed to this request, only to realise a little later that this was a mistake. What would she do in case the woman dies during childbirth? Whose death certificate would she sign—would it be the death certificate of the sister, in whose name the woman had registered herself, or would it be the death certificate of the woman herself? This is an outstanding example of lack of proper documentation leading to extremely difficult situations.

Another relevant issue that is exercising the minds of people in our country in regard to surrogacy is whether or not surrogacy in India should be considered ethical if the reason is only convenience of the couple. There is a view that surrogacy by assisted conception should be considered only for those for whom it would be physically or medically impossible or undesirable to carry a baby to term, and not for those who are perfectly capable of producing a child in the normal way but desire a surrogate mother because the woman does not want to go through pregnancy for the sake of convenience or for reasons such as a break in professional service or simply the risk of having one's vital statistics affected. I am personally in favour of allowing surrogacy for whatever reason the couple consider important.

Germ Cell Donation

Then there is the question of the right of the child born through donation of a germ cell to know who his/her biological father or mother is when the child attains adulthood, assuming, of course, that the sperm or the egg donation has been anonymous. In the Indian environment, it would, perhaps, be both impractical and unethical to give this right to the child. Given the closeness of relationships in India, this right would be psychologically unfair to the child, to the donor and to the couple who have brought up the child; the child, of course, must continue to have the right to know everything else (except the name and address) about the person who donated the oocyte or the sperm.

However, we have the technique of DNA fingerprinting available today which establishes biological parenthood without any doubt. If a need arises for DNA fingerprinting to be done on the child, it would become obvious that the couple who brought up the child does not comprise both the biological parents. Such a discovery for the child, all of a sudden, could alienate him from his parents whom he could accuse of deliberately hiding the truth from him. Therefore, there may be no harm in the couple's telling the child at an appropriate time that he/she was born following anonymous sperm or egg donation.

There are also several other issues that have still not been resolved in respect of the practice of ART in India. For example, we still have not yet finally decided on the age limits—upper and lower—for germ cell donation or surrogacy, and the number of times one can act as a surrogate mother.

The silver lining is that the Indian Council of Medical Research (ICMR) released, on 4th September 2002, a draft of national guidelines for accreditation, supervision, and regulation of ART clinics in India, following the recommendations of a high-power committee it set up. These guidelines have been publicly debated in the country.This has set the stage for an appropriate Act passed by our Parliament.

Ethics of GMOs

There are two types of GMOs (Genetically Manipulated Organisms)—one that is used in a factory to make a product such as Hepatitis B vaccine or human insulin, and the other that is released in the environment as such. The first kind poses no problems at all and, as has been already mentioned, has provided a number of extremely valuable drugs which have changed the face of medicine. In fact, at least three of the ten largest selling drugs in the world market today are made through GMOs. These GMOs are used under highly contained conditions; even if they happen to get released they would not survive in the environment on account of their special genetic makeup. They, therefore, pose no problem. However, the release of GMOs in the environment is another cup of tea altogether, as a living organism, once released, can never be recalled. It, therefore, becomes extremely important to ensure that before any GMO is released in the environment, all the risks that such a release poses are meticulously assessed. I have listed these risks and the manner of assessing them in great detail in two recent articles.[7] I would, therefore, not repeat them here. What I would like to say is that even though we have over 100 million acres of agricultural land planted with GMOs around the world (which include genetically engineered cotton, soya bean, canola, and corn), the fact is that in no case have all the risks that should have been assessed and could have been assessed, actually been appropriately assessed.

The marketing of these organisms by multinational corporations (MNCs) around the world has had two purposes: first to make quick money, and second, to obtain control of agriculture in the developing countries and erode the rights of their farmers. If, today, someone wishes to control the destiny of a country like India or Nigeria where 70 per cent of the population derives its total income from agriculture or agriculture-related activities, all that one has to do is to obtain control over the seed and agrochemical businesses in the country. If this happens for India, we would no longer be a free nation. This is precisely what the MNCs have been wishing to do through a nexus between them, the concerned governments and the bureaucracy. And new biotechnologies such as genetic engineering, which hold great promise for the benefit of mankind (as already mentioned earlier), also happen to be the tools that the above nexus would use to lure unsuspecting farmers (specially of the Third World countries) into their net, to control world food production. In this context, we should take note of the fact that, as of today, the US is the biggest bribe giver in the world. And one of the purposes of such bribe giving is likely to be to obtain control over world's food resources through the nexus mentioned above.

The proponents of release of GMOs in the environment, especially the GM crops, say that there are no examples of any damage caused by GMOs. This is not true. Let me give a few examples.

In the last decade, Japan developed a GMO that produced large amounts of tryptophan, an essential amino acid that is widely used as a nutritional supplement, especially in the affluent West. It turned out that over 30 persons in the United States fell sick, suffering from a rare disease, Eosonophilia mylangia, after consuming the Japanese tryptophan-based preparations. It was fortunate that this happened in the vicinity of the famous Mayo Clinic in Rochester, Minnesota, which is one of the world's best-known centres for identifying rare diseases. If this would have happened in a country like ours, or Zambia, the people would have simply continued to die for long, without anyone knowing what the cause of the deaths was.

To cite another case in point, an American company put a gene from Brazil nut in soya bean to make up the deficiency in the soya bean protein of an essential amino acid called methionine. It turned out that a number of Americans were allergic to the genetically engineered soya bean, which was, therefore, never marketed in the US. However, the GM soya bean, was sent by the US, against all ethical principles and even the Cartagena protocol to which both the US and India have been a signatory, to Orissa, to be distributed to the Orissa famine victims a few years ago. (This happened even though we had 60 million tonnes of grain in our stock with the Food Corporation of India at the time).

In late 2002, in spite of widespread food shortage and starvation in Zambia and Zimbabwe, the governments of these two countries refused to allow genetically engineered corn to be given as a gift by the US. The US refused the request by these two countries for cornflour instead of corn, so that no one could plant the GM corn and thus contaminate the corn produced in these countries. In this context, it is important to realise that Europe has totally banned the import of GM food; if the food in the African countries gets contaminated by foreign genes, Europe will stop importing any food from these countries, thus affecting these countries' long-term economic interests. This is, perhaps, what America has been wanting to do by, again, establishing a nexus between, on the one hand, its own government and the MNCs who have been virtually exclusively marketing GM seeds, and on the other, the government and bureaucracy of the recipient developing country which would have no hesitation in selling their country for their own personal interest.

Even Bt cotton has these kinds of concerns. Bt cotton, one of the most widely used genetically engineered crops, has a gene from a bacterium, *Bacillus thuringenesis* which contains codes for producing a toxin protein that can kill certain pests. (*Bacillus thuringenesis* was transferred through genetic engineering into cotton to make it pest resistant, thus not requiring the use of pesticides). In the United States, after the fifth generation, as much as 40 to 50 per cent of the plantation has necessarily to be of non-Bt cotton. The non Bt cotton has to be planted as a refuge to which the insects could go, sparing the Bt cotton, the reason being that over the years, insects develop resistance to Bt cotton.

Further, according to a recent study,[8] about 65 per cent of the cotton farmers in the particular geographical area that is contiguous must plant Bt cotton for it to be economically viable—a situation unlikely to occur in countries like India where the holdings are small. (The cost of Bt cotton seeds in India currently is at least five times the cost of good non-Bt seeds).

Then there is the risk of the foreign gene put in a GMO being transferred to non-GM crops, or even across species. Such horizontal transfer of genetic traits is now widely known and has also been established for GMOs in the market today; it seems possible even in the oral cavity (and rumen) in the case of cattle.[9] In fact, it is estimated that between 10 to 20 per cent of all genes in today's living organisms have come about as a result of horizontal gene transfer. An outstanding example of such a transfer is the recent contamination of non-GM, wild type corn in a region in Mexico which has the world's largest corn biodiversity, by GM (genetically manipulated) corn grown nearby.

Both developing and developed countries are, in fact, already beginning to pay a price for the use of improperly assessed GMOs in agriculture. For example, in China, where Monsanto's Bt cotton (which has been genetically engineered to be pest resistant) and their own Bt cotton have been used on a substantial scale, it has been found that, over the years, the proportion of insects that are not killed by the toxic gene in the genetically engineered plant has increased, thus affecting the promised yield.[10] China has also decided recently—causing great annoyance to the US—that it will not import any GM technology from abroad but develop its own as and when it considers it necessary to do so in the country's own interest.

We must also remember that the developed countries may be able to absorb any long-term damage through the use of GM crops. This, however, would not be so in the case of most developing countries.

Having said all this, I do not wish to argue for one moment that we should not engage in genetic engineering of plant and microorganisms with the eventual objective of releasing them in the environment. However, our objective should not be to exploit and/or only to make money. There should be the larger objective of national or international good—an objective in which the requirements for sustainable development are met. For example, there should be no objection to putting in new genes that would delay ripening of fruits that are otherwise fragile—such as custard apple. As of today, this delicious fruit cannot be transported over a long distance. Similarly, it would be worth looking at the possibility of putting in new genes that would allow plants of economic importance which cannot normally tolerate high salinity, to grow in semi-arid or arid areas. In this context, what is most important is that nations like ours, China or Nigeria must make sure that seed business is our own national business. If we need to develop a genetically engineered crop for a valid reason that is in our interest, we should do it ourselves. The fact is that such capabilities exist in certainly the three countries I have named above.

What is equally important is that before we release any GM crop, we must have in place an appropriate risk assessment procedure which we do not have anywhere in the world today—least of all in our country. In addition, the entire risk assessment data must be put in public domain, which has not happened in our country so far.

Before commercial or public release, any GM material (be it a drug or a crop) has to go through two committees in India—the RCGM (Review Committee on Genetic Manipulation) of the Department of Biotechnology (DBT), and the GEAC (Genetic Engineering Approval Committee) of the Department of Environment and Forests. The first applicant for such release of a GM crop through these committees has been Monsanto, which sought approval for release of its Bt cotton that would be resistant to the common cotton pest, the bollworm.

As it turns out, both these committees are unknowledgeable, self-centred, unprofessional, socially and politically insensitive, (probably) corruptible, and without any commitment to the country. Fortunately, on account of many protests from responsible quarters, no permission was granted by the GEAC for the release of Monsanto's Bt cotton through their Indian associate, Mahyco, in which Monsanto has a 26 per cent stake, till June 2001, in spite of DBT's unwarranted pressure on GEAC for permitting such release. Yet it was found that in Gujarat, in the latter half of 2001, Bt cotton seeds were sold by a company called Navbharat, and planted in some 10,000 acres; a similar plantation was also made in a much smaller area in Andhra Pradesh. (I would not be surprised if Monsanto had a direct or an indirect stake and/or role in these plantings). What is amazing is that even though these plantations were totally illegal and the GEAC did issue a (weak) directive that the crops should be burnt and the seeds confiscated, nothing of the sort happened, and the farmers who used the seed, as well as those who sold the seeds, have been living happily since then, in spite of their contravening one of the important laws of the country. This incident substantiates what I have said above: that a nexus between the multinationals, the government and the bureaucracy is very much alive and kicking in our country.

In March 2002, Mahyco was finally granted permission by the GEAC to market their (that is, Monsanto's) Bt cotton. Reports from Andhra Pradesh, Maharashtra, Madhya Pradesh, and Gujarat where Bt cotton was planted in the last season after the permission from GEAC in March 2002 have established unequivocally that the Bt cotton in these States has been largely a failure.[11] The reasons for the success of the illegally planted Bt cotton in Gujarat in 2001 are not clear, as the powers that be did not wish to investigate the matter. It is quite possible that this success was manipulated (perhaps with the knowledge of the authorities concerned), for example, by putting in several Bt genes (instead of just one that has been approved so far) in the cotton plant; such an unauthorised and unlicensed procedure, although providing possible initial advantage to the farmer, could be a disaster subsequently. The purpose of such an exercise could have been to pressurise the professionally incompetent GEAC to grant the permission it did a few months later (in March 2002) to Mahyco (indirectly, Monsanto) to market their Bt cotton in India. No risk assessment of any kind—even rudimentary—has been done for cotton having more than one Bt gene.

The unfortunate fact is that in spite of our asking the Indian Council of Agricultural Research (ICAR) and the Council of Scientific & Industrial Research (CSIR) that they jointly set up an agency to test the seeds using modern DNA fingerprinting techniques, no trustworthy organisation exists in the country which could even determine routinely whether a particular seed has a Bt gene in it or not. Nor have our governments—State or Central—encouraged and popularised Integrated Pest Management developed in the country (first for cotton) and shown to be effective, again indicating collusion with the multinational corporations (like Monsanto) that are marketing GM seeds and pesticides in the country.

Contrast the situation in India with that in China that has already been mentioned, and in Nigeria—the seventh largest country in the world in terms of population. I had a meeting with the President of Nigeria, Mr O. Obasanjo, on September 9, 2002 and, at his instance, subsequently with the senior officers of the Nigerian National Seeds Service, in Abuja on September 12, 2002. Nigeria has been convinced that it is not in their interest to permit any MNC to have any control of any kind on their seed business. If they wish to use a GM crop, they have the ability to make it themselves. Further, they have realised the need for putting in an appropriate and fair risk assessment system before release of any GM crop, either their own or an imported one, keeping in mind the long-term interests of the country. And China—if we need the example of a scientifically advanced developing country—is exercising immense caution in regard to GM crops; it is not permitting the growing of GM food crops, and ensuring that if any GM crop has now to be introduced in China, it would be their own and not that of an MNC.

Conclusions

I hope I have underscored the tremendous promise that modem biotechnology holds for us, as well as immense and wide-ranging implications of the progress in modem biology and biotechnology. The challenge before us as informed and responsible world citizens is to ensure that we use the new bio-technologies in such a way that their use is ethically defensible, and in the largest interests of mankind, both in our country and around the world. In the present context, this will not happen unless responsible and socially sensitive citizens understand what modem biotechnology is about and what its various implications are, and then build pressure to break the existing nexus between the MNCs, the politicians and the bureaucrats.

I must, to be fair to all of science and technology, reiterate what I said in the beginning—that it would be not only modem biology and biotechnology that would bring about dramatic changes in our lifestyles and the way we think and deal with problems, but also several other areas. For example, in course of time, the world store of fossil fuels such as coal and petroleum would be exhausted. We would, by then, have to learn how to exploit the virtually inexhaustible sources of energy such as biomass, solar energy, nuclear energy and wind energy. Sooner or later, the mineral wealth of the planet would also be depleted. The only inexhaustible source of materials would be carbon-containing (organic) compounds. We would, therefore, have to learn to replace minerals with suitably designed organic compounds.

One would like to believe that, as man becomes more knowledgeable, it would become increasingly difficult for him to be exploited. This belief, however, may be erroneous, for one is likely to see an increase in sophistication in the techniques of exploitation. The techniques of exploitation of man by man and of nation by nation have undergone a dramatic change in the last one hundred years. On the other hand, it would be unwise to underestimate the ingenuity of man to find solutions. Perhaps, the only insurance against exploitation in the world of rapidly advancing knowledge (especially in science and technology), would be to work towards reducing the gaps in people's knowledge around the world, to as insignificant a level as is possible.

That is a major social challenge we all face today. It is in this context that discussions such as this become relevant.

NOTES

1. Genetic disorders can be diagnosed in three ways: by using DNA-based probes, chromosomal analysis, or enzyme analysis.
2. Proteins are made of 20 naturally occurring building blocks called amino acids strung together in a chain, like pearls in a necklace. Proteins have generally more than 100 amino acid moieties in each of their molecules. The sequence of the amino acids and the number of each amino acid in a protein molecule is what defines the particular protein.
3. P.S. Venkateswaran, I. Millman and B.S. Blumberg, US Patent numbers 4673575 (June 16, 1987) and 4937074 (June 26, 1990).
4. Verlinsky*et al. 2000. Reproductive Biomedicine Online.* Vol. 1, pp. 31–32.
5. "Designer baby wins court go-ahead" *The New Indian Express,* April 10, 2003.
6. The articles appeared in *The New Indian Express* of November 7, 14, 21 and 28 2001 and December 5, 2001
7. P.M. Bhargava 2002. "GMOs: Need for appropriate risk assessment systems", *Economic and Political Weekly,* April 13, 2002; and P.M. Bhargava, 2002. "The perils of mutant food", *Down* to *Earth,* April 15, 2002.
8. *Nature,* March6, 2003, Vo1.422, p.5.
9. (P.S. Duggan et*al.British Journal of Nutrition,* 2003, Vol. 89, pp.159–266).
10. *DaynanXue.*2002. A summary of research on the environmental impacts of Bt. cotton in China, The State Environmental Protection Administration of China, P.O. Box 4202, Nanjung 210042.

11. "Bt cotton leads to losses: farmers say there was no increase in yield", *Deccan Chronicle,* March 4, 2003; "Cotton ryots a confused lot", *The Hindu,* March 5, 2003; "Government promises compensation to Bt cotton farmers", *The Hindu,* March 2003; "What ails Bt cotton" (by D Banerji), *The Hindu,* March 18,2003; "Government to move cautiously on Bt cotton", *New Indian Express,* April 24, 2003; "In Gujarat, Bt cotton seed loses out to illegal Navbharat", *The New Indian Express,* April 25, 2003.

4

Towards a Spiritual Society*

Swami Agnivesh

I knew that Durgabai Deshmukh, who I had heard much of, was the wife of C.D. Deshmukh, but I mistakenly thought she was a Marathi lady. When I discovered she was, in fact, from Andhra Pradesh, my Andhra pride was awakened. On learning that she was from Rajamundry, which is close to my birthplace (Srikakulam), I was thrilled no end. Indeed, the fact that I hold Durgabai in high regard makes me delighted to contribute to this series of discourses organised by an institution she founded—the Council for Social Development. When I was invited to do so by the Council's President, Professor Muchkund Dubey, however, my reactions were mixed—I felt joy mingled with surprise. Joy, because I was considered worthy of the task, and surprise, because someone like me, who had been so immersed in social and political struggles that he has had very little time to read, and none at all to write, was expected to prepare a text of nineteen to twenty pages. Notwithstanding my disquiet on this score, I accepted the invitation. By making a commitment, I reasoned, I would get to think and reflect.

I however stipulated that I would express myself, not in English, as the others before me had done, but in the mother tongue, Hindi. My delight knew no bounds when Professor Dubey unhesitatingly agreed. The clout of the anglicised in Independent India is something I could never bring myself to accept and whenever I have had the opportunity to flout their traditions, I have seized the moment. It has been a matter of pride and self-respect. Consequently, it was with deep respect that I read of how, at the tender age of 11, Durgabai Deshmukh, responding to Mahatma Gandhi's boycott call, had her name struck off the rolls of the school she went to, because English was taught there, and of how she then went on to found her own school—the *Balika* Hindi School. If today's anglicised in our country have any shame left in them, they should take a page from Durgabai's life. Those who today stand ready to give thousands of lakhs of rupees worth of bribes to get their children

* Edited transcript of the July 15, 1998, Durgabai Deshmukh Memorial Lecture by Swami Agnivesh. Translation from the original Hindi into English by Dr Rajiv Balakrishnan.

admitted to English medium public schools must surely think of Durgabai as someone who was truly mad. Today, 50 years after Independence, if only such madness would revisit the children of my country!

The Flame

In the past 30 years of my public life, most of my time has been spent fighting two forms of slavery—bonded labour and child labour. In the course of this struggle, I have found that in places of worship in our country, young, unmarried girls, reduced to slavery as *devadasis* ("servants of gods", that is, temple servants), were physically exploited. I cannot express the pride I felt when I read that at a mere 12 years of age, Durgabai fought to eradicate the hateful practice of the *devadasi* system, as also, the custom of *burqa* or the veil, prevalent to this day among Muslim women.

In standing up to social evils and arousing pride in nation and language at a tender age, Durgabai metamorphosed from an ordinary girl to a veritable Durga who struggled all her life to shatter the shackles of helplessness, powerlessness, blind belief, and ignorance. The rebellious spark within her was, in my view, the most distinguishing feature of Durgabai's life. It was a spark that, in due course, burst into a flame that posed a challenge to the extensive exploitation, disparity, and apathy in society. May the light of that flame inspire us to transform into an erupting volcano of purpose aimed at social transformation.

The Varna Order

If we are to storm the bastions of conservatism, we must, however, exercise caution, lest we throw the baby out with the bathwater. We talk of 'transformation' in a manner of speaking, but the fact is that neither a society nor an individual is entirely transformed. An individual and a society have some foundational values, some *sanatan dharma* that harkens back to time immemorial. There is a need for society as a whole and for individuals who stand firm in this value-based legacy from the past to treat the institutional structures that have grown up around it as means (of guiding our behaviour) rather than as ends of ritualistic observance. There is a need to purify and refine those means with discernment and propriety, so that the values endure even as the encapsulating structures change. Things go awry when, in the name of institutional reform, the eternal values themselves get eroded. When this happens, outward dazzle corrupts our inner being. The family breaks up, society disintegrates, and all that is left is an elusive mirage.

The fashion now-a-days is such that whenever there is a debate about transformation of the social order, the discussion gets focused on capitalism, communism, and the market. Communism as an alternative to capitalism captured the imagination of millions, but since the disintegration of the Soviet Union, the role of the market has occupied centre stage.

I propose today to contribute to this discussion by drawing your attention to an arrangement that is either considered synonymous with casteism and hence adjudged undesirable and unacceptable, or is seen as impractical and insufficient, so much so that it is not even considered worthy of ideological discourse. The arrangement I speak of is the *varnashram vyavasta* or the *varnashram* order. Though aware of the prejudice against *varnashram*, I see it today as overwhelmingly practical. I am neither knowledgeable of sociology, nor am I a student of history, but as a humble comrade in the ongoing struggle for freeing the oppressed and the exploited—the bonded labourers and child workers, of the fetters that shackle them, I have time and time again sensed a sense of restlessness, a lack of moorings, which I attribute to the social, economic, political, and moral order in its entirety. Whenever I have reflected on this, I have seen the light in the form of the foundational principles of *varnashram*, which I elucidate below.

Etymology and Symbolism

The term "varna" in Vedic etymology, is derived from the root "*vra*", which means, "to select" or "to choose". In the *varnashram vyavasta*, which I refer to here also, in abbreviated form, as the *varnavyavasta*, children will be motivated to choose their life mission themselves. Mothers, fathers, and teachers can help them make their choices, but the child himself will have the full freedom to mould his life in terms of his talents, his nature, and his karma. At the same time, the endeavour will be to shift the focus of attention from selfish desires to the greater or spiritual good. The more this feeling is fostered, the more the individual orients to the wider society rather than to his own selfish needs.Though engaging in strenuous efforts and achieving the highest excellence at work, he is not attached to the fruits of his actions—he does not think of it in terms of *his* achievements. Life becomes sacrifice.

It is in this context that the ceremony of *yagnopaveet*, or investiture with the sacred thread, acquires importance.The word "*yagnopaveet*" is a combination of two words—yagna and upaveet. *Upaveet* is the term given to the thread. *Upaveet* can have many meanings: the thread (or rope) used for hanging is called the *pashopaveet—pasha*, meaning noose, combined with *upaveet*, becomes *pashopaveet*. Similarly, the rope used to tie the feet of the cow at the time of milking is called *dohanopavceet*, that is, *duhan*, meaning milking, combined with *upaveet*. So also, the thread that is associated with *yagna*, or sacrifice, acquires meaning and radiance as the *yagnopaveet*.

It is worth noting here that this word *yagna* is rooted in *yaj*, which means giving, worship, and joining or mixing with others. Roughly, *yagna* means to build social ties or union, and to sacrifice oneself to the mandates of that bigger entity or union. This is symbolised by the sacrificial fire. In the *havan-khund*—the pit in which the fire sacrifice is performed, a fire is kindled and the kindling material is consumed by the flames, leaving behind nothing but ash. In the same way, if you are to bring light and fragrance into your life, kindle the fire of your resolve, and yourself become the kindling material that is devoured by the flames and reduced to ashes.

Distinguishing Features

Listed below are a few of the distinguishing features of the *varnashram vyavastha*:

- No one will be a Brahmin, or a Kshatriya or a Vaisya by birth. As per the dictum *janmana jayate shudrah, sanskarat dvij ucchyate*, every child will be in the shudra category, to start with. Only by virtue of his *samskaras* or tendencies will he be invested with the sacred thread and so become *dvij* or twice-born; it is his acquisition of knowledge and worth that will usher in his second birth, as a social being.
- As far as possible, every boy and girl will be given equal opportunities for acquiring knowledge and being given *diksha* (consecration or initiation).
- In the schemes for imparting *shiksha* (knowledge) and conferring *diksha*, from beginning to end, every child will be emphatically enjoined to be firm in adhering to his vows or *vrat*. On the basis of his aptitude and talent, his nature, and his karma, every child would be free to choose whether to fight against ignorance, against injustice, or against want. Those who resolve to fight ignorance and light the flame of knowledge and truth will be Brahmins; those who resolve to remove wrongs and fight to establish justice will be Kshatriyas; and those who resolve to banish want and produce food, clothing, etc, in sufficient measure will be Vaishyas. Children who are not found suitable for any of these three categories will remain in the category of Shudra and will have to try again. In time, they will acquire the necessary qualities and capabilities to achieve their goals.

  Since an individual's *varna* category in the Vedic *varnavyavasta* was based, not on birth, but on aptitude and talent, nature, and karma, it was not cast in stone. There are many examples to prove the point. Visvamitra was a Kshatriya, but he acquired Brahminical qualities and was initiated into the Brahmin varna. The authors of those two great tomes—the Ramayana and the Mahabharata, namely, Valmiki and Ved Vyasa, were from Shudra families, but by virtue of their *samskaras*, they were acknowledged as Brahmins. Rishi Aithray, author of many works on the Rig Veda, was a gambler and the son of a slave. He was once forced out during the course of a sacrificial rite being performed on the banks of the Saraswati. But later, after he reformed himself, he was once again instituted as an *acharya* officiating at sacrificial rites. Satyakam Jawal was the son of a Vaishya but by dint of his noble *samskaras*, he was able to attain the Brahmin varna. Prishag, who killed a cow, became a Shudra. On account of prostitution, Nabag was exiled, but her children became kings again. Visvamitra's sons, because they wronged their father, were demoted to the Shudra varna. Parasuram, Dronacharya, Kripacharya, Aswatamma, Indra—all fell from the Brahmin to the Kshatriya varna. On the other hand, like Visvamitra, the sons of Emperor Sharyati and Emperor Rishbdev ascended to Brahminhood.

History bears witness to innumerable such examples from the *varnavyavastha* of antiquity, but even to this day, so called preceptors of the *sanatan dharma* go by the doctrine that one's varna is determined by that of the family one is born into—which is entirely at odds with the Vedic *varnavyavastha* and undermines its scientific basis and efficacy. Today, *varnavyavastha* stands martyred at the altar of *jati*, or caste—which is what is, in fact, determined by birth. The irony is that the evils of the institution of caste are attributed to varna, whereas, in fact, *jati* and varna are fundamentally different. They are contrary to one another. There is a heaven-and-earth difference in their distinguishing features and aims. It was to provide deliverance from the hold of *jati* that Maharishi Dayananda campaigned to revive the ancient and neglected Vedic *varnavyavastha*. This unfortunately is not understood.

- The most important thing in *varnavyavastha* is for the individual to rise above his selfish interests and to live and work for the good of society. To that end, every individual is to be given *diksha*, educated about the means at his disposal, and moulded into a missionary. In brief, the objective would be to effect a transformation in the mercenary order of our times. In the missionary order that is the goal, every individual would be given suitable resources. For the Brahmins, to facilitate their calling of teaching, research, reading, and writing, provision will be made for classrooms, libraries, research centres, etc. The kshatriyas would be provided suitable weapons to support their struggles against injustice, and the Vaishya youth would have the use of productive resources like land, machinery, factories, and so on. Only *access* to resources would be allowed. No individual would be permitted the right of ownership, that is to say, no resource could be bought or sold, mortgaged, or bequeathed. Today, resources pertaining to education and defence are, to a great extent, not privately owned—but in the sphere of production and distribution, private ownership prevails to a great extent. Under the market system, private ownership has reached its apogee, and holds sway in production, distribution, and exchange. It includes intellectual resources, biological resources, etc. The exploitative capitalist system has assumed such fearsome proportions that without any commodity even being traded, market speculation entails business worth approximately 1.3 trillion dollars transacted every day.

- A noteworthy feature of the *varnashram vyavasta* is that it divides the average 100 years of human life into four divisions. The first—the *bramacharya ashrama*, is a phase marked by restraint, simplicity, and ascetic practices. Then comes the *grihastha ashrama* phase of marriage, children, and the service of society as determined by one's varna. In the third phase of life—*vanaprastha ashrama*, one distances oneself from one's family and private possessions, while devoting oneself to the service of society. In the final phase of *sanyasa ashrama,* one gives up every luxury and enjoyment—enjoyment of children, of money, of worldly pleasures—and one dedicates oneself to the worship of God. In this stage of life, one plays the role of a world citizen and strengthens in oneself the community sentiment of *vasudeva kutumbamb*—the world is a family.
- While every individual will be free to choose his varna, based on his talents, his nature, and his karma, the *varnavyavastha* would extend to all. Everyone will have to mould their lives on the lines of the four *ashramas*. The *varnavyavasta* will be instituted more by people-power than the power of the State. With every individual subjecting himself to the eternal spiritual values, a new society and a new human culture will flourish.

The Precipice

In contrast to the *varnavyavasta*, capitalism, communism, and the market, based as they are on the prioritisation of materialistic concerns, are confined solely to the gratification of needs. The grander the world view that goes with this, the more, in the name of development, is the merciless milking of nature, and the more hideous and destructive the exploitation of man by man. Today, on account of the rapacious, unjustifiable and arrogant exploitation of 82 per cent of the earth's resources by 18 per cent of the world's population, humankind stands on the precipice of environmental disaster. Yet, there is not even the slightest trace of any change in the materialistic orientations of the powerful 18 per cent. At the Rio World Summit in 1992, the then American head of government, President George Bush arrogantly boasted that even thinking about changing the American lifestyle was unacceptable. Apart from America, Canada, England, France, Germany, Italy, and Japan (the G7 nations) too adopted a belligerent posture. It is these very nations that dominate the International Monetary Fund, the World Bank, and the World Trade Organisation. Multinational companies situated in these countries bank on their monopoly in cutting edge technology, and in the name of intellectual property, seek to hold sway over all of civilisation.

The powerful nations dominate the world not only economically, but militarily as well. America, as proprietor of a nuclear weapons stockpile, keeps Russia, England, France, and China (the P 5) in tow as it exercises control over the United Nations Organisation and acts as a bully by threatening countries with economic blockade.To make its nuclear capability even more deadly, America annually spends 400 million dollars on missiles, 3,300 million dollars on nuclear weapons, and God knows how many million dollars on computerised testing. It is because of this that if 82 per cent of the world's population has one share of technology, then 18 per cent has 50 shares (50: 1).These "developed countries" spend recklessly on science and technology, on new research and new discoveries, and the biggest share of this spending is on making weapons technology even more deadly. The developed countries then strengthen their own economies by selling their weapons to developing countries at exorbitant prices. What is truly comical is that it is those very countries that produce and export the maximum weaponry which preach human rights the most vociferously.

Today, America has at least 8,650 missiles fitted with nuclear warheads on 24 hours alert. At the touch of a button, the American president can unleash, on the entire earth, such a catastrophic dance of death that for thousands upon thousands of years, no living creature, let alone human beings, will inhabit the planet. Like hideous demons gnashing their teeth, these deadly weapons stand ready to strike. Russia has 6,240 of them, France has 450, England, 260, and China, 600. Who is to tell these caretakers of the world, who spend 85 billion dollars every year on weapons alone, that even a 10 per cent to 15 per cent cut in this expenditure can release the resources to end hunger, disease, helplessness, and powerlessness, and that if the entire amount is spent, not on warmongering but to build peace and happiness, then the world can be more beautiful than any heaven one could imagine. The question is: Is this possible? Can the world be pulled back from the precipice of destruction? The answer is: Yes, on condition that we are humble before the lord of this creation, the most compassionate supreme Spirit, treat as paramount our aims for our future, and build anew our individual, economic, and social life.

Root Causes

The gist of the four Vedas, the eleven Upanishads and the six philosophical systems of Hinduism[1] is that *prakriti* (nature), the *jivatma* (the individual soul), and the *paramatma* or the supreme spirit are eternally existent. *Prakriti* is existence, *jivatma* is existence and consciousness, and *parmatma* is existence (*sat*), consciousness (*chit*) and bliss (*ananda*), that is to say, the *parmatma* is *satchitananda*. The *jivatma*, in human form, wanders about in search of *ananda*, which it can get by worshipping the *parmatma*, but due to ignorance, it is attracted to this worldly happiness, mistakes momentary pleasures for supreme *ananda*, and remains unhappy and dissatisfied. At the root of this ignorance is the fact that it mistakes the ephemeral for the eternal. This forms the basis of its attachment to what is transitory, which is the main source of its sorrows.

How is one to gain deliverance from this root cause of human ignorance?

One answer lies in being perceptive to the realities of one's body and mind. Aided by this perceived or experiential truth, one moves ahead an inch at a time. Knowing the melody within yourself to be eternal, be detached, still your mind, achieve a calm state, and practice watchfulness. In proportion to how calm he becomes will the individual be freed of tensions and strains and be in an uplifted state until, one day, crossing the final frontier, he experiences *nirvana* or *moksha*—that is, the eternal, inexpressible *ananda*.

Failings of Religion

But is the practice of meditation in the seclusion of a mountain cave the only way? Is Brahman the only truth, and is the world and its activities a falsehood? The one-sided conception of Brahman as the truth and the world as an illusion has been a source of many defects in society. A handful of people who practiced religious chicanery set themselves up as agents of not only religion but of God as well. In course of time, they made worship, ceremony and ritual complicated and difficult to understand. Such individuals, establishing their monopoly of the sacred by virtue of birth, took upon themselves the responsibility of sending the rest of society to either heaven or hell. Instead of creating heaven on earth, they portrayed an imaginary heaven, with the passport and visa office in their own hands.

As the seed of birth-determined *jati* sprouted and began to flourish, these agents of God and religion sought to make access to the meditative path—the *sahaj gyan* and the *sahaj sadhna*, even more restrictive by closing the doors of meditative practice to women as well as to those who were not Brahmins, Kshatriyas or Vaishyas and were classified as Shudras. Those who proclaimed themselves to be Brahmins by birth were dull and lifeless in the roles they played. They also became willful and egotistical. Their arrogance reached a peak when they issued a fatwa to the effect that should women or Shudras unintentionally utter a mantra, their tongues were to be cut off; should they listen to a mantra, their ears were to be filled with molten lead; and if they were to keep a mantra in their hearts, then their hearts were to be riddled with holes. For 5000 years, tens of millions of Eklavyas had a finger chopped off by the Dronacharyas of the Brahmin dispensation, who sought to pave the way for their Kshatriya sons and the sons of kings. In between, one Siddhartha Gaumata emerged on the scene, raising revolutionary questions about the rights of women, of Shudras, and even of animals. Then Sankaracharya burst forth, waving the flag of *advaita*. In the *Vivek Chudamani*, he queried as to what constitutes the doors to hell, and himself providing the answer, proclaimed: 'Woman'!

When, like Gautama Buddha, Lord Mahavira, imbued with compassion for all living things and inspired by the light of justice, challenged the Brahminical order's monopolistic principles, the so-called upholders of the flag of dharma declared them to be heretics and sought to eradicate them from the root.Throughout history, we see this phenomenon at work: appropriate jurisdiction over "God" and "God Knowledge"; make the worship of God complicated rather than simple; make an individual's standing in life dependent on birth, and not ability, aptitude, and nature.

On the basis of such a dispensation, access to nature and its resources is circumscribed and controlled by an elite, setting the stage for the exploitation of the many by the few, and the establishment of an inequitable *status quo*. Whoever raises the flag of revolt—label him a heretic and an enemy of God's creation! If that does not work, then infiltrate the rebel camp and transform the kindled flame of intellectual revolt into the apathetic worship of stone idols! When religion becomes so pathological that, contrary to its basic and essential character, it gets transformed into hypocrisy and stone worship, oppressed society stands up in violent revolt to destroy that decayed dharma and to establish a new dispensation, one that is hostile to the inequitable *status quo* of birth-determined privilege and exploitation. But the fortress of vested interest is not fully destroyed. It hides in the shadows, and assuming a disguise, stealthily takes command of the new environment. As the lava of resentment against injustice begins to cool, a new dharma, new traditions in the hands of a new generation, new idols, and new shackles once again emerge and provide a fertile ground for injustice to take root.

Five thousand years ago, to break the back of Dronacharya's inequitable social order in which privilege was conferred by birth, Krishna thundered in the Bhagavad Gita: *Chaturvarnya mya srishta, guna karma vibagashah*. Krishna, the great revolutionary, whose death warrant was issued even before he was born and whose birth took place behind bars, was still in his adolescence when he organised a group of exploited cowherds and milkmaids against his own uncle, Kamsa. It was the very same Krishna who exhorted Arjuna to destroy the misrule of evil Duryodhana and Dussasana brick by brick, even if Arjuna's own blood relations, his guru, and his grandfather, took the side of injustice and stood in the way. Indeed, this is the essence of the Gita: warding off injustice and demonic tendencies is what constitutes dharma.

The same Krishna, who, till his death, waged struggle after struggle against injustice, who, rather than going to a temple and ringing the temple bell, rang the death knell of his enemies, destroying them brick by brick, who, rather than performing the *arti* ceremony before a temple diety, performed a different kind of "ceremony" in which he chopped off the evil Shishupal's head—that very same Krishna of revolutionary vision was reduced to a temple idol by his disciples. On his feet, they tied dancing bells; from his hands, they snatched away his *sudharshan chakra* (his favoured weapon, the discus) and replaced it with a flute; and with mincing, delicate steps, they performed the *rasleela*—the circular dance depicting Krishna's dalliance with the milkmaids of Brij. What easier way for the priests of the Brahmin order to induct the daughters of the poor and powerless as *devdasis*, or female temple servants, and to physically exploit these women?

When, for two years, we waged a relentless struggle in order to see to it that the oppressed (the Dalits) were allowed access into the historical temple of Nathdwara, we discovered that no Dalit was allowed to even cast eyes on, let alone touch, the Krishna idol that had been brought to Nathdwara some 600 years ago from Brivandan. The ones who *could* cast eyes on the idol, who could touch it, were those rich men from Mumbai and Gujarat who offered patronage to thousands of *pandas*—priests officiating at pilgrimage centres, whose daily work it was to pump out ghee from storage wells; grind saffron into a paste; offer five *laddoos* costing Rs 500 each to the Krishna diety in the temple; and confer benediction on disciples, reassuring them that even if they were to loot the country and suck the blood of the poor as much as they possibly could, they only had to bow their heads in the temple to qualify for a passport and a visa to heaven.

Rama, who in his childhood itself resolved to destroy Ravana proclaiming: *neshechar heen karhun mahe bhuj utayae pran keenha,* also was reduced to an inert idol. Even today, there are 15 temples in Ayodhya whose chief priests claim that Rama's true birthplace was in their own respective temples, even as Rama's spurious caretakers flail about for a sixteenth temple. "Rama" was synonymous with "struggle against injustice", "Krishna" was synonymous with "struggle against injustice", but the priests of Rama and Krishna, engaging themselves in shouting *Hare Rama, Hare Krishna, Krishna Krishna, Hare Hare*, comfortably acquiesce to injustice instead of fighting to remove it. In the festival of Dushera, there is a big hullabaloo over the victory of justice over injustice, but instead of destroying a real-life Ravana, amidst dancing and rejoicing, it is a Ravana made of paper that is set aflame. What more could the Ravanas who exploit society ask?

It is not merely the Hindus who are the victims of the flaws of religion. Islam, which arose on the wave of a vigourous revolt against stone worship and idol worship, countenances the veneration of tombs and the custom of donating *chadars* (shawls) at shrines. Similarly, Haj pilgrims kiss a stone, or circumambulate a stone seven times. Or they throw gravel at a *shaitan* (devil), thus betraying the essentials of their religion. I feel the most pained when, on the occasion of Bakri Id, in the name of "sacrifice", instead of renouncing sensuality and raising aloft the banner of revolt against the culture of indulgence, Mussalmans catch hold of a meek lamb or a goat, and slowly cutting it up, say to the hapless and thrashing creature: *Bismillah O Rehman O Rahim*! If this is the measure of mercy, sacrifice, and compassion, you can imagine what the rest of it is like. On the occasion of Muharram, *Tajiye*—paper models of the shrines of Hasan and Hussain, are taken out in procession to the cry of: *Haye Hussain, hum nahuay*! Like Hazrat Iman Hussain, who martyred himself in his struggle against the gluttonous and tyrannical Yajidin at the maidan of Karbala—in the same way, may people challenge the corrupt Yashids standing on street corners, and if need be, be martyred in struggle, like Iman Sahib. In proportion to which the burning of Ravana in effigy and the custom of *Tajiye* being taken out in procession are on the rise are society's real-life Ravanas and Yajids growing in numbers.

In the Roman empire, the irrepressible Jesus Christ, martyred on the cross, kindled the fire of struggle in hundreds of thousands of the exploited—but with what brashness do the padres and the Pope divert attention from his martyrdom with their story about the resurrection of Jesus; instead of urging the crores of followers of Christ to struggle against injustice, they only tell them to have faith in Jesus. Alas, like every other sect, religion and path, the history of Christians too has been one of hypocrisy, blind faith and infatuation with miracles. These religions have, in fact, changed the definition of belief. It is for this reason that every religion is divided into sects. Not just the Hindu religion, but Jainism, Buddhism, Islam, and Christianity have all been victims of this divisiveness.

The followers of the resplendent Guru Gobind Singh, who made his four sons don the yellow robes of martyrdom, today compete with each other in adorning their Gurudwaras with expensive marble stone and polishing the gold cupolas on top, rather than fighting injustice in the name of the Sikhs and the Sikh brotherhood.Rust has accumulated on the swords of Guru Tej Bahadhur's soldiers and all their dharma and karma remains focused on the five K's.

All these are indications that behind the ostentatious display of religious observance, adharma flourishes, while in adharma's shadow, injustice abounds.The glitter of religious observance and the influence of the unrighteous come into play to keep in force an unwritten code, namely, that one share of the wealth wrongly acquired by the exploitation of man by man and the merciless loot of nature is to be allocated to the preservation of religious ostentation, which in turn nurtures an unholy *status quo* alliance of the ruler, the *mutt* (religious establishment) and the wealthy. Perhaps finding God and his servants reduced to this sorry state, the poet weeps:

Khudakebandhokodekkar, kuda se munikarhuiehaiduniya
Ki aisebundehaijis Khudake, voh koi accha Kudhanahin

(Seeing the lot of the servants of the God, the world has wearied of Him,
For a God who has such followers cannot be a good God).

Failings of Isms

Perhaps that is the reason why savants like Karl Marx revolted against organised religion. When communism's revolutionary fervour blazed forth like an erupting volcano, the priests of organised religion trembled with fright and decided that regardless of their differences, they would equate communism with atheism and unite against a common foe. They very conveniently forgot the fact that the communist scheme of things, based as it was on compassion, justice, and equality, was far more spiritual than the aforementioned religious paths—it was far more grounded in human values. Besides, if Marx and Lenin's communism was to be seen as atheist and contemptible merely because it denied the current conception of God, then how could Siddhartha Gautama's Buddhism and Lord Mahavira's Jainism be considered dharmic?

We can also discern other commonalities between communism and religion. Thus, just as, according to Buddhist doctrine, inner watchfulness and attentiveness to the most subtle of mental perceptions induces an evenness of mind, which leads to equanimity, so also, the abolishing of private ownership in accordance with the understandings of the scientific principles of Marxism leads to the eclipse of the capitalist order and the birth of a socialist dispensation based on equality. In one case, the equality, or the evenness, is within, and in the other, it is outside, in force in society.

It needs to be pointed out, though, that neither by way of spiritual resources alone can equanimity be made to fill the heart of every individual, nor can the individual's heart be transformed by changing the relations of production. On the one hand, despite religion, unjust disparities of an intense kind are extensive. On the other, notwithstanding the establishment of a revolutionary socialist order, the individual, caught in the grip of hatred, lust, anger, greed, and so on, is fragmented from within. Consequently, in China and other countries, even after the socialist revolution, the individual has not been liberated from capitalist and consumerist yearnings. It is because of this that the foundations of communism remain hollow.

The question arises, then, as to whether there can be any such order by which the evenness of mind within and the removal of disparity in society can be in accord. On the one hand, the individual rises above sensory desires and consumerist tendencies and on the other, becomes the moving force by which the structural disparities and injustices in society are brought to an end.

This perhaps is the greatest challenge of our age. That we might rise up to the challenge, there is a need, throughout the world, for people who can break free of the traditional thinking, ceremony, and ritual of religion. On the other side, Marxism, as an economic religion, has also become tradition bound, and its slogan of scientific socialism rings hollow today. A third development of note is that science itself has grown by leaps and bounds and every day throws up new discoveries. The Darwinism of the time of Karl Marx is not chiming in with intellectual analysis of the ground realities of today, and the minutest atom of Newton and Dalton has remained but a wavelength in the scientific world after having traversed the realms of Einstein's theory of relativity and quantum physics. The idea of the solid particle has been given up. Science, which at one time considered the cosmos to have limits, has been forced to acknowledge that it is infinite.

Claiming the Future

So why can't flexible and authentic savants from religion, Marxism and science, sit together and, instead of regarding each other with suspicion, establish an open discussion in which each complements the other? Rather than onesided thought, comprehensiveness and concord are what is called for. Such a discussion would mark the beginning of a new spiritual socialistic order. It is for such a great, historical initiative that, with utmost modesty, I offer some suggestions, based on the Vedic *varnasharam vyavastha*. This social order, described in the Vedas, has no explicit recorded history but some signs are certainly visible here and there. In course of time, when the *varnasharam vyavastha* became corrupt, there was a revolutionary attempt to revive it from the root. Five thousand years ago, Krishna attempted to do this through the medium of the Gita.

In more recent times, some 150 years ago, the revolutionary visionary, Sanyasi Dayanand was an important figure to emerge on the scene. His thoughts have been elucidated by the incomparable Vedic scholar Samarpanand (formerly Buddhadev Vidyalankar) in his celebrated work *kayakalp*. I present here what I learnt sitting at the feet of Samarpanand-ji as his disciple.The founder of the Arya Samaj, Swami Dayanand, was a staunch opponent of tradition and fanaticism, which is why, of the 10 rules of the Arya Samaj, a special one is: *Be ever eager to embrace truth and abandon falsehood.* My entreaty is that we adopt this as the foundation of our thinking too. Along with this, I list below the three mantras Swami Dayanand elucidated as *sine qua non* in establishing a vigorous thinking tradition. I enunciate these in the form of the three D's of the English language, namely: to doubt (to question), to debate (to argue), and to dissent (to express disagreement, if need be).

In turning to the Vedas as a source of wisdom from antiquity, we need to steer clear of obfuscations. If we are to free ourselves from the misguided stubbornness of a few Western scholars, then it becomes clear that it is futile to look for history and geography in the Vedas.The Indian Aryan scholars proclaim, with one voice, that the God-knowledge of the Vedas is meant for the welfare of all of humankind. Neither is there caste or high and low in the Vedas, nor is there any special ranking of India or any other country. The meaning of "Arya" in the Vedas refers neither to north India nor to any race. The word "Arya" comes from the root *rgthow*, which, simply put, means knowledge, dynamism, and achievement. In this worldly creation of Ishwara (God), whoever is active, dymamic, and conscientious is an Arya. Throughout the Vedas, the Arya's struggle is not against any Hindu or Mussalman, but rather, against the *dasyu*, or the wicked person. Who are these wicked ones? The answer, according to the Yajurved, is "*akarmaha dasyu*", that is, one who does not labour, one who livesby exploiting others, is a *dasyu*, or a dacoit. Roughly speaking, an Arya is a labourer or a worker and a dasyu is a plunderer or a robber.

The Vedas explicitly state:

Indra vardantho apthuraha krinvatho vishvamaryam apadnantho aravanaha?
(Rg. 6.63.5)

(O you labouring ones of the world, unite to destroy the miserly and exploitative). Some may find in the above quotation a resonance with Karl Marx's famous utterance: "Proletariat of the world unite, establish the dictatorship of the proletariat and expropriate the expropriators". The resonance is a mere coincidence, though; neither were the Vedas composed after Karl Marx, nor is Marx's proclamation likely to have been inspired by the Vedas. The reference to karma in spiritual discourse, it is generally alleged, is meant to justify the disparities of rich and poor, of high and low, in terms of the fruits of past-life karma.The Vedas, however, explicitly enjoin: *kritmmay dakshinay hastay, jayo me savya aahitaha* (toil with the right hand and receive the rewards with the left).

But what if someone were to get work out of you and not pay you for it, then what are you to do? Blame it on the inauspicious karma of a previous life, with arms folded in resignation? Or struggle to wrest your rights? With what clarity is the viewpoint of Vedas illuminated in this verse: *yasay vishvani hastyo; Panch kshetenam vasaha; Spash yasv vo asmdyug; Divyae pasha nirjhe.* Translated into Hindi by the celebrated poet, Bashir Ahmed Myook, the Vedic verse proclaims: "Those exploiters of society who have accumulated wealth, count five of them on your hand. Destroy those enemies of the people. Become a divine thunderbolt that strikes them down". What greater proclamation can there be against disparity and exploitation? Consider also this mantra that censures individualism and consumerism: *kevaladho bavati kevaladi*—one who eats alone incurs sin.

In any social order, the most important question will be: who is the master of the means of production and distribution? In other words, will wealth be privately owned, or will it be owned by the State or by society? On this issue, the Vedas make explicit, not once, but a thousand times, that wealth is to be collectively and not privately owned.Thus, the Yajurveda 40.1 states: *Eeshavasyam edam sarvam yatkinch jagtyaam jagat, tayn tytkayn bhunjeethaha ma grdaha kasya svidhanam?* Again, in the Atharvaveda (3.30.6) it is stated: *Samaanee prapaa pjaa sahvo anna bhaagaha samaane yoktre sahno yunijm samychow agnim saparyatara nabhim evabe taha.* When Guru Nanak said "*Vandkay kha to dab kevah*" distribute and eat and stand firm in earnest endeavour, he was reiterating this verse of the Upanishads in the language of the common man: *Sahanaavavatu sahanow bhunktu sahaveeryam karva vahay tejasve naavdeetamstu. Ma vidveshavahay.* (Katho Upanishad: 2/6/19).

Rejecting and denying today's individualist ideology that is based on exploitation, injustice, and disparity, *varnavyavastha* comes through as a holistic world view of justice, partnership and equality. In place of today's values of consumerism, materialism, and mechanisation, *varnavyavastha* promotes a culture of sacrifice, simple living, and high thinking. *Varnavyavastha* will be such that every individual, be he a child or an elder, every second adopts, towards his life, apart from his faith, spiritual values that sustain the axis of the social, economic, and political order. Most important of all, *varnavyavastha* liberates God from the prison of traditional religion, and worshiping the virtues of God—justice, equality and truth, becomes the stimulating power of social transformation.

I conclude with these reverberating words of Maharishi Dayanand.

> Be not fearful of the powerful who are unjust, but fear the righteous, even if they be powerless. With all your ability, work for the protection and advancement of the righteous, and treat them lovingly, be they utterly powerless, weak and without capability. Work for the destruction and decline of the unrighteous and treat them harshly, regardless of whether they are kings or powerful and strong. In other words, as far as possible, always work to undermine the unjust and to strengthen the righteous. No matter how painful the suffering you have to endure in this endeavour, even if you have to give up your life, never relinquish this humanistic dharma.

NOTES

1. *Vaisesika* (Kanad), *Memansa* (Jaimini), *Yoga* (Patanjali), *Nyaya* (Gautam), *Sankhya* (Kapil) and *Vedanta* (Ved Vyas).

5

Democracy at Work*

Aruna Roy

I have known about Durgabai since I was three years old. This was not only because many institutions were named after her in those days, but also because I had heard my parents talk of her with affection and respect. She was somebody I grew up with. Perhaps mine will be the last generation to remember Aruna Asaf Ali, Durgabai Deshmukh, Sarojini Naidu, Kamala Devi Chattopadhay, and so many others, not merely as photographs of important women in a gallery, but as persons who peopled the milieu of our childhood. In some remote but definite way, they shaped our values.

Durgabai and Aruna Asaf Ali were women who worked in a political context wherein politics and social work were interwoven. Durgabai has been described as the mother of social work, but she also led the Salt March in Madras and spent time in a "C" class prison, having refused the special privileges granted to political prisoners of her stature. As political and social activists, women like her occupied an important space, influencing and shaping not only women's issues but those of mainstream politics as well. Even as a member of Parliament, or as chairperson of the Central Social Welfare Board (CSWB), Durgabai never became a ruler. She remained, in essence, a political and social activist.

So, who are our real leaders today and what do they do? Who are our role models—are they the film stars, glamorous women, and glitterati portrayed by newspapers, who are themselves monitored by manufacturers of cosmetics and by fashion designers? Are they Chief Ministers, Prime Ministers, and CEOs of multinational companies? Or, is there in fact a different type of role model for leadership? There is, even today, a kind of glamour in working for poor people, and fighting for causes. Medha, despite all the controversies about big dams, is an icon with her own kind of glamour. She is a famous and a familiar face. She is a popular figure in India. She is what many would aspire to be—someone known for tenacity and commitment.

* Edited transcript of the July 15, 2006, Durgabai Deshmukh Memorial Lecture by Aruna Roy.

Democratic Spaces

This brings us to the issue of democratic spaces and the opportunities they present us with. To some, democracy is about no more than electing a government to power every five years. In India, we have done this quite ably. For many others, democracy comes alive only with a deeper understanding of the texture of responsibilities and participation; when it is seen, not only in terms of electoral politics, but also in terms of issues of development and meeting people's basic needs. Sadly, demanding accountability of the State to the people is still often regarded as a threat to the sovereignty of the country. But this caricaturing of dissent is now questioned by large numbers of people, and despite many acts which lead us to question India's capability to govern itself through the prevalent democratic structures, there are numerous examples of remarkable collective actions that reinforce a different and more meaningful understanding of the underlying principles of democracy. Even those of us who see the intolerant face of the State on a regular basis realise that India still has large democratic spaces one can use.

In many ways India has greater democratic space than the so called "mature democracies" like the USA. This was forcefully brought home to us when my colleague and friend, Nikhil Dey and I went to the US in March earlier this year. We had taken with us a brilliant five-minute video called "America America". It was made by K.P. Sasi and was a song and dance spoof on President Bush. The short film very creatively and sarcastically deals with war and jingoism. Practically everyone we met was appreciative of it in private viewings, but was apprehensive about showing it in public. Despite all the suppression and oppression in India, our space to voice sharp criticism in the public domain seems to be more a part of our political culture than in the US. We owe a lot to leaders like Durgabai, who were the architects of the independence movement, and who, through their commitment to democratic values even after Independence, helped create a political culture of plurality, with space for dissent.

One example comes from a first-hand encounter we in the MKSS had when the *Ghotala Rath Yatra* was created in 1997 to lampoon politicians who had used the religious imagery of the *rath* (chariot) to procure votes, while they were being exposed in scam after scam. When the *ghotala rath* (the "chariot of scandal") barged into the grounds of a prominent temple in Jaipur, amidst chanting to the tune of a *bhajan* (a religious hymn) but with the words changed to *ghotala raj ki jai jai bolo, bhrashtachar kar hari hari bolo* ("victory to the chariot of scandal, practice corruption and take the name of the Lord"), we saw the expression of people change from reverence (in response to our evocation of the *bhajan*), to shock (when they realised the words had been changed), to delight.

There is, of course, the other face of the Indian ruling establishment. There are daily reports of atrocities against Dalits, women, children, and anyone who is vulnerable, of violation of human rights, of economic crimes against the poor, of State violence and negligence. Sometimes it requires enormous optimism and hope to continue to struggle. It is, therefore, essential to be aware of the democratic spaces that exist and to make sure that those spaces can be expanded. That is the true legacy of people like Durgabai.

The skepticism about the future of democracy and a reluctance to make any effort forces our middle class into cynicism and apathy. Our intellectual middle class is silent more often than not. It is not that they do not think or are not concerned, but the immediate condition of their lives does not force them to act. This silence is going to lead to a huge deficit in the political, economic, and social well-being of the country in years to come.

Whatever the issue—the slums being cleared in Bombay or the removal of hawkers in Calcutta, it is this deafening silence that is most worrying. On the other hand, in the face of the greatest of odds, the poor speak out in large numbers. They have the courage born of despair—the courage to face the police and the threat of violence in order to make their voices heard. The silence of the progressive middle class is all the more tragic because it can make a discernable difference.

Ground Realities

There are tragedies occurring in this country on a daily basis that are greeted by a deafening silence. We read of farmers' suicides, and seem to want to push the issue out of our minds, out of conversations, and out of the pages of newspapers. How many of us feel concerned enough to go to the root cause of the farmers' desperation, and see what we can do about it?

All modes of production in this country are getting hijacked and eroded. I wonder how many of you know that Banarasi saris and rakhis are being made in China and being sold in India at half the price. If you go to any way-side *dhaba* (eatery) between Delhi and where I live in Bhim, ordinary consumer items now come from China. The much sought after "foreign goods" now dominate our local markets. Since they are cheaper, wrist watches, pens, battery cells, and so on are sold quicker. What's going to happen to the production capacity of this huge country, for which we all fought during Independence? And what of Gandhiji's *charkha* (spinning wheel), the symbol of Indian self reliance and economic independence? What we see is economic suicide. This is not to question the need for trade and imports, but you cannot finish off the production capacity and consequently the livelihood of large numbers of the people of the country, and still call it development.

What are the options in front of the farmers who go to the market in Bhim, when *tuar ka dal* (lentil) from Australia is sold much cheaper than our own indigenous variety? I heard from a reliable source that the seed for *tuar ka dal*, imported from India, is being planted in Australia with the sole intention of exporting the harvest to India. What will happen to the farmers in Madhya

Pradesh and other States who grow *tuar ka dal?* Will it not also affect the consumer when the local farmer stops growing it and imports become very expensive?

These are not part of the concern of our political mainstream. We are so busy buying our cars and other consumer goods, we do not have time to examine or question these trends. If we do not question the terms and conditions of our growth today, I do wonder about our future capacity to chart our own course. What kind of democracy is it if the decisions about our local markets and production are being decided from beyond even our national parliament?

I remember at the World Social Forum in Bombay, Captain Lakshmi Sehgal said: "One East India Company came to India and for hundreds of years we were slaves, now there are hundreds of East India Companies coming into this country. I don't know how long we are going to be enslaved now". This may not appear to be so and we may retain the vestiges of our Independence. The appalling question is: how can our own politicians surrender their minds and souls to the economic designs of a few powerful people? What are our options for action?

In some way, every one of the farmers who commit suicide is really speaking truth to power. He is saying, "I cannot live; you are forcing me to commit suicide". We tend to see the farmer who commits suicide as a nuisance. We have ceased to realise how important a contribution farming makes to the self reliance and independence of India. The primary producers are the unsung heroes of our times. Women's groups that made *rakhis* will no longer be able to make them; men and women who make *papad* or chips will be out of jobs. All our little hawkers in the streets will soon be displaced by giant malls with "kilometres of shopping". Where is justice for all these displaced people?

Speaking the Truth to Power

Jeremy Cronin, the deputy leader of the South African Communist Party, who writes poetry, spent several years in jail during Apartheid rule, and is now part of the ruling coalition in South Africa, said that we have to face the democratic challenge of "speaking truth to power, making the truth powerful, and making the powerful truthful". I would like to use this as a reference point for our discussion today.

Justice and power are divided by a huge chasm. "*Speaking truth to power*" is an attempt to bridge that chasm, but it is hard to imagine the challenge this entails. It requires tremendous courage. It requires doggedness, tenacity and above all, it requires continual effort. That's why so many of these efforts are quite aptly called *struggles*. Before my days as a social worker and activist, I could not fully comprehend the nature of this "struggle". One has to simultaneously deal with external exigencies and the inner voices of doubt. Every inch is a battle. Whether it is going to the Collector and waiting outside his office for hours, or going to the BDO (Block Development Officer) asking for minimum wages for wage workers, or battling for forest rights or living spaces, or going to the Information Commissioners who are supposed to be the allies of the people, and whose power and position itself has come out of peoples struggles—it is a struggle with no end in sight. It begins with trying to re-establish an entitlement which is, more often than not, already written into law. How does one establish a legitimate entitlement? That these demands are just is as plain as day for all to see. But who will listen and who indeed, will provide justice? In the persistent speaking of the truth, one hopes that the indifferent will also be moved to support those who are suffering and are at the receiving end of an unequal battle for justice.

Let us start with the controversy surrounding the Sardar Sarovar Dam. The dam, as we know, became controversial because of its potential to inundate the Narmada valley and displace the people living there. Many of us have been concerned for years about what's happened in the Narmada valley—and there are so many who have struggled, fought, written, argued, and debated for the rights of the displaced people of the Narmada. The Narmada has become symbolic for all displaced people in India, and across the world. It is also a factual situation relating to the lives of people who are being displaced in the valley. The contribution of the NBA—the *Narmada Bachao Andolan* (Save the Narmada Movement) to the country has been in its strength to stand up and speak truth to power. The country and the whole world has benefited from this struggle, which has forced us to confront and acknowledge the fundamental dilemmas in the development choices and paradigms we have made. We fashion progress on the debris of human lives, without even acknowledging the human costs. The struggle that the NBA is engaged in now is to try and make us understand that policy, no matter at what stage, can be questioned, argued and debated, and if necessary, even revoked.

While we stand at a point of comparative despair in this *andolan* (movement), we must also take stock of its extraordinary achievements. People in this country have demonstrated across the board that they can support a campaign like this. International participation has bridged communities and people across the world and forced powerful institutions like the World Bank to withdraw funding for the Sardar Sarovar Dam. Today the *andolan* is at a point where things are very bleak because the ruling classes have turned their backs on the people of the Narmada valley. This country's rulers and their institutions have retracted on their promises to the people. Even the Supreme Court, which had so far ruled that rehabilitation must precede forced displacement, has now found the easy way out; it has turned its back on the reality of the lack of rehabilitation, and has said that displacement and rehabilitation can take place simultaneously.

Making the Truth Powerful

We know that the powers that control "democratic India" do not reflect the will of the people. They act under the influence and control of what money can buy. To regain control requires one kind of strategy, but there is also a battle on today to create space for a certain universal set of ethical norms. This is a more basic battle than the struggles defined by ideologies, because truth and ethics are important allies against exploitation. There is also a need to unmask the kinds of exploitative policies that are often ideologically dressed up. These are actually smoke screens to divert attention from cruder interests of private profit and gain. It is self-interest that often dictates policy in this country today. To resist this, people who want to lead ethical and honest lives need to speak out, to enter into debate, even to argue in the public domain.

So we have to *"make the truth powerful"*. Gandhiji's constant emphasis on ethics has much to teach us about establishing ethics in public life. His emphasis on how public figures need to live and delineate norms of an active public life was a part of making the truth powerful by establishing its centrality in political decision making. He died when I was a year and a half old, but reading about him, and understanding his thought processes has helped shape my understanding of the role of honest and open democratic debate in public life. Gandhiji understood the importance and value of bringing all these debates into the public domain. When intellectual giants like Rabindranath Tagore, Ambedkar, and even Nehru disagreed with him, he made sure the debates and the differing opinions were out in print for people to read, to understand, to take positions. He gave central place to the concept of dissent, which is an important and vital democratic value. This commitment to democratic dissent, even at a time when the struggle against the larger adversary was at its peak, created the space for public debate, which helped our generation form its opinions.

Today, the movements that are trying to use democratic spaces to draw attention to issues of survival are finding themselves crowded out of a public domain that does not want to acknolwedge its poorer side. It is not just the Narmada Bachao Andolan which is trying to draw attention to the plight of the displaced. There are today women's groups, Dalit groups, human rights, civil rights, and democratic rights groups screaming for attention to be paid to the exploitation of the vulnerable, the atrocities perpetrated on innocent people, and the suppression and violation of the basic democratic rights of those at the political margins who dare to question the *status quo*. It is not that the movements only have what is often described as a negative agenda. The Right to Information (RTI) campaign or the Right To Work campaign are reflections of an effort to forge a kind of politics which is responsive to peoples concerns.

We have in fact very few choices. We must make democracy work, not in the limited way it has, by going to the polls, or because some of us have been able to get some space to express ourselves. There are some who argue that democracy has only worked up to a certain point, for containing dissent. They point out that misuse of power and lies are given legitimacy by the system. The ruling establishment, regardless of the party in power, bribes, kills, and terrorises the courageous into silence and claims that this is in the interest of peace, law, and order.

If democracy has to be sustained in India, we will have to make people in power hear the truth and take it into account. To force the ruling elite to listen, we will have to state our views from where movements and deprived people stand. This articulation has to come from people like those who read these words. The privileged will have to recognise that in more fundamental ways than they perhaps realise, their freedom and their space is also linked to the circumstances of those being displaced from the Narmada valley and from *jhopad patties* (shacks) in Delhi and Mumbai.

Martin Niemöller's poem continues to make a deep impression on me since I heard it 30 years or so ago.

They came first for the Communists,
and I didn't speak up because I wasn't a Communist.
Then they came for the Jews,
and I didn't speak up because I wasn't a Jew.
Then they came for the trade unionists,
and I didn't speak up because I wasn't a trade unionist.
Then they came for the Catholics,
and I didn't speak up because I was a Protestant.
Then they came for me,
and by that time no one was left to speak up.

It is important for those of us who cherish democracy to perceive that when somebody's powers are being whittled away, when self expression is being limited, the right to live is being questioned, and we keep quiet, we become party to those crimes, we acquiesce to these acts and give strength to their architects. Neutrality is a strange concept in politics. Bishop Desmond Tutu, who has a host of fables to unmask our hypocrisy, points out: "If an elephant has its foot on the tail of a mouse and you say that you are neutral, the mouse will not appreciate your neutrality." There is an important role for a privileged and affluent class who are unhappy with injustice they see around them. They must face the truth, and ensure that the voice of truth is heard. It means actively forming alliances with those fighting for justice. Otherwise, as Paulo Freire said, "Washing one's hands of the conflict between the powerful and the powerless means to side with the powerful, not to be neutral."

We have to speak truth to power, and make the truth powerful, not merely for the poor but for ourselves as well.

Civil Society is a new term being used these days, which people like Durgabai did not have to deal with. It also seems to be, a deliberate attempt to depoliticise processes of socio economic change. A political worker cannot be a part of civil society—supposedly by definition. A social worker is. So, those who are a part of civil society should never be political. What would Durgabai, who was considered the mother of social work, but a person who led *andolans*, went to jail, and was later a member of Parliament be described as? In today's context she would have to shed her political side, I suppose, to be accepted as a member of civil society. The movements of the marginalised and those who represent them are not accepted as part of civil society either. Sometimes we are literally seen as "uncivilised" and therefore unacceptable. Civil society certainly consists of those who can enter the India International Centre. Some of us merge, chameleon-like, into the cultural ambience of either world. But we are a small minority.

The passage of the Right to Information Act and the National Rural Employment Guarantee Act were important breakthroughs. Their passage was not dependent on the support of "civil society" alone. While the Right To Information Act did receive important support from civil society, and is now being used extensively by members of civil society, we must remember that the *andolan* in both rural and urban areas was the result of the struggles of the poor. While we owe the Act to the poor, the voice and interest of the progressive middle class did contribute to the enactment of a very fine piece of legislation aimed at uncovering the truth.

I urge you all today to face the truth, to take sides, to become more political, even if it means shedding the garb of being a part of civil society. As citizens of a democracy, we have to speak out clearly without worrying about the consequences. It is only then, that we can help "make the truth powerful". And at moments when this happens, unexpected changes do take place, and important breakthroughs are made.

Right to Information Act

Two acts that have come into effect—the *Right To Information Act* and the *National Rural Employment Guarantee Act* provide us some space to make the truth powerful.

Let us look at recent experiences of the Right to Information campaign. In the last fortnight, there has been a campaign launched called the "Drive against Bribe". It was a media and citizens campaign to bring the Act to everybody's doorstep. The act of forcing disclosure will go a long way in replacing the apathy and indifference to bribe giving and bribe taking.

The bureaucracy, for its own reasons, does not want this Act even today. If you go into government offices, you will find that the Public Information Officer is not in his seat. If you do find the Public Information Officer, he most often does not even know the Law. When I went to the SDO's and the Tehsildar's office in Beawar and I looked at their files, they did not have a copy of the Law, nor a copy of the rules. All they had was the Tata Consultancy Service's note on using IT for implementing the RTI law. What could he use IT for, if he was not familiar with the law? There is a greater vested interest in the use of computers, and obviously far less in the use of the Right to Information!

In every single government office, there should have been a board outside telling you everything about that office on the October 13, 2005, when this Law came into force. Information required to be posted at a public place under Section 4 of the Act is absent at almost all places, even in Rajasthan. In Jaipur, the government says it does not have the money to paint the boards. The real reason is that once the boards are in place, information will be out, and there is much to conceal.

Then people who apply for information are denied it in many different ways. A famous Rajasthani folk story which my friend Shankar loves quoting comes to mind.

> There was once a Thakhur who was a drunkard. He used to go to sleep at night in a state of intoxication. His wife told his kamdar, the manager of his estate: "Brother, give him a glass of milk every night". The kamdar thought: "The Thakhur is in a state of intoxication at night, so he won't know if I add water to his milk. I'll drink a fourth of his glass of milk and offer him the rest after topping up with water". He did this for a few days. Then he started helped himself to half a glass of milk, giving the Thakhur the remainder after adding an equal measure of water to it. A time came when the kamdar began consuming three fourths of the glass of milk, with the Thakhur getting only a fourth share, diluted with water, as before. Eventually, the kamdar himself consumed the entire glass of milk meant for the Thakhur. The Thakhur got no milk, only water. The kamdar however took the precaution of smearing the Thakhur's moustache with cream from the milk. Waking up in the morning, the Thakhur told his kamdar: "You gave me no milk last night". The kamdar said: "Sahab, you are laboring under a misconception. You did indeed consume milk at night. See, the cream from the milk is on your moustache".
>
> This is exactly what the government has done to us, and now that we have become articulate, they feel disturbed.[1]

The authorities simply do not like the fact that the people are demanding their right to know the reasons for their suffering. Like the Thakur, people were unconscious of the ways and means by which they were defrauded of their right. Today they know, and they demand the full glass of milk that is theirs.

The resistance is mounting. The Right to Information Commission is wanting in activism, but the government is even more guilty. The Commissions themselves have been set up with so much reluctance, that many of them are mere tokens. Despite that, about 850 applications have been filed in Rajasthan in the last 15 days. A woman who was a rape victim was allotted Rs 1,25,000 from the Chief Minister's Fund, and she had not received it. In Beawar, there was a man who's been fighting for the entitlement (*patta*) to his land—a small plot in an urban colony, for many years. He filed an application under RTI and he got the *patta*. There are many examples of poor people who have got wheat quotas denied to them for months and a year or more. They have got the right to scrutinise their land records, the right to see file notings, to examine the process of procuring caste certificates, and so on. The key to all this is the penalty clause that makes an officer liable for a personal penalty of Rs 250 for delaying or denying information to any applicant without adequate reason.

But the RTI is about more than fighting corruption. It is an attempt to reclaim democracy and make democratic institutions work for the majority of the people in this country. When we sat in *dharna* in Beawar in 1996, a lawyer came and said to us in Hindi: "*Your demand is an excellent one, but you will never in all your life get what you're asking, for you expect vitality from a rotting and decayed system.*"[2]

The law gives us hope. It gives everybody a chance to engage and intervene with governance. If you sit back, nothing will happen. We will wait like Godot, forever. The middle class has always wanted to fight its wars by proxy. In a democracy, you and I have to fight our own battles, and every battle strengthens the movement to protect democracy. To begin with, each one of us needs to file one application each, and test the system and strengthen it.

NREGA

The second extraordinary piece of legislation which was passed by Parliament in 2005 is the National Rural Employment Guarantee Act. NREGA guarantees every rural household 100 days a year of manual work at minimum wages within a 5 kilometer radius. A failure to provide work gives the applicant a right to draw an unemployment allowance. NREGA, the first piece of social legislation in India which gives such a legal guarantee, provides the poorest in this country some measure of security to guard against hunger, but even more importantly, it provides the unorganised in rural India a platform for mobilisation. NREGA has immense significance in the context of neo-liberal globalisation where the State, in countries around the world, has been withdrawing from all manner of social commitments.

How will people be able to ensure implementation of this important entitlement? Given India's socio political rural scenario of feudalism, caste and other inequalities, how will the rural poor ensure they get what is their due? How will they stop leakages and fight corruption? It is here that the two pieces of legislation come together. Transparency provisions and the right to information are important means for workers and their organisations to exercise control over delivery systems. The now popular mode of *Jan Sunwais* or public hearings have emerged from the public audits of rural public works programmes designed and controlled by workers organisations in rural Rajasthan. Social audit measures and processes are emerging as important means and platforms through which citizens control can be exercised as an example of participatory democracy. One simple form of social audit is a public assembly where all the details of a project are scrutinised. However, "social audit" can also be understood in a broader sense, as a continuous process of public vigilance.

The first stage of the Right to Information is the proactive disclosure of information, where the government has a duty to inform people. The NREGA and its guidelines lay great emphasis on proactive disclosure, underscoring, and strengthening certain provisions contained in the Right to Information Act. It is an indication of how one movement and campaign affects another leading eventually to a change in the culture of governance.

The principle of granting a legal entitlement for work has been conceded under great duress, and it is still a battle every inch of the way. There are attempts to reduce minimum wages, and the increase in number of districts where scheme is in force has been sluggish. People have not yet realised that the work is demand driven and that they can ask for work at any time of the year. They do not also understand in most parts of the country that the government is bound to give them employment within 15 days, failing which they must be paid an unemployment allowance. There is in fact only one instance in the country of unemployment allowance being paid to a group of workers who had to engage in a protracted agitation to get it.

But implementation of progressive laws is the most difficult part of Jeremy Cronin's trilogy of challenges in an unequal democracy like India's. Having these two laws passed was a part of *"making the powerful truthful"*. The RTI faced massive bureaucratic resistance, and the NREGA was fought with doomsday predictions of fiscal collapse flooding the pink papers and English media. The great outcry against allocation of funds for the NREGA has to be both economically and politically challenged. There seems no earthly reason why 60 per cent of the people cannot claim 2 per cent of the GDP. For a family or household in Rajasthan, it means Rs 7,300 a year. This sum of money is spent in 15 days, may be 10 days, and may be even in a day by the affluent elite. And it is that very class that bitterly opposed the passage of the NREGA.

NREGA and the RTI will not change people's lives in a revolutionary manner, but they have already demonstrated their capacity for mass mobilisation. The *Soochna Evam Rozgar Adikar Abhiyan* (Right to Information and Employment Campaign) set up as a platform to monitor RTI and NREGA in Rajasthan decided to conduct a mass social audit in the district of Dungarpur in Rajasthan in April 2006. Every work site was visited and 1,000 people—workers, representatives of mass organisations, people's organisations and NGOs, academics and researchers, government servants, and others, along with the active support of the State and district administration, did a *pad yatra* (walking tour) of the entire district in a week.

It was seen that almost all households had job cards, knew the basic provisions of the Act, but were unclear on the details. Many did not know about the procedure for filing an application, nor of the facilities available at the work site, or the minimum wage. Of the 1,25,000 strong work force, 70 to 80 per cent were women. There were very few contractors, and no machines were used on the work sites. Muster rolls were available at 99 per cent of the work sites—a phenomenal improvement in the last five years in Rajasthan since the implementation of the state RTI Act in 2000. The social audit process, greeted with protests by local level functionaries, and elected representatives, have demonstrated a means by which the people can confront the powerful with the truth, and eventually force the powerful to be truthful. It is an indication of how democratic spaces can be created even within an otherwise hostile environment.

The passage of the RTI and the NREGA has enabled people in mass organisations understand some facets of the bargaining power of the vote. Many of us are still surprised that laws like these were passed. We have seen some of the weaknesses and vulnerabilities of the political establishment, and we have understood that the vote, with all its imperfections, does, at least occasionally and in a limited way, express the will of the people. People's movements have been very ambivalent about the electoral process. Despite accepting the political nature of their work, they have kept a distance from electoral politics. Can the RTI be used as a means of demanding accountability from political parties and democratic institutions? Can we, for instance, use the RTI to force power structures into accountability, and, by disclosing information in the public domain, make ethical conduct a necessity for governments and citizenry alike? Can the process of transparency help cleanse electoral politics, so that the vote is not so open to blatant manipulation?

If we want civil and democratic rights to be protected, and we want to avoid using violence as a means of change, we have no option but to strengthen political processes and promote participatory democracy. We have to build on small victories to bring ourselves closer to revolutionary change, step by step. It is pointless and counter productive to wait endlessly for the revolution.

Making the Powerful Truthful

Forcing political parties and governments to be truthful is an uphill task. Our failure to do so in some obvious cases makes the task seem impossible. The most recent example is the issue of the displacement in the Narmada valley. In spite of the government's own fact finding teams having established that it was not possible within the next six months to rehabilitate people properly, and the Group of Ministers upholding this stand, people in government still insisted that these were not "accurate" facts and the Prime Minister delayed long enough for the pro dam lobby to distort the facts and the court to give an order that in effect left the oustees with no more than empty promises, rhetoric and platitudes.

Let us also look at an example of success. The Delhi Right to Information Campaign and *Parivartan*, a Delhi-based organisation, exposed the contradictions and the lies behind the Delhi Jal Board and the World Bank proposal to privatise the supply of drinking water. When the 4,000 pages of relevant information was sifted and analysed, it came to light that the facts quoted were technically and otherwise untenable. There was a book I read when I was young called *How to Lie with Statistics*, and that was succinctly what the whole project was. It also proved why access to the decision making processes and opinions contained in file notings were so important for the people to know the truth. The affluent colonies joined the cause of the poorer parts of Delhi, to protest against the project.

Documents are powerful communicators of the truth. Opinions and oral statements do not have the sanctity of papers and records. The use of the RTI Act has generated fear and discomfort amongst the ruling elite. They are uneasy at the prospect of having to share power and be accountable. There are moves to amend the Act. There may be attempts to add to the list of agencies which should be exempted from disclosing information. Many people who are powerful and influential—retired civil servants, eminent economists, members of political parties, important social activists—can make a difference in Delhi. One hopes they will use their clout to fight any measure that might weaken the Act.

Last but not the least is the engagement with electoral politics. How are we going to speak and get our voices heard through the electoral process? In this debate, there are questions, but no one seems to have any solution. But one thing that we have used and found useful in Rajasthan is that a credible commitment to transparency can elect *panches* and *sarpanches* (members of local government bodies) to power. This is a strong deterrent to bribing/ corrupting the process. If people can win elections in India with a very modest budget, is it possible in the larger scenario for people to get elected in a similar fashion to Legislative Assemblies and Parliament?

Epilogue

I will end with quoting Lal Singh, my colleague and a symbol of the extraordinary common sense of the ordinary citizen. Shankar, Nikhil, Lal Singh, Narayan and I were addressing civil servants on a cold winter morning in Jaipur. While Nikhil and I were certainly not *mazdoors* (labourer) or *kisans* (farmers), Shankar fell in the ambivalent category of a man who had done 17 jobs in five years. He worked on all sorts of jobs, from vending to making *pakoras*. But it fell to Lal Singh to truly represent the working *kisan*. When it was his turn to speak, the organisers gave him three minutes. They said it was time for lunch. He responded saying he would need just a minute to say what he wanted to. What he said has the same ring of genius and perception as Jerome Cronin's statement which has been the paradigm of this lecture. He said in Hindi: "*We wonder if we will live if we are denied the Right to Information. You are worried whether you will stay in power if we are granted the Right to Information. Friends, we should all be collectively concerned about whether our country will survive without the Right to Know.*"[3]

Lal Singh went on to conclude:

> And friends, if we do not have a genuine democracy, if all we have is a mockery of it, all our lives will go for a toss. It's not just those of us in the Narmada Valley who will have to pay a price, or those of us in the slums of Mumbai, or the mine workers or the bonded labourers, or the people dying of starvation in central Rajasthan. Friends, it's not only they who will suffer. There are many of us, and if you push us to the wall, there will be civil war in this country, there will be demands, there will be violence, your lives will be spoilt, our lives will be spoilt too. Time gone by cannot be recalled, and so, these are worrisome times. While we still have time, let us use it wisely. As far as we can struggle, let us do so. Let us not forget that we have gained our independence after a formidable struggle for freedom. We need to bring the true meaning of that independence into our midst, and to that end, you need to speak out—speak where you will, speak how you will, make whatever pressure groups you need to.[4]

NOTES

1. Translated into English from the original Hindi by Dr Rajiv Balakrishnan, the editor of this volume.
2. Translated into English from the original Hindi by Dr Rajiv Balakrishnan.
3. Translation from Hindi to English by the author of this chapter.
4. Translated into English from the original Hindi by Dr Rajiv Balakrishnan.

6

Social Development and the Girl Child*

Leila Seth

Durgabai Deshmukh, a young girl of great courage and determination who flowered into a woman of immense strength and dynamism, created institutions that helped women at the grass roots. At the age of 12, she influenced *devadasis* to change their way of life and Muslim women who wore *burqas* to do away with this degrading social custom. While still a little girl, she persuaded Mahatma Gandhi to address a group of these women in Kakinada for a few minutes. Gandhi spoke for more than half an hour, much to the annoyance of the local leaders who had arranged for him to speak at another locale and had conceded to Durgabai only a few minutes of his time. Gandhiji said that it was such constructive reform programmes for the emancipation of women he liked best. When she was only 14 years old, she started a Hindi medium school—the *Balika Hindi Pathasala*. Later in life, Durgabai went on to become a young committed freedom fighter and, in that role, she learnt Hindi and taught it to 400 women who needed to know that language in order to function as volunteers for the Congress session in 1923. I salute her spirit of social service and nationalism.

Child Marriage and Age at Marriage

The reasons for my choice of topic (Social Development and the Girl Child) were twofold. First, when I read Durgabai's autobiography, I was reminded of the tragic trauma of child marriages. This is what Durgabai, who was married in 1917, says:

> When I was young, the social conditions in India were feudalistic. Child marriages were in great vogue. And I myself was a victim of this primitive social custom.[1]

She goes on to add:

> The only mistake my father had committed was to marry me off when I was eight years of age, to an adopted son of a zamindar who had estates

* Edited transcript of July 15, 1997, Durgabai Deshmukh Memorial Lecture by Justice Leila Seth.

> yielding a large income. Later my father had regretted this. He died in 1929 at the early age of thirty-six. The words he spoke to my mother, Krishnavenamma, before he breathed his last, were that he had ruined his daughter's life by marrying her at an early age, and that my mother should give her consent if and when I wanted to marry someone else.
>
> When I grew up to the age of fifteen, I realised the significance of marriage. I told my father that I could not treat the man to whom I had been married as husband. I also told him that I would tell Subba Rao (that was his name) that I could not accept him as husband, and that I would be prepared to give him in writing to that effect. I also told him that he could marry any girl he liked. This was before the marriage was consummated.
>
> In fairness, I must say that Subba Rao was a decent and liberal man. He understood my point. After a couple of years, his elders pressed him to marry again, especially because he himself was an adopted son and there had been no children in the family for three generations. They wanted me to give a letter to the effect that I would not object to his marrying another girl. This was understandable as no parents would like to give in marriage their daughter as a second bride.[2]

The second rationale for the topic I have chosen links up with a recent meeting I had with the well-known sociologist, André Betéille, who made a totally unconnected remark at the Lal Bahadur Shastri National Academy of Administration, Mussoorie, when we were together there. He said he was often asked by students as to what he saw as the single most significant favourable social trend in India in the last 100 years. Replying, he said that though it was difficult to prioritise, he felt that the fact of the age of marriage of girls having steadily gone up, especially in the higher castes, where it was particularly low, was an extremely important trend. He mentioned that his own Bengali grandmother from a *kulin* Brahmin family was married before attaining puberty at the age of 10 to a much older widower with a couple of children. These step-children eventually appropriated the property on her husband's death, leaving her a defenceless widow with young children and no learning or earning capacity. She did not return to her natal family and somehow fended for herself, selling her jewellery, etc. till one of her sons was employed. On hearing this tale, the tragedy and the vulnerability of the girl child struck me anew and forced me to the conclusion that unless her condition improved rapidly, there could be no real social development.

Why child marriage was so prevalent in the past and why it still continues to this day, though to a much lesser extent, depriving girls of the chance of education and growth, are pertinent questions. The answer lies in the patriarchal system and the socialisation process in India, which has been to make boys independent and get girls married. When a girl attains puberty, she becomes sexually vulnerable and requires protection, and the parents want to shift this burden as soon as possible. So marriage is considered a priority. Since the girl is not educated, she is dependent on others, and this is what society envisages.

This has been the way things were, from olden times. Manu, the law-giver, said: "She should do nothing independently even in her own house; in childhood, subject to her father; in youth to her husband; and when her husband is dead, to her son. She should never enjoy independence...". Moved by the plight of women, Rabindranath Tagore lamented: *"O Lord why have you not given woman the right to conquer her destiny? Why does she have to wait head bowed by the roadside, waiting with tired patience, hoping for a miracle in the morrow?"* Has that morrow now arrived and is that miracle now taking place?

As noted, attainment of puberty has traditionally played an important role in determining age of marriage for girls, but despite this, the mean age of marriage for females rose from 13.2 years at the beginning of the century to 16.1 in 1951–61. It went up to 17.2 years by 1971 and to 18.3 by 1981. By 1992, the mean age of "effective marriage" for females was 19.5. However, while more than 90 per cent of women were married in the 25 to 29 year age group in 1992, about 30 per cent were married while still in their teens, that is, when they were in the age group of 15 to 19 years.

Early marriage is a social evil which affects the growth, both physical and mental, of the girl and also results in high infant and maternal mortality. As pregnancies often took place before the girl was physically mature, it led to a high rate of maternal mortality. In the early decades of the twentieth century, women, unsure of their children's survival, and also because of the desire for sons, bore a very heavy burden of repeated pregnancies. Child bearing and child caring started from the early age of 15 and continued all through the reproductive span, up to 45 years. The marriage age was low and rarely did someone remain unmarried. There were miscarriages and still births and infant mortality was also very high, resulting in a great deal of wastage in reproduction.

The Child Marriage Restraint Act 1929, amended to become The Child Marriage Restraint (Amendment) Act 1978 (Act 2 of 1978), raised the minimum age of marriage of girls to 18 years from 15, and for boys, to 21 years from 18. This was designed to strike at the evil of early marriages of girls and the ensuing early pregnancies, which resulted in undue strain on young mothers and the birth of premature babies. Despite the law, however, child marriages continue.[3] To cite cases in point, Ameena, a young Muslim girl of 12 from Hyderabad was married off to Sheikh Yahaya, a 60-year-old Arab, who was taking her out of India; and Chhoti was married off to Manjit Singh, a 45-year-old deaf and dumb Sikh from Western UP. Many child marriages are performed even now during the festival of Teej in Rajasthan and during the festival of Mahashivratri at Deoghar in Bihar.

Maternal Mortality

As is apparent from the figures cited above, the mean age of marriage has risen from about 13 years at the beginning of the twentieth century to 16 and 19 at around the middle and end of the century respectively. This is certainly a healthy sign, more so because early childbearing increases the risk of maternal mortality. However, despite the increase in the minimum age of marriage of girls, maternal mortality continues to be high in the country. In the nineties, the Maternal Mortality Rate (MMR) in India was as high as 750 (per 100,000 live births). Sri Lanka, by comparison, brought down its MMR from 813 in 1948 to 140 in the 1990s. In the Indian context, gender discrimination in conjunction with poverty seems to be the main factor acting to weaken women and make them less able to withstand the rigours of childbearing. Girls are breastfed for shorter periods than boys and given less food and medical attention, which result in widespread malnutrition and anaemia among girls. Poor health care and sanitation and lack of education are other factors. Sri Lanka's success has been due mainly to free health care and free education which has led to 80 per cent literacy among women.

Girls Schooling in India

At the beginning of the nineteenth century, there was hardly any provision for the formal education of girls. The position was not much better even at the beginning of the twentieth century. In 1901, the percentage of literacy amongst women was only 0.8. The number of girls enrolled for every 100 boys was only 12 at the primary stage and 4 at the secondary stage. The total enrolment in higher education was only 264, which included 76 girls studying in medical colleges and 11 in colleges of education (Education Commission Report 1964–67). Subsequently, notwithstanding increase in overall literacy levels, girls continued to be disadvantaged. The literacy rate in India increased from 18.33 in 1951 to 52.51 in 1991. In classes VI to VIII, the enrolment ratio went up from 21 in 1950–51 to 35 in 1965–66, and in the case of enrolment in classes IX to XI, the ratio rose from 15 in 1951 to 26 in 1965–66. However, sex differentials have been consistent and pronounced. Thus, in 1950–51, there were 3.9 girls for every 100 boys in classes I to V. In 1965–66, the figure rose to 55 girls for 100 boys.

Notwithstanding the disparities, over the four decades 1951 to 1991, female literacy went up about five times, from 8.86 in 1951 to 39.29 in 1991. There are, however, wide regional variations, ranging from near universal literacy in Kerala to 20.8 per cent female literacy in Rajasthan. Rural-urban differentials in literacy are also wide. The literacy rate in 1991 for rural areas was 44.7 against 73.0 for urban areas. Female literacy in rural areas—30.4 per cent, was still very low. Overall, it is true that the enrollment of girls in schools has increased nine fold at the primary level—from 5.4 million in 1950–51 to 46.44 million in 1993-94, and over 30 fold at the middle stage—from 0.5 million in 1950–51 to 15.7 million in 1993–94. At the higher secondary stage, the increase has been from 0.2 million to 8.1 million over the same period. However, a high rate of dropout from schooling continues to be a major problem. In 1993–94, a little more than one-third (39 per cent) of the girls who enrolled at the primary stage dropped out, before completing the primary level. More than half of them (about 57 per cent) dropped out before completing the middle stage. Of the remainder who reached the higher secondary stage (43 per cent), another 10 per cent dropped out before the school completion stage. Thus, only about 32 per cent of girls entering the primary stage completed their schooling. Such high dropout rates are because of social, cultural, and economic factors.

The Accursed Daughter

One of the reasons why a daughter is not educated is that she is seen as *paraya dhan*—another's wealth—and is considered only a transitory member of her natal family. Her whole upbringing is oriented towards that end. She is taught to be timid and submissive so that she can adjust to the ways of her new home. Consequently she hesitates to take decisions. Her training to be self-sacrificing and subservient to age and authority results in producing an apathetic person who suffers in silence and does not even speak out when constraints are removed. Further, ignorance of her rights and the fear of returning to a home where she is not wanted keeps a young girl tied to these early marriages contracted without consent.

Discrimination against the unwanted daughter starts even before birth. Amniocentesis is being misused for sex determination of the foetus so that if the foetus is female, it is aborted. A survey conducted in Bombay some years ago found that out of 8,000 reported abortions, 7,999 were female foetuses. Subsequently, the use of tests for sex determination was banned in the country by the Pre-natal Diagnostic Technique (Regulation and Protection of Misuse) Act 1994 (Act 57 of 1994).[4] Under the law, such tests can be used only to screen for genetic defects. But sex determination tests are continuing because there is no political will to enforce the law ... not a single doctor has been convicted for conducting these tests.

Infanticide—by choking the baby girl to death or giving her opium or by other means, is not uncommon. On November 22, 1995, an article in *The Pioneer* referred to infanticide in certain parts of northern India where the eldest female member of the family would ask the male head of the household: *Baraat rakhni hai ya lautani?* The response decided the fate of the new born girl. If the male head said *"baraat rakhni hai"*, the baby girl survived—otherwise she had to leave the world without opening her eyes. It is believed that this practice of murdering the new born is still prevalent in Sitamarhi, Bhagalpur, and Katihar in Bihar, Salem in Tamil Nadu, Bhind in Madhya Pradesh, and a few places in Haryana and Punjab.

In *The Pioneer* of October 23, 1996, there was another article about female infanticide. It was a heart rending account of the anguish of the women of the Khallar community of Tamil Nadu. One of these women, losing consciousness in the aftermath of childbirth, did not see the face of her child. "My neighbours told me she was very beautiful. My mother and the nurse buried her alive ... I did not even hear her cry". Another woman, recounting her experience, said: "I had to cross the river to reach my husband's house. I was carrying the child on my shoulder and I lowered her slowly as I was getting into deep water. By the time I crossed the river, I knew my new born child was dead ... That is the burden I will carry within my conscience. But at least my daughter will not go through what I am going through ...".

The article also talks of other methods of killing female babies. One method is to feed the female infant with poisonous milk of a wild plant (calotropic gigantea) or the oleander berries known for their lethal poison. It is reported that almost every Khallar household has this plant growing in the courtyard for use at an appropriate time. Another method was to stuff a few coarse grains of paddy into the baby's mouth. On breathing the grain into her windpipe, the infant chokes to death. But the easiest way is simply to starve the girl child or place a flower on her throat and suffocate her to death.

On an average, of the 1,200 deliveries per year to women belonging to the Khallar caste, nearly 600 are female babies. Out of this, an estimated 570 babies along with their mothers vanish as soon as they open their eyes. Hospital sources estimate that nearly 80 per cent of these vanishing babies become victims of female infanticide. Though a "cradle baby scheme" has been started where parents can quietly deposit their unwanted female babies, only a negligible number are taking advantage of this scheme.

Though the infant mortality rate has shown a great improvement since Independence, gender violence and discrimination, both societal and domestic, continue unabated. A most telling demographic symptom is the persistence of an adverse sex ratio. The number of females per 1,000 males has fast declined from 972 in 1901 to 934 in 1981 and 927 in 1991. This led the famous Harvard economist Amartya Sen to ask: "Where are the missing women?" He estimated that in 1990, 100 million fewer women were alive than the number projected by demographic studies.

The Curse of a Daughter

In the words of Rabindranath Tagore: "Every time a child is born, it brings with it the hope that God is not yet disappointed with man." But it appears to me that when a girl child is born in India, more often than not, man is disappointed with God. The birth of the first daughter is often considered bad luck, the second a disaster, and the third a catastrophe. Indeed, it has been said in *Atharva Veda* VI-2-3: "The birth of a girl, grant it elsewhere, here grant a boy." Why is a daughter considered a curse? Mainly because she is seen as an economic liability, as the difficulties faced by her parents in getting her married with adequate dowry are considerable. This results in parents' treating their sons and daughters differently—loving one and neglecting the other; doting on the son and depriving the daughter; educating the boy and letting the girl child suffer ignorance, while making her do domestic and other chores, including looking after siblings and cattle.

The Promise of Education

So what is the girl child asking for? A fair deal. A right to be born. A right to be nourished and loved. A right to education and a homogeneous environment. A right to choose, and a right to excel. In the poem below, I give voice to the girl child's plea.

Where have all the young girls gone?
Some are aborted before they were born;
A few are buried or choked with coarse paddy,
Others are smothered, starved or drowned in a well;
Poisoned with berries of oleander till dead,
So that dowry need not be paid or in-laws fed,
Or daughters raped, beaten or burnt—
This is the sad story of the girl child's hell.

Father, why do you discriminate against me,
When I can be as good as my brother?
Mother—nurture, nourish and educate me, and you will see
That I will not be a burden but will control my own destiny.
And you will have nothing to fear (if brother is not there),
I will look after you both when you are old and worn with care;
I ask only to be treated equally—will you not dare?

O Father, give me a chance,
Just give me a chance!
O Mother, break the bonds of tradition
And let me into the sunlight to dance.

For us to heed the girl child's plea, education of all children is essential, for children are the parents of tomorrow and can eliminate the evils of dowry and discrimination. This must be given top priority as it is a very important factor in bringing about the attitudinal changes necessary for treating girls on par. Moreover, the education of girls and women is a necessity, for it is only then that they become aware of their rights, assert themselves, and change perceptions in society both for themselves and their children. The fact that more girls are now getting educated and have greater employment opportunities has also played a role in raising their age at marriage. In fact, many have started questioning whether marriage is the main aim of a young girl's life, especially because of the evil of subjugation.

Many parents feel it is better for the girl child to look after her siblings and do domestic chores rather than go to school; they also feel they have no choice;

they need the services of the girl child and do not appreciate the advantage gained from schooling. But the girl child, when asked, feels differently. Myron Weiner, in his book *The Child and the State in India*, talks of a group of girls in a village near Pune who had been enrolled and then taken out of school at the request of their mothers to look after siblings, fetch water and firewood, and care for cattle. On being queried, these children said that they would ensure their own daughters went to school. They said they would, if necessary, send their babies to their mothers-in-law or to a crèche or arrange for someone to watch over them so that young girls could go to school. The cattle could be herded together and someone hired to look after them. As such, the children did not regard their parents' decision about their schooling as a correct one, nor did they regard the parents as not having a choice in the matter.

A study conducted at the Giri Institute of Social Sciences in Uttar Pradesh indicated that there was a direct relationship between enrolment in school and the number of children in the family, especially in the case of girls. If there were many young siblings, the elder children stayed home to take care of the younger ones. The study found also that if there was even one educated member in the family, then the children were more likely to be kept in school; and that they stayed in school if the school was attractive and had play facilities and programmes that held their interest. Thus, a child-friendly school environment is important. Indeed, in Lalima Gupta and others *vs.* State of Himachal Pradesh and another AIR (1993), H.P. (Page 11), it was held that the best way to educate small children was for the school to be an extension of the home so that the child could develop in a natural and holistic manner. A teacher who knows the culture and language of the child is the best person to provide the participatory environment. He should have a child-centered approach and a warm welcoming attitude, especially when the child is a first-generation learner.

In a significant development, the right to primary education has now been held to be a fundamental right. In Unni Krishnan J.P. and others *vs.* State of Andhra Pradesh and others, AIR (1993), S.C.,[5] three out of the five judges held that though the right to education is not stated expressly as a fundamental right, it is implicit in and flows from the Right to Life guaranteed under Article 21. Consequently, construing Articles 45, 46 and 41 of the Directive Principles of Part IV of the Constitution, the Supreme Court held that every child/citizen of this country has a right to free education until he (she) completes the age of 14; thereafter his (her) rights are circumscribed by the State's economic capacity and development. More specifically, the Constitution of India adopted in 1950 not only grants equality to women but also empowers the State to adopt measures of affirmative discrimination in favour of them. The Constitution further imposes a duty on every citizen to renounce practices derogatory to the dignity of women.

Towards Gender Equality

India's search for an organisational structure to coordinate efforts towards gender equality and gender equity began with the establishment of the Central Social Welfare Board in 1953. Durgabai Deshmukh was responsible for its conception and its coming into existence and was appointed its first chairperson. The concept of a national machinery has been evolving ever since. In 1971, the Government appointed a Committee on the Status of Women in India (CSWI). The CSWI raised basic questions about the socialisation process inherent in a hierarchical society. Its report *Toward Equality* led to a recognisable shift from viewing women as targets of welfare policies in the social sector to regarding them as critical groups for development. This was reflected in the Sixth Five year Plan (1980–85) which, for the first time in India's planning history, contained a chapter on Women and Development. It conceived of a multi-pronged strategy as essential for women's development relating to employment and economic independence; education; access to health care and family planning; support services to meet the practical gender needs of women; creation of an enabling policy, and an institutional and legal environment.

In 1985, a Department of Women and Child Development was set up under the newly created Ministry of Human Resource Development, and in 1990, the National Commission for Women was set up by an Act of Parliament. In another significant development, the Eighth Five Year Plan (1992–97) promised to ensure that the benefits of development from different sectors did not bypass women. Consequently, the three core sectors of employment, education, and health care were to be monitored very closely. Notably, the approach of the Eighth Plan, which regards women as equal partners in the development process, marks a progress from the goal of development to that of empowerment of women. Also auspicious is the 73rd and 74th Constitutional Amendment Acts of 1993, which constitute a watershed for the advancement of Indian women. These amendments ensure that one-third of the total elected seats and positions of chairpersons in rural and urban local bodies go to women. About one million women are estimated to emerge as leaders at the grass root level in rural areas alone, and of these, 75,000 are to be chairpersons. Despite such an achievement, women still comprise the largest section of population living in absolute poverty and represent the poorest of the poor.

Alas, despite the specific schemes and programmes of the government, despite the enthusiasm and activities of voluntary agencies, the benefits of development have not yet reached women and girl children. Gender equality is still a distant dream. But there is no premium on dreaming!

Gender Stereotyping

The mother and wife, who is required to take care of the physical needs of others, seldom has time to develop her own higher faculties of the mind. As a young girl, she is most vulnerable to the insults of poverty and deprivation. As an infant, she is likely to be breastfed for a shorter time than her brother, and be neglected when she falls ill. As she grows up, she becomes the victim of discrimination in access to education, skill development, and recreation. Her entire socialisation tends to make marriage the ultimate goal of her existence, and subservience to the males in the household, her initial and final destiny. Women have carried out the domestic work for centuries without being given any credit for it. Men have not changed their lifestyle and have been brought up to expect service and care as an integral part of domestic life. Consequently, women who have tried to achieve something in other spheres have had to make most of the adjustments and carry out their domestic work along with any outside work they have done. Now that women are realising their potential, caretaking has to be shared or else there cannot be any equality of opportunity. The ideology of patriarchy and the accompanying culture of silence need to be challenged and broken if development is to touch the lives of women. Without equity in the family, there cannot be equity in society. The girl child is entitled to a right to justice. Gender justice must start from the womb. The unique empowerment strategy which is emerging can only be effective if patriarchal perceptions are altered and an expanding network of support services built up so that women are freed from some of their assumed gender related shackles.

Gandhiji suspected that women resist male exploitation and domination by refusing to marry, refusing to have sex, and even refusing to cook. According to him, collective resistance would be the way for women to liberate themselves from the chains of gender apartheid. He said, "Marriage is an institution designed by men to tyrannise women. More often than not, a woman's time is taken up not by the performance of domestic duties but in catering to the egoistic pleasures of her lord and master." This "domestic slavery of the kitchen" was, to Gandhi, a remnant of barbarism. A believer in harmonising and equalising, Gandhiji persuaded men to cook, sew, clean dishes, etc.—to do what was known as "women's work". The idea was to "shift mental perceptions of the difference between men and women by transporting traditional roles".

The need of the hour is the immediate implementation of compulsory education and the creation of an environment leading to equality. An educated child, especially a girl child, will eventually result in an educated family and a just society free from superstition and prejudice. When children play and study together, caste and religious differences do not seem to matter; even economic differences are obliterated as the bonds of friendship flourish. Apart from this, an educated woman will be anxious to implement family planning, health care, and sanitation. She will have the capacity to earn and thus not feel suppressed and subordinate to men. She will be self-confident and not view marriage as the only option, thus hopefully resulting in the decline and death of the evils of dowry.

Contradictions of Development

In 50 years of Independence, things have changed but not sufficiently. It is true that foodgrain production has increased and famines have been virtually eliminated, yet 50 per cent of children under four (60 million) remain undernourished. Though literacy has more than doubled, almost half the population remains illiterate. Life expectancy has more than doubled and infant mortality more than halved (74 per 1,000 live births), yet there are 2.2 million infant deaths, most of them avoidable. More than 90 per cent of the population has access to safe drinking water but declining water tables, resulting in poor quality of water and its contamination, are raising problems.

Income poverty has been reduced, especially in Andhra Pradesh, Haryana, Kerala, and Punjab, but 50 per cent of India's rural income-poor live in the States of Bihar, Madhya Pradesh, and Uttar Pradesh, where the reduction has not been so good. These three States, along with Rajasthan, have also not been too successful in family planning and reproductive health programmes. The population has continued to increase and illiteracy is high. Deprivation hits women worse than men, and though the gap has been narrowing, wide gender inequality still exists. The political commitment to put primary education, health and gender justice on top of the agenda has been strong in words but not in action. Despite national and international laws, plans, schemes and conferences, true gender justice has not been reached. The Convention on the Rights of the Child and the Convention on the Elimination of All Forms of Discrimination against Women has made but a dent.

Building Capabilities

The Human Development Report 1997 published by the United Nations Development Programme states that poverty of choices is far more crippling than poverty of income. It speaks also of working towards gender equality as a means to end poverty. It calls upon people to commit themselves to gender equality in order to unleash the energy and productive capacity of women around the world.

Many of the things that have been touched upon here are known to most of us, but we need to constantly to feel the anguish to stir ourselves into action. The shocking facts regarding discrimination and neglect of the girl child which still exist are not really known to all sections of society. We need to make people aware of the prevailing situation and mobilise a mass movement to change it. The political commitment to provide primary education and health services must be enforced. It is important to highlight the situation of the girl child, and bringing it centre stage, force political parties to take a stand.

NOTES

1. Deshmukh. 1980. *Chintaman and I.* New Delhi: Allied Publishers Private Limited, p. 1.

2. Ibid. pp. 1–2.
3. The Child Marriage and Restraint Act applies to all religions but it does not make marriages which are performed below the minimum age null and void. It merely provides for a punishment of the parents, of the guardians and of the bridegroom, if he is an adult, as also of persons who conduct, perform or direct a child marriage. The question of annulment, repudiation, divorce, etc., however, depends on the personal law of the parties.
4. The Act replaced a similar legislation passed by the State of Maharashtra in 1988.
5. p. 2178.

7

Women and the Political Process*

Vina Mazumdar

While younger generations perhaps know Durgabai as a pioneer social worker, older women and men still remember her as the indomitable freedom fighter who created and managed an institution at the age of 12, and brought Mahatma Gandhi to address a meeting of devadasis in the face of reluctance and resistance from the local leaders organising his programme. As I was to discover in a village in Nagaland in 1973, she could even make an impact on women otherwise cut off from any knowledge or contact with the national mainstream. When the Committee on the Status of Women arrived at the village to talk to the women there, one old woman came forward to ask, "Do you know Durgabai?" We said we knew her slightly, but that our Chairperson, Phulrenu Guha, had a long experience of working with her. "Oh then, we shall tell you all you want to know. Durgabai came here 20 years ago, and told us to organise a *mahila mandal* [women's association] so that we could resolve our problems. We have done something, but there are many new problems; now that you people have come, we can tell you all about it."

A Rebel at Twenty-One

Durgabai's early life epitomised the struggle of many upper-caste, spirited women to whom the freedom movement provided an opportunity to break out of oppressive social norms, and seek creative avenues for self-fulfillment and leadership without the opprobrium of being perceived as "selfish" or "self-centered". A rebel constricted by inherited values that ran counter to placing her own dreams and designs before her obligations to the family, she could take on the needs of the bigger family—the nation, without feeling guilty. Within the national context, her priorities were clear and consistent—her obligations were to all those oppressed by poverty, ignorance, and oppressive social institutions. In her own words, the political awakening of the freedom

* Edited transcript of the July 15, 1993, Durgabai Deshmukh Memorial Lecture by Professor Vina Mazumdar.

movement provided "the renaissance of Indian womanhood".[1] The value of equality had to be internalised by all who preached it, so the young rebel, at the age of 21, was challenging her own party leaders for allowing the Raj to divide political prisoners into A, B, and C classes for the identical offence of breaking the Salt Law.

Two decades later, she challenged two successive Finance Ministers (including the one she was to marry later) for drawing up "rich men's budgets, with no provision for the poor".[2] Since the Constitution designed India as a "welfare" instead of a "police" State, she told the Legislature[3] as well as the Prime Minister and the Finance Minister that "there was no use talking about the need for bringing up the weaker sections of society, and giving better status to women unless we had a budgetary provision to help them and to save the institutions working for their welfare from being closed down".[4] From her autobiography, *Chintamani and I,* it is evident that she was acutely aware of the responsibilities of the State in this regard. "The Chapter on Directive Principles places on the State a wide range of obligations," she notes.[5] Her insistence on the obligations of the State as well as of individual men and women—a lesson she learnt from Gandhiji, stoked the fires of rebellion in her, and though she used the term "welfare" in describing her life work, by her own definition, she was talking about social reform which "aims essentially at change, a *change that may sometimes involve the basic values and the social institutions in the community* ..." (emphasis added).[6] Social reform, as she understood it, included: "Fighting for the equality of rights of women, pleading for a better deal for Harijans, and launching a movement for a change in the manner of handling juvenile delinquents..."[7] The rebel was thus fully aware of the hurdles in the way and was impatient with the two men she admired so much for being so insensitive to them.

Central Social Welfare Board

I intend to interpret Durgabai's creation and development of the Central Social Welfare Board (CSWB) from this perspective. Durgabai had an intimate understanding of the obstacles that would hamper the women she knew best from actively participating as equals of men in the political process—a responsibility that came with equal political rights. Upper caste, middle class women were rooted deeply in their family roles and obligations to traditions, and to caste and religious norms, and would not find it easy to free themselves from those values. The excitement and slackening of controls that had come during the freedom struggle were already over. The women's movement, mostly confined to elite women in urban areas, was beginning to flag. Younger generations with greater advantages of education and/or professional experience who could have been expected to swell its ranks appeared to be keener on taking up jobs as the first generation beneficiaries of the equality clauses of the Constitution. Women's organisations were beginning to break down under ideological and/or personality tensions. The relatively better known leaders with broader popular support were picked up by the government for high offices, a move which could not be opposed but was certainly going to denude the women's movement and the organisations of a sense of direction, purpose and much needed challenge, excitement and leadership.

Realist enough to know that the women's movement had a very narrow base and had never really reached the grassroots except perhaps for short spells during the great national upheavals, Durgabai also knew that her lieutenants would need considerable exposure to the variety of problems at the grassroots as well as skills to create new institutions to manage nation-building activities. One such lieutenant—Sarojini Varadappan, told me how Durgabai dragooned them into learning account-keeping, maintaining records, being ready to face audits, and still maintaining touch with the actual work going on among women, children, and the needy at the grassroots.

The CSWB was a unique institution whose real purpose and status baffled many political and administrative pundits over the years. Twenty years after the birth of the CSWB, even members of the Committee on the Status of Women in India (CSWI) remained confused. While the relatively younger, professional academics accustomed to neat classifications and categories saw the CSWB as an official agency, a creation and extension of the State, the serving Chairperson of the Board—Neera Dogra, who was also member of the CSWI and some of the older members who had served on it earlier, perceived it primarily as a non-official women's body engaged in assisting other voluntary organisations, most of which they believed were run by women to carry out nation-building tasks which, in the CSWB's opinion, could be done much better by them than by the bureaucracy.

In hindsight, after the experience of the last 20 years, I am compelled to admit that what I dismissed then as lack of understanding by older colleagues was in fact the message that Durgabai had sought to imprint on their minds—to view themselves not as agents of government, but as constructive workers in nation-building, and mobilisers of new groups of women, especially in rural areas, for similar tasks. As a teacher of formal politics decades ago, I would perhaps not have regarded such mobilisation as political action, but in today's context, I find strange parallelisms between some aspects of the post-emergency women's movement and the vision and efforts of Durgabai. I would, therefore, describe her first steps unhesitatingly as efforts to expand avenues for women to participate more efficiently and effectively in the political process.

Three Themes

The objective here is not to analyse the work of the CSWB or of Durgabai, but to present the changing perspective of the inter-relationship between women and the political process that has been evolving through the revival of the women's movement since the 1970s. In my view, this re-interpretation of

Durgabai becomes not only an important analytical tool, but provides some critical answers to a few of the dilemmas that face the present women's movement.

I shall concentrate on only three:

(a) nature and purpose of the role that women do or should play in the political process;
(b) meaning and implications of the frequently used term "women's perspective"; and
(c) in the face of earlier lessons from India and elsewhere in the world, how do we ensure the sustainability as well as sustenance of the women's movement?

Being born a woman or being trained as a political scientist did not help me identify these issues. What did was the process of unlearning, new learning, and redefining—a process that began, in my case, with the investigations of the Committee on the Status of Women in India (CSWI) and has continued with the rebirth of the women's movement. I believe my formulations will find echoes in many hearts.

Many Voices

The CSWI's investigation of changes in women's status since Independence left us with more questions than answers. Why had the whole process of change—economic, political or otherwise—deviated so far from what the women's movement had dreamt of when it demanded total equality? Why had the government, political parties, other institutions of our political system and constitutional and political pundits of all hues ignored the gender dimensions of such deviations? Why had the women in active political life, including many who achieved positions of great power and influence, not done anything about it, not even registered any protest? Above all, why, despite the steadily increasing participation of women in the voting process,[8] had no one had taken the responsibility to inform them of their rights and responsibilities in free India?

In the absence of a movement, the Committee's recommendations could only be addressed to the formal institutions—the government, the judiciary, political parties, the educational system, trade unions, etc. But we—educated professional women—did not spare ourselves for our failure to ensure the extension of these rights to other women. We, too, had contributed to the increasing devaluation and marginalisation of the majority of women by society and by policy-makers by ignoring our broader responsibilities. Neither could we absolve ourselves of the guilt for the collapse of the women's movement or the total lack of understanding, knowledge or sensitivity among educated middle class women of the appalling situation of women in poverty and the courage with which they faced their utter powerlessness.

The voyage of discovery—of the diversity of women's situations, roles, traditions, values, constraints, and strengths despite powerlessness—a voyage that began for some of us 20 years ago, is nowhere near completion. It would be futile to attempt even a summary recital of all that we have learnt from our attempts to come closer to the lives of different sections of women in our vast and diverse population. The rebirth of the movement has not been either a painless or a simple, unified, linear one-way process. Our society is plural and diverse as well as iniquitous and unjust. The last two features had to be fought, undoubtedly. But was it necessary to regard the plurality and diversity as points of weakness? Could we not view them as potential sources of strength instead? That question, forced on us while grappling with the multiplicity of issues, perspectives, ideologies, priorities, and information and communication gaps that revealed themselves with the growth of the movement, has today been answered by science. Years ago, some peasant women asked us:

> Why does the sarkar [government] allow felling of a variety of trees in the forest that supplied so many of our needs and then replace them with only eucalyptus? Don't all these learned people know that it is not good for the soil, apart from not meeting our needs for food, fodder, fuel and a livelihood?[9]

We had not then heard of bio-diversity as essential for sustaining the planet. Indian peasant women were ahead of the scientists and heads of powerful States of the world by at least two decades, if not more! We also know now that they had resisted intensive cropping of only HYV seeds with heavy doses of chemical fertilisers and pesticides.[10]

But no one had given them a hearing. They had no voice because the political process has not ears to listen or avenues through which they might communicate their opinions, knowledge or priorities. This deafness is at all levels—in families, the community, and other parts of the socio-political system. All of us in north India are familiar with the word *char diwari* which we interpret as the four walls of the home that traditionally confined women. An illiterate village woman taught me a totally different meaning. She explained:

> We have four walls to scale before we can even acquire an identity as women in our own right—the family, the caste or the community (this is a tribal region with multiple ethnic groups), the village, and then religion. These have been the barriers that kept us divided, unaware that we had any rights as women, as citizens, as workers. Now that we have our organisation and know our rights, we shall ensure that every woman we come across knows that we do not have to feel powerless. We shall force the panchayats to listen. If we fail there, we shall go to the higher-ups, but we are not going back to our earlier state of suffering, silent, powerlessness. Rights also mean responsibilities and our responsibilities now go beyond our own children and the family.[11]

In another instance, Tustu Sardar, a peasant woman from the Bhurkura Mahila Samiti [Bankura Women's Society], District Bankura, West Bengal, commented:

> All children need care and a chance to develop. Why do we not have child-care centres in every village? They would make our work easier, release our daughters to go to school and give the kids some chance to have a better life than ours. They will learn something in the Centre and will not feel frightened or handicapped when they go to school.[12]

There are many other such voices. For instance, factory workers, asked as to why the creches provided by a few employers according to the labour laws were empty, answered with counter questions:

> Would you hand over your children to be cared for by those who exploit you? And, how do we bring them all this distance when we have to face a daily struggle to reach here ourselves?[13]

In another instance, a peasant woman at an Asian Development Bank Workshop on Gender Issues in Agriculture heard the word 'mainstreaming' being used repeatedly by the participants and asked her interpreter for its meaning. When it was explained, she made her intervention:

> What do you mean by mainstreaming? To make some room for us in all that is going on? But that is not what we want. We want no part in planting thousands of eucalyptus trees that rob our soil of water and other plants, leaving our children and cattle hungry. We want to change these processes. If we have our way, we will call the scientists to work with us, adding their knowledge to ours, and look for solutions that would be good for everybody.[14]

A delegation of national women's organisations which visited Bhopal, Ahmedabad, and Surat in February 1993 to talk to the women affected by the recent communal riots heard even more unexpected voices:

> Our present plight is a direct consequence of the moving out of our Harijan neighbours from the mohalla (neighbourhood) five years ago. They were our neighbours and friends. We celebrated all festivals together. Many of us did the same work. The society (housing society) moved them out. After that, the Hindus started attacking us.
>
> We would all have been killed if our Hindu behenen (sisters) had not hidden and sheltered us in their homes, fed us, given us saris, mangalsutras and bindis before escorting us to safer areas ... But women are not included in the Mohalla Peace Committees.[15]

These few examples illustrate, on the one hand, the strength of diversity, and the potential role that such women can play in shaping the path and direction of development. *But the political process had failed to tap this energy, knowledge and sense of human and social responsibility.* After reviewing women's role and status in the political process over a quarter of a century, the CSWI concluded:

> All the indicators of participation, attitudes, and impact come up with the same results—the revolution in social and political status of women for which Constitutional equality was to be only the instrument, still remains a very distant objective ... the large masses of women continue to lack spokesmen who

> understand their special problems, and [are] committed to their removal, in the representative bodies of the State ... though women do not numerically constitute a minority they are beginning to acquire the features of a minority community by the three recognized dimensions of inequality: class, status and power.[16]

The CSWI also commented rather sharply on the resistance from political elites to measures aimed at promoting gender equality, and "contradictions in the regard and concern" among women elites—social or political—for the inequalities suffered by women in every sphere.

Women's Movement

The revival of the women's movement has changed that bleak picture to some extent. But the dilemmas still remain. The right to political equality is an individual right, but the institutional forces that are arraigned against gender equality are all powerful collectives that exert control on people's minds and behaviour—class, caste, community, religion, locality, family, occupation, etc. These controls affect women and men both, making them accept gender inequality as a value *per se.* Sometimes it persists as an unconscious bias, even among persons committed to progressive secular and egalitarian ideologies.

Another source of resistance comes from the calculations of electoral arithmetic. Since women are not perceived as an organised interest or pressure group, it is the anticipated reaction from a community or voters at large that influences decisions on measures that would affect women's status directly.

The political situation has worsened with a deepening of identity politics—politics that taps an identity based on race, caste, ethnicity, culture or religion. All such movements require greater control over women's freedom, as women are viewed as the first and major carriers of this sense of an identity, defined by the accident of birth.[17] Another role thrust on women is to be "custodians of traditional cultural values". Contemporary history however proves conclusively that in defining the values meant to be preserved, neither women nor history have any say, only the perception of political imperatives by male political elites.

Let me illustrate this from some less known examples. In 1983, a *Times of India* reporter interviewed the leader of a team of lawyers commissioned by the Akali Dal to draft a Bill for a separate personal law for Sikhs. The story suggested the possibility of withdrawal of the Punjab agitation if the Bill was accepted by the Union Government. The draft provisions would have deprived Sikh women of their rights to a share of parental property and to divorce provided under existing laws. Another clause sought to give legal approval to the custom of *chaadar andaazi* (widows being married to a brother-in-law, irrespective of the latter's age or marital status), which was claimed to be a Sikh custom. We have found it to be a custom among peasant communities in many parts of the country, which has nothing to do with the Sikh religion. Secondly, as reported to us by many village women in Punjab belonging to the

Sikh community, it was a dying custom not practised since their grandmother's times. A protest meeting called by national women's organisations and civil rights groups was announced in the national press. Before that meeting, the Centre for Women's Development Studies received resolutions from several village *mahila mandals* (women's societies) in Punjab, stating that they had not been consulted on this move and had very strong objections to such erosion of their rights, especially to "bringing back polygamy by the back-door". They requested that their resolutions be conveyed to the Prime Minister, and also made public at the protest meeting. We carried out both their requests. While it is not possible to provide evidence on the impact of these actions, the objective fact remains that no such personal law bill, to which the women were opposed, was initiated by Prime Minister Indira Gandhi.

Women researchers have identified the customs of some tribes, prevalent as late as the mid-nineteenth century, guaranteeing usufructuary rights to land to women for subsistence food production. Words defining such customs in the particular tribal language, e.g. Santhali, recorded in earlier ethnography and judicial records[18] have gone out of use, and have been replaced by terms like *khorposh* which do not obviously originate from any tribal language. The issue of women's ownership or control of land, both as the basic production resource and the root of any status or entitlements in rural society, has been voiced by peasant women from many communities—tribals, Scheduled Castes, Muslims, and others—repeatedly through the last 20 years. [19] In fact, peasant women's struggles for their right to have a voice in the management, and especially, distribution of natural resources like land, water, and forests, which are essential for their survival, provide one of the best examples for the observation in the Human Development Report 1993 that "the forces of democracy are not likely to be so obliging as to stop at national borders."[20]

The political fall-outs from the Shah Bano and the Roop Kanwar cases are too well known to require discussion here. [21] What is perhaps less known and therefore worth emphasising is the role played by the women's movement, and especially the large mass-based national women's organisations, in forcing policy changes, even Constitutional amendments, during the last 20 years by bringing these diverse but clear, articulate voices of women from the grassroots into the political process. Research, or women's studies too has played its role when it has responded to the issues and priorities articulated by grassroots women, and approached the issues from the latter's perspectives instead of imposing pre-conceived frameworks, concepts, and categories. It is this feature of Indian women's studies that led M.N. Srinivas to describe it as "the most significant development in Indian social sciences" during the seventies and eighties, and as "a thrust from below."[22]

This mutually reinforcing relationship between, on the one hand, grassroots mobilisation, the building of large-scale organisations, networks, or joint fronts cutting across individual organisational identities with their respective claims, and, on the other hand, the demands of academic research, which can claim validity before academic peer groups, has also not been without tensions and difficulties. But the relationship has persisted. The capacity that the women's movement has displayed to overcome recurring identity crises perhaps legitimises its claim to be recognised as one of the most powerful forces against the destructive, fascistic, and criminalised elements that seem to be overtaking the political process in the country and many other parts of the world.

Movements, however, are seldom efficient in recording their struggles, changing priorities and perspectives in response to changing political situations. Consequently, a need has arisen for the women's movement to defend itself against the misinformation that is being spread about it. The misinformation campaign about the nature, origin, and aims of the women's movement have become even more virulent since its declaration of war against communalism, and it is essential to record some authentic information before we are defeated by the "politics of memory".

The most common charges against the movement have been of being west-inspired, against Indian cultural traditions, divisive of people's democratic aspirations, and dominated by a small number of urban, educated middle and upper class women. Such charges ignore basic historical facts. I list only a few of them.

(i) Movement politics is virtually as old as India's recorded history, and very few movements from the ancient, medieval or modern periods can be named which did not receive massive support from women—as followers and as leaders. Poor recording by historians or chroniclers does not eliminate the objective fact of women's participation.[23]

(ii) Association or dialogues with women's movements outside the country does not make it subordinate to or inspired by the former. On the other hand, the Indian women's movement played a major role in incorporating third world perspectives and priorities into the international women's movement, thereby enriching and revitalising the latter. The World Congress of Women for a Healthy Planet at Miami in November 1991 perhaps represents a far greater triumph for the third world than the efforts of NAM or G-77 for a new international economic order.

(iii) Even exercises of the wildest imagination would fail to attribute such characteristics to manifestations like Chipko, SEWA, the WWF, etc., their smaller, localised counterparts in different corners of India, or the current waves of anti arrack, anti-political terror or anti-dowry movements in the country.

(iv) Most of the reluctant, hesitant but highly publicised policy decisions of the Government of India in favour of women did not emanate from altruism or a belated acceptance of Constitutional obligations, but under pressure from the women's movement. The amendments in Criminal Law relating to rape, suicide, dowry deaths, etc., the establishment of the National Commission on Women, the introduction of a minimum quota for women within the anti-poverty programmes, and finally the introduction of one-third reservation for women in panchayat institutions and urban elective bodies come within this category. Since attempts have already begun to use misinformation to make political capital out of these measures, I will seek to set the record straight in these few instances.

Women's Lobbies

The Criminal Law amendments took place only because of a carefully constructed alliance between women's organisations, legal academics, activists and the Law Commission, with considerable support from the Press.

The setting up of the National Commission on Women, recommended by the CSWI in 1974 and the UN's World Plan of Action for the International Women's Decade in 1975 were resisted by the Government right up to 1989. The much publicised NPP (National Perspective Plan) for Women up to 2000 AD, prepared by the Government of India in 1988, suggested only the appointment of a senior officer within the Department of Women and Child Development as Commissioner for Women's Rights. National women's organisations called for a debate on the NPP and reiterated their demand for an autonomous statutory Commission.[24] The National Front included this in its election manifesto in 1989 and introduced the Bill early in 1990. The final Act passed in August was substantially different from the original bill because of intense lobbying by women's organisations and the emergence of a virtually all-party women's lobby among the members of Parliament.

Introducing a Special Component for Women within all anti-poverty programmes was first recommended in 1977–78 by a Planning Commission Working Group on the Employment of Women appointed by Prof. Raj Krishna when he was Member, Planning Commission during the Janata government. The recommendations of this as well as other working groups on women's issues appointed by the Janata government went into oblivion after the general elections of 1980, which brought the Congress back to power. The framework document produced by the new Planning Commission made no reference to the Working Groups or the findings of the CSWI, despite a parliamentary resolution after a full debate on the report, requesting government to mount necessary legislative and executive action programmes "to remove all disabilities that Indian women continued to suffer from." A formal request from the Ministry of Social Welfare, which then included the Division on Women's Welfare and Development created in 1975, to have a separate chapter on Women and Development, was rejected.

It was at this stage that a joint front of seven national women's organisations—some old, some new—was formed to demand that government should live up to its Constitutional obligations.[25] The leadership included many freedom fighters, members of several political parties including some in Parliament, former members of the CSWI, and several former members of the CSWB. The public rebuke from the white-haired freedom fighters,[26] and lobbying by the group of women MPs assisted the Ministry of Social Welfare's efforts to ensure consideration of some of the alternative strategies recommended by the earlier Working Groups and by the Joint Front of Women's Organisations.[27] A chapter on Women and Development entered the 6th Plan (1980–85) document with some promises of government's 'endeavour' to provide assets to poor women, including joint titles to land. The Special Component Approach for all anti-poverty programmes had to wait till the 7th Plan and another general election following Indira Gandhi's assassination in which, by all estimates, the women's vote had something to do with Rajiv Gandhi's landslide victory.

There is a persistent effort to misinterpret and trivialise women's motives in relation to the way they exercise their vote. The underlying idea is that women do not understand and are not interested in politics, and that, therefore, they vote for non-political reasons. The popular interpretation of the 1984 election was that "women had voted for Rajiv out of sympathy for his bereavement at his mother's death." This interpretation ignored the fact that very few women had demonstrated any support for that mother in 1977 when they too decided to punish her for the anti-democratic interlude of the Emergency. Prannoy Roy's study of the 1984 elections offered a far more substantial reason for the way women voted. In his pre-poll survey, he had asked 11,000 respondents to identify the three greatest problems facing the nation in order of priority. He had expected most women to identify inflation as the first and was taken aback when 64 per cent of women placed national integration as No.1, whereas only 13 per cent of the men gave it that much of priority. Unfortunately, such findings are not followed up or even publicised by their authors, and research on women's political participation continues to be inadequate and influenced by false assumptions and stereotypes. Political parties also need to clear their minds of obsolete ideas rooted in western interpretations of Indian society. They need to re-examine the issue, or they will continue to be shocked by demonstrations of women's political choices, as the Congress was in the recent Tripura elections.

Constitutional Amendments

I now come to the two recent constitutional amendments. Discussions on them in the capital during the last few months have displayed such blatant ignorance or misinformation that I take this opportunity to present a straight history. The debate on reservations for women in elective bodies did not begin with the NPP (National Perspective Plan) or the 64th Amendment Bill introduced by Rajiv Gandhi, but in the Constituent Assembly itself. One section of the women's movement had at that time suggested continued reservation of seats on the lines of the Government of India Act of 1935.[28] Women members in the Constituent Assembly, however, rejected this as against the principle of total equality.[29] A group of social scientists consulted by the CSWI—Upendra Baxi, Lalit Sen, Iqbal Narain, and V. M. Sirsikar strongly advocated reservation, especially in panchayats, and accordingly, the CWSI recommended "statutory women's panchayats at the village level to ensure greater participation by women in the political process as an integral part of the Panchayati Raj structures". [30] The recommendation was passed on to State Governments, received mostly negative responses, and was thereafter buried within the Government of India (GOI). However, some States, undertaking steps to entrust more powers and responsibilities to the panchayats, began a gradual process of inducting more women in the panchayat bodies. The most daring was the Karnataka Zilla Parishads, Taluk Panchayats, Mandal Panchayats and Nyaya Panchayats Act 1983, which provided for 25 per cent seats reservation for women.

The Government of India's National Perspective Plan (NPP 1988) proposed 30 per cent reservation in all elective bodies, to be filled, at least in the initial years, by nomination or co-option. The debate organised by the National Women's Organisations rejected this as "subversion of the Constitution". They refused any reservation in State assemblies or in Parliament, but recommended 30 per cent reservation in PRIs (Panchayati Raj Institutions), "with due precautions to ensure representation of the poorer sections of women, especially Dalits and adivasis". The organisations were, however, emphatic on the need for election to ensure the emergence of a new leadership from the grassroots.[31] The 64th Amendment Bill, therefore, did not invent the wheel. The 72nd Amendment Bill, introduced by the National Front government in 1990, proposed to increase the reservations for women to one third, with an additional provision of one third for the reserved categories of SCs/STs, and among office bearers. This, with minor changes, is the 73rd Amendment to the Constitution. The Governments of Orissa (a National Front Government) and West Bengal (a Left Front Government) however did not wait for the constitutional amendment. They amended their Acts in 1991 and 1992, and held election in 1992 and 1993, electing about 25,000 women in each State to these bodies. Despite the gloomy forebodings of various political pundits, and the high rates of female illiteracy in rural areas in both the States, neither has reported lack of enthusiasm among women to participate—as voters or as candidates.

Women's Perspective

Like all other movements, the women's movement too is fragmented by ideological, organisational, educational, class, regional, and personality differences. But, on certain issues, there has been remarkable unity and solidarity.

What began as a protest against increasing violence against women—an issue around which women could rally, has gradually expanded to a principled opposition to social, political, and State violence as destructive phenomena to be opposed. On the issue of rising communalism and communal violence, the movement's reaction has been spontaneous and openly critical of political parties and some women's flirtations with communal organisations. This is no mean achievement in a country where the majority of women are deeply religious through their socialisation. Despite its disillusionment with the political process to fulfill women's dreams of equality, justice, and dignity, the movement has remained staunch in its defence of the ideological foundations of the Indian political system—secularism, socialism, and democracy. The same ideology has driven it to oppose the new economic policies which it firmly believes will hurt the poor and the unemployed, be inimical to human development in general, and aggravate existing inequalities and divisions.

If we accept the theory that the dream of building an Indian nation required "radical departures from the inherited social system" which institutionalised inequalities at all levels—vertical and horizontal— then the women's movement's general opposition to hierarchies of all types, oppressive and exploitative social institutions, and to being "co-opted" by the State or other powerful groups, offers at least a partial answer to the first of the three dilemmas that I posed in the beginning. The most critical role for women in the political process should be to oppose all those barriers that resist human equality, dignity, and justice, not merely for women but for all. To quote from the CSWI's guiding principles:

> Any policy or movement for the emancipation and development of women has to form a part of a total movement for removal of inequalities and oppressive social institutions, if the benefits and privileges won by such action are to be shared by the entire women population and not be monopolised by a small minority.[32]

As for the implications of the term "women's perspective", I am forced to submit that this is a typical method of obfuscating and mythifying gender into an all-pervasive homogeneous category. As long as people are divided by various forms of inequality and diversity, by class background, life experience, culture etc., how can there be one uniform perspective for women or for men? The commonality of subordination, or the "nurturing quality of women" that are often advanced in defence of this theory, tend to oversimplify the complex social factors that influence and govern the social construction of gender roles at different levels of society, or the dimensions of personality that they tend to promote. Could any of us— urban, educated middle-class women—be able, spontaneously, to produce the kind of ideas and voices I quoted earlier? Do we have either the knowledge or the experience?

But at an ideological level, any rational, sensitive person can recognise the value and significance of such voices, and make a deliberate choice to identify with them. Many in the women's movement have chosen to do so. Some have even conceded that the transformational effect of this closer identification is empowerment, for both the privileged and the marginalised women at the grassroots. I cannot say that such a view is shared by all. Its implications are far-reaching and would include being prepared to accept not only the rights of the marginalised majority to participate as equals, but even their right to lead in areas where they have far greater competence and expertise than us.

I am convinced that this mutually reinforcing empowerment was the dream that Durgabai tried to institutionalise through her network of women's organisations, by pushing them to work with underprivileged women, mobilising them for "self-improvement" and "nation-building" tasks. However, like Mahatma Gandhi, she underestimated the influence of class differences and the "sanskritisation process" in strengthening the power of patriarchy. Neither could she anticipate that the process of planned development would increasingly give less priority to over all social and human development and accelerate, rather than reduce, economic and social inequalities. Nor did she visualise the power of the co-optation process that would affect men and women in public life.

But her dream remains as valid today as it was 40 years ago. The current women's movement has, for the time being, obtained a grudging recognition from a minority that the women's question is basically a political question, being linked to changes in power relations across and within all levels of society. Building on this fragile foundation, strengthening the ties with the currently powerless women at the grassroots, and learning to grow stronger along with them through a mutually supportive process of empowerment are the challenges as well as the source of sustenance for the women's movement in the coming years. Without that strength, women's capacity to influence and redirect the political process would crumble. There are plenty of examples before us. If we ignore them, then we have learnt nothing from the past or the present.

NOTES

1. Durgabai Deshmukh.1980. *Chintaman and I.* New Delhi: Allied Publishers, p. 27.
2. Ibid. pp. 29 and 33.
3. The Constituent Assembly also functioned as the Central Legislature until the 1st General Elections in 1952.
4. Durgabai Deshmukh. 1980. *Chintaman and I.* New Delhi: Allied Publishers, p. 62.
5. Ibid. p. 60.
6. Ibid. p. 53.
7. Ibid. p. 53.
8. Government of India. 1975. *Towards Equality: Report of the Committee on the Status of Women in India.* GOI: Ministry of Education and Social Welfare. Chapter 7: *Women in India,* GOI, Department of Women and Child Development, 1985; Prannoy Roy, *India Votes.*

9. Jhilimi women's camp organized by Department of Land Reforms, Govt. of West Bengal, June 1980. See D. Bandyopadhyay—Travails of Tribal Women, *Mainstream,* 1980; ILO, *The Bankura Story;* V. Mazumdar, Peasant Women organize for Empowerment, *The Bankura Experiment,* CWDS 1989; also *Women of the Forest* (CWDS forthcoming).
10. *National Summits of Peasant Women, India, Bangladesh, Nepal, Pakistan, 1991*-92, UNIFEM; Synthesis paper by V. Mazumdar, FAO-FFHC.
11. Rasi Mudi, Peasant woman from village Korapara, Dist. Bankura, W. Bengal, *Women of the Forest.*
12. *Women of the Forest, op cit.*
13. Statement made to the CSWI by women workers in a Jute factory, Naihati, West Bengal
14. Malati Mandi, Secretary, Nari Bikash Sangha (Women's Development Society), District Bankura, W. Bengal at Manila, ADB workshop on Gender Issues. in Agriculture, 1991; interpreter was myself. For other similar statements, see Voices of Peasant Women, Report of a National Conference of Peasant Women on Management of Natural Resources: *A Wider Role for Peasant Women,* CWDS, 1993
15. Muslim women in Ahmedabad—*Women Against Communalism,* Report of the Delegation of National Women's Organizations–AIDWA, NFIW, MDS, CWDS, JWP, YWCA–1993.
16. Government of India. 1975. *Towards Equality: Report of the Committee on the Status of Women in India.* GOI: Ministry of Education and Social Welfare, p. 301, paragraphs 7.97–7.98.
17. *Women and Fundamentalism:* Papers presented at (i) World Congress of Anthropological and Ethnological Sciences, Zagreb, 1988; (ii) World Congress of Sociology, Madrid, 1990; (iii) Workshop on Women, Equality, and Reproductive Technology, WIDER, Helsinki, 1992
18. Manoshi Mitra in *Samya Shakti,* 1989-90. Also Govind Kelkar, 1985.
19. State Conference on Women and Development, 1978–79; Jhilimi Camp, *op cit,* 1980; Indian Women in the *'80s-Development Imperatives, Joint Memorandum by National Women's organisations,* AIWC, 1980; Kishwar and Vanita (eds.), In search of Answers, London, 1984; V. Mazumdar: *Peasant Women organize for Empowerment,* CWDS, 1989; ILO: *Women, Resources and Power*—Report of an Afro-Asian Workshop, 1984; UNIFEM and Aurat Foundation, *Report of Regional Conference on Women and Environment,* Lahore, 1992; CWDS : *Voices of Peasant Women, 1993*
20. *Human Development* Report, 1993, p.7: NAM Conferences on Women and Development, Baghdad, 1979 &. New Delhi.
21. The Shah Bano case refers to a woman, Shah Bano, who was divorced and then denied maintenance under Muslim Personal Law (*The Times of India,* January 31, 2004). Roop Tanwar was a woman who allegedly committed Sati (Wikipedia).
22. M.N. Srinivas, Inaugural Address to World Congress of Sociology, Delhi, 1986
23. CWDS: Samya Sakti, 1984 and 1993; *Manushi:* Special Issue on Women in Bhakti Movements; Sunil Sen: *Women in Popular Movements in Bengal;* L. Kasturi and V. Mazumdar (eds.): *Women and Indian Nationalism,* Vikas (forthcoming); Sujata Gothoskar: *Struggles of Women at Work,* Vikas, 1992.
24. National Perspective Plan for Women: A Perspective from the Women's Movement, Delhi, August 1988 (mimeo).
25. All India Women's Democratic Association; All India Women's Conference; All India Coordination Committee of Working Women; National Federation of Indian Women; Indian Federation of University Women's Associations; YWCA of India; Centre for Women's Development Studies; Institute of Social Studies Trust.
26. At a public meeting on September 10, 1980, India International Centre, Delhi. See press reports in national dailies on September 11.

27. *Indian Women in the Eighties: Development imperatives, op cit.* See CWDS, *Women's Work and Employment: Struggle for a Policy*, 1983.
28. Geraldine Forbes in V. Mazumdar (ed.), *Symbols of Power*, Delhi, 1977.
29. Renu Chakravarty in her discussion with CSWI. See *Towards Equality*, Ch. 7.
30. *Towards Equality*, p. 304.
31. *NPP: A Perspective from the Women's Movement, op cit.*
32. *Towards Equality*, p. 8.

8

The Nautch Girls of Purulia*

Mahasweta Devi

In December 2006, on my way to Nandigram, I went to Purulia. The Sabar tribals were there for the *Sabar Mela* festival just like in the yester-years. The *Nat* performed their martial dances, and the Sabar, their *Chho* dances. It was on this occasion that, for the first time, I saw a live performance by the nachni girls. To *naach* is to dance, and nachnis are dancing girls.

The origin of the nachni dance can be traced to Ayodhya Prasad Singdeo of Baghmundi, one of the many feudal estates in Purulia after the Permanent Settlement of 1793. Ayodhya Prasad Singdeo was a patron of dance and song. He composed songs, and encouraged musicians and dance-girls. The type of song he composed later came to be known as the Jhumur, and the girls who sang and danced came to be called the nachnis.

A Nachni's Life

I do not know enough about the devadasis of the south but whereas the devadasis dance, the nachnis dance *and* sing. Today, the nachni and the jhurmur singers are found mainly in West Bengal's Purulia district. While the custom of keeping dancing and singing girls goes back to twelfth century Bengal, it is today prevalent mainly in Purulia, according to Deepak Barpanda of *Durbar,* a leading sex worker's organisation. Purulia is a very neglected and poverty-stricken part of West Bengal and remains so because of the state government's cruel indifference.[1] For the last 30 years, the State Government has deliberately failed to do even the minimum for the people of Purulia. There are no roads, there is no electricity, and there are no doctors in Purulia. In fact, the government does nothing at all for the people. The different branches of the State government in Purulia are utterly non-functional. Only two days ago, one Sabar tribal died of starvation in Amlasol in West Medinipur. In the North Bengal tea gardens, labourers die in the hundreds. The panchayat system is a total failure in Purulia.

* Edited transcript of the July 15, 2007, Durgabai Deshmukh Memorial Lecture by Mahasweta Devi.

The nachnis of Purulia come from Dalit and tribal society. Many of them are sold in childhood because their parents are too poor to feed them. In some cases, parents sell them to avoid money demands from husbands. Girls are sold in their childhood to the *rasiks*—the masters of the nachnis. A nachni remains perpetually bound to her *rasik*. Whatever she earns goes to her *rasik*. The *rasiks* marry and beget children and the nachni has to support the *rasik* and his family. Sri Barpanda writes that the Nachni girls are treated like untouchables. The *rasik's* wife and her children do not allow the nachni to enter the kitchen. In the heart of West Bengal, a Left Front ruled state for 30 years, this cruel practice of purchasing a young girl, making her sing and dance to please her male clientele, taking all her money and treating her like a pariah, goes on and on.

A *rasik* can keep more than one nachni, but a nachni cannot leave a *rasik* and live with another. Usually the nachni, like a married woman, touches her forehead with vermillion, and wears special bangles, the way married women do. A nachni's life is, perhaps, tolerable, as long as her *rasik* lives. But after his death, a nachni is neither cremated nor buried. Her legs are tied to a rope, she is dragged to a distance and thrown in the garbage heap. Rajubala's life story illustrates:

> Kartik Jantubai, a weaver by caste was Rajubala's *rasik*. He loved her so much that he did not marry. Rajubala too, was very loyal to him. They lived in a hut in village Jugidi. When Kartik died, Rajubala was thrown out of the hut. She left Jugidi and went to Urmahat. Here she sat under a Mowa tree and begged. This is where she died, in 2006. Rajubala wanted to be cremated, like a Hindu. Instead, she was dragged to the nearby railway lines and left there.

The nachnis mostly come from Dalit society, while the *rasiks* are usually from the so-called upper classes. The nachnis are usually from poor Dalit homes, and because they are Dalits, their *rasiks* and their clientele demean them, for, after all, they are "lowly born." They are physically tortured too, which is why the *rasiks* do not allow their daughters to become nachnis. The nachni women sing, dance and earn, but their earnings go towards maintaining the families of their respective *rasiks*. The nachni, a woman, earns, and her *rasik*, a man, keeps the money.

Thanks to West Bengal's 30-year-long Left Front rule's abysmal neglect of Purulia, the nachnis do not get any rights—social or human. The nachnis accept it too. Twenty-year-old Kajol thinks she is happy. She earns, she is young. She is loyal to her *rasik*. Surely, the *rasik's* family will take care of her once she becomes old. Or so she thinks.

Is the nachni song and dance legitimate art? I do not know. Some nachni women have achieved recognition. One might say, they forced the outside world to recognise and honour their talents. Sindhubala Devi received the Government of India's *Lalan Puraskar* award for her songs.[2] Malabati, a nachni, performed her nachni dance on Republic Day in 1986 before an all-India audience. Rajbala too was an artist of excellence. She performed the nachni dance in different cities of India. Bimala Devi was acclaimed as a teacher-instructor in nachni dance and jhumur songs. But name and fame could not keep the nachnis from being reduced to a life of beggary and destitution. Rajbala died on the streets, and Hajari begs from door to door on the streets of Manbazar, Purulia.

Nowadays, jobless youths are becoming manager *rasiks*. They keep nachnis, give them shelter and food. They earn a lot by forcing nachnis to go to places to dance and sing. The nachni receives nothing. No account is ever opened for a nachni in a bank or a post office.

Case Studies

- KESHAVATI, 50, is renowned as a skilled and popular nachni. She hails from village Charaikella. Her father, Shatrughna Kalindi, is a Dalit (a Dom). In 1973, Keshavati, along with the mother, elder sister, and sister's husband went to Rajkharswan, to *rasik* Bauri Bondhu Mahajato's house. Keshavati wanted to be a nachni—hers was one of the rare instances of a self-chosen vocation. Not many avenues were open to her. She put her thumb impression on a blank sheet of paper and Bauri Bondhu kept her as his nachni. This happened in the year 1973. To Bauri Bondhu, Keshavati was his property. However, Sreedhar Sharma, the assistant station master of Lotapahar Station, a friend of Bauri Bondhu, intervened when Bauri Bondhu slapped Keshavati and she protested. Sreedhar was sensitive to Keshavati's predicament and offered to take her away. Keshavati left Bauri Bondhu, her *rasik*, and went off with Sreedhar. The incident angered Bauri Bondhu, who filed a case in court, and lost. The story did not end there. Sreedhar had a wife and family, so Keshavati had to leave him. Thereafter, she became a nachni of Dhiraj Mahato of Ratgidi village, district Charaikella. After Dhiraj's death, she became the nachni of Anand, Dhiraj's cousin. Anand became her *rasik*.
  Keshavati is someone who truly loves dance. Her daughter Meera was married to a Mahato youth of District Chhapra (now Sean) of Bihar, but he died in an accident. Amidst all these ups and downs, Keshavati continued to dance. Meera's father-in-law, Ram Ikbal Mahato, respects Keshavati, and says: "Dance is a performing art. Why should she stop?" Keshavati is really a remarkable and praiseworthy woman, a truly liberated one.
- MALAVATI, 42, is the daughter of Jagannath Karmakar, a small farmer from Kaki village, District Mayurbhanj, Orissa. Jagannath had 4 daughters and many *rasiks* came to his house. Her father tried to stop Malavati from becoming a nachni, but she had a mind of her own, and at the age of 14, she went off with the 60-year-old Bauri Bondhu

Mahato of village Udalkham, P.S. Parsana, District Paschim Singhbhum, Jharkhand. Malavati was given dance and music lessons and she excelled at both. Rajiv Gandhi, the then Prime Minister of India, saw her perform in 1986, on the occasion of Republic Day. The Bihar State Government gave her an award. There are cassettes available of her songs.
Malavati's *rasik*, Bauri Bondhu, was a teacher and had a social conscience. Malavati learnt and practiced dance and music for eight years. Her *rasik* arranged coaching lessons for her. His wife Pelavati accepted Malavati, allowed her to help in the kitchen and attend to guests and visitors. Pelavati is childless. Malavati has one daughter, Sevati, who is a high school student, and a son, Godadhar. Bauri Bondhu is now dead. He left his property to Malavati, Pelavati, Sevati, and Godadhar. Bauribondhu's is an exceptional instance in *rasik* society.

- BIMALA, 60, is from a Sardar family of village Amdiha, District Bankura, West Bengal. She became a nachni to Raghunandan Kumar of village Amda, P.S. Arsa, District Purulia. After Raghu's death, his brother Gour became her *rasik*. Bimala, who performed at Panchkot Raj palace, Purulia, with the renowned singer Sindhubala, is quite well known and her songs are available on cassettes. She has a son from Raghunandan—Amit Kumar, aged 32. Bimala is respected in the family. Gour Kumar boasts: "We in this family do not look down upon the nachnis."
- BUTAN BALA, 42, is the daughter of Panchanan Lohar, an ironsmith from village Tetola, P.S. Sonahar, District Purulia. At the age of 15, she eloped with Laxmicharan Singh Munda. She now lives in village Tao, P.O. Bundu, District Ranchi, Jharkhand. Butan has made some cassettes. She gets invitations to perform throughout the year. Jharkhand's anti-AIDS committee has asked Butan and her troupe to conduct anti-AIDS awareness programmes. Butan supports Laxmicharan, his wife Gouri, and their three children. Her daughter has passed the secondary school examinations. Laxmicharan admits that thanks to Butan's earnings, he has a brick-built house and a car.
- SARASWATI, 42, a Bhumij tribal with the surname Singh-Sardr, hails from village Jathadi, P.O. Mathaforest, P.S. Baghmundi, District Purulia. She now lives in Dhobghata, Purulia town. Khepu Singh purchased her as his nachni when she was 12, and gave her training. Saraswati has given open air *yatra* performances. On one such instance, she met Hrishikesh Mukherjee, a Brahmin, and became his nachni. Saraswati lives with Hrishikesh. She has 3 daughters, all married. One died after marriage. Now Saraswati and Hrishikesh compose and sing songs of resistance.
- PUSHPA, aged 30, is the daughter of Sukhram Karmakar, village Limba, P.S. Tamar, District Purulia. Thirty-year-old Benoy Majhi, a

graduate from village Paromdi, District Ranchi, asked Sukhram for Pushpa to keep her as a nachni. Sukhram agreed. Pushpa became a nachni at the age of 25. Benoy and Pushpa live together. Benoy is still unmarried. The couple has a child.

- Forty-five-year-old FULAN of village Bonkati, P.O. Barabhum, P.S. Barabazar, District Purulia, fell in love with Gobindo Mahato of the same village. They went to court and registered their marriage. Then Fulan underwent coaching and started earning. Gobindo and Latika, his wife, have three children. Fulan and Gobindo have three. Fulan works in the fields when she does not have programmes.
- 65 year old BIROLA of village Berali, P.O. Sirum, P.S. Ningri, District Purulia, the daughter of Kuka Lohar, an ironsmith from village Madhupur, P.S. Ningri, District Purulia, made off at the age of 15 with Lalmohan Singh Munda. Birola's father followed in pursuit, armed with bow and arrow, to teach Lalmohan a lesson. Birola faced the crowd that gathered and publicly declared that she would stay with Lalmohan, her *rasik*. Lalmohan subsequently died. Birola now works as an agricultural labourer to support her two sons.
- Fifty-year-old CHINTAMONI SINGH MURA of village Deoli, P.O. Atna, P.S. Baghmundi, District Purulia is the daughter of a *rasik*—Falari Mondal of village Ilu, P.S. Jhalda. At the age of 12, Chintamoni had fallen in love with Rampada Singh Mura, who made her his nachni. Rampada arranged to have Chintamoni trained by the famous jhumur singer, Abani Singh Deo. Rampada and his wife Sankari have five daughters. Chintamoni has one daughter, who is now married.
- ADARMONI, 65, joined her *rasik* Bauribondhu Mahato and stayed with him for 10 years. Then they separated and Adarmoni joined Surat Mahato. Adarmoni is a renowned jhumur singer. Her cassettes are available and she has sung in many languages, such as Bengali, Oriya, Panchparganya, Naghuri, Mundari, and Santali.
- Fory-five year old PURNIMA is the daughter of a Purulia cycle rickshaw puller. Her father died when she was 6. Eventually she became a nachni. Durgacharan Mahato is her *rasik*. Durgacharan has two sons and one daughter by his wedded wife. Purnima is childless.

A Charter of Demands

The *Durbar Mahila Samanoy Committee* is doing unique work in West Bengal, Bihar, Jharkhand, Orissa, and Chhatisgarh to organise sex workers to fight for their rights. They have organised the Purulia nachnis to form their own organisation—the *Mandhum Loksanskriti & Nachni Samsad.*[3] The demands of the nachnis are listed below.

- Nachni dance and songs must be socially and officially recognised as art, and the performers as artists.

- A Nachni Academy must be established.
- The right of nachnis to their earnings must be officially ensured.
- Children born to nachnis have a right to the property the *rasiks* acquire from their nachni's earnings. This right has to be recognised by the State.
- Children born from nachni-*rasik* relationships have to have medical and educational benefits.
- Social ostracism of nachnis must be stopped by legislation.
- Each nachni has to have a personal (or postal) bank account, a savings account, in her name.
- The nachnis must be given every benefit from government Acts and laws.
- They must be given monthly pension when they retire.
- Each nachni must be entitled to a proper funeral, according to her belief.

I conclude with these words of Deepak Barpanda of the *Durbar Mahila Samanoy Committee*: "The demand of the rights of the nachnis is very much a part of the human rights movement. One cannot isolate the nachnis from the rest of society and judge them. Once, society treated earning women with contempt and suspicion. Times are changing. Once, women who went out to earn were treated with mistrust. Now the scenario has changed. Now is the time to shake off the old taboos. The nachnis earn, but they are not allowed to touch the money, since *rasiks* live off them. The 21st century is very much a woman's century. We have to work hard, very hard to get the nachnis their legitimate rights".

NOTES

1. Purulia is the district where the Sabar, or Kheria Sabar tribals, who were notified by the British in 1871 as born criminals, were killed by non-tribals and the police. In 1952, the Government of India declared the Kheria Sabar de-notified. Since the 1980's, together with activists like G.N. Devy of Baroda and many others, I have fought against the stigma these tribal people continued to carry.
2. Lalan was a great folk-singer. Rabindranath Tagore admired Lalan as a people's singer.
3. *Mandhum Loksanskriti & Nachni Samsad*, Shabari, Munsef Danga, Purulia 723101. Phone: 9732114569.

9

Caste in the Indian Census*

Gail Omvedt

For the first time since Independence, there are questions on caste in the 2011 Census of India. This appeared, in a sense, to be sudden. Indications were that the government would, as it had done before, avoid the issue. However, when the Yadavs—Sharad Yadav, Lalu Prasad Yadav, and Mulayam Singh Yadav—raised the issue vociferously, and when all the opposition parties and many Congress ministers supported the proposal, questions on caste in the 2011 census began to appear inevitable. The main justification, as Law Minister Veerappa Moily put it, was to gather caste data for carrying out pro-OBC policies. Indeed, a general groundswell of opinion supporting the move had been building up, with increasing aspirations of the subaltern castes supporting it.

The decision to collect census data on caste was however greeted with a good deal of concern and even resentment among the elite. The press coverage, by and large, was not favorable. *India Today* saw the government as simply giving in to populism and headlined its cover story "The Curse of Caste"; Asha Krishnakumar, writing in *Frontline*, cited "social scientists" (primarily writing in the early years of Independence) who argued that "even assuming that caste data are relevant, enumeration of the population on the basis of caste is bound to be vitiated by vote-bank and reservation politics";[1] and Bal Thackeray, opposing the proposal to enumerate caste, mocked the idea thus: "How will you record the caste of a couple if the husband is a Brahmin and the wife is either an OBC or from another caste? Will you record the caste of the husband, or the wife? Enough is enough! Do not divide the country further".[2] Finally, Jug Suraiya, lampooning "competitive casteism" (I should have more quota than you), rejected the problems of backward Muslims and Dalit Christians, and argued, in the age-old fashion of the elite, that it would be better to count "economic backwardness".[3]

* Edited transcript of the July 15, 2010, Durgabai Deshmukh Memorial Lecture by Dr Gail Omvedt.

Many of these objections have been rebutted in a recent article in the *Economic Times* by sociologist Satish Deshpande, one of the most insightful writers on caste issues, particularly issues concerning the OBCs.[4] Deshpande points out that "on the other side is the vast majority of the so-called 'lower' castes, which, having been massively shortchanged by six decades of supposedly caste-blind development, now insists that caste is all-important and all talk of abolishing caste is mere humbug". He notes that the paucity of data on caste is not accidental, but results from a policy of "willful if well-intentioned neglect", and further, that the practical difficulties in the way of a caste census are exaggerated. To all those loudly proclaiming that caste is irrelevant and that they do not want to be counted, Deshpande says that when questioned on their caste by the census enumerator, they could indicate "no caste" as a response; "The number and class composition of those who can afford this luxury will itself be educative," he opines.[5]

Keeping these differing viewpoints in mind, let us look in more detail at some of the issues pertaining to caste in the census.

Caste under Colonialism

Caste censuses, which originated under colonial rule, have acquired something of a negative connotation associated with the colonial government's need to classify and categorise, so as to dominate through its divide and rule policy. Nonetheless, important documents were produced: the various caste and tribes volumes for many provinces; the gazetteers, and the censuses themselves. These, however, were vitiated by a good deal of racism. The British adopted fairly wholeheartedly the Aryan theory of caste, seeing the three upper varnas as of Aryan-European descent, the shudra castes as non-Aryan, and those they called "primitive tribes" as aborigines.[6] This was interpreted in terms of a descending level of race and of civilisation. The last half of the nineteenth century, when the approach flourished, saw intensified racism, with—among other things—the propounding of the theory of "martial races" and the expulsion from military service of Dalits, who previously provided many fine soldiers. Many of the more enthusiastic racial theorists used clippers and other instruments to measure facial features such as the size of noses, length of foreheads, and so forth.One of the proponents of the racial theory of caste, H.H. Risley, the British ethnographer and colonial administrator who was known for his earlier work on the castes and tribes of Bengal, became Census Commissioner in 1901. Risley's concern was not only to count castes in the census, but also to order them in terms of existing hierarchy. He believed that varna established order of precedence. The furor he produced brought in its wake a flood of petitions about names and order, and led to the approach being dropped in the 1911 Census. But the thrust remained.

There were a great number of caste tracts published by people at all levels of the caste hierarchy, taking varying stands ranging from rejection of traditional caste positions and nomenclature to justification of the existing order.[7] For the subalterns, the effort was either to claim a traditional "high" status—Brahman descent, turned into untouchables by some fluke or trickery—or, very often, an entirely new identity.The old caste names were often rejected; even relatively modern, elite-assigned terms such as Panchama began to go out of favour in a new wave of radical organising that began to take place from the 1920s. Groups began to call themselves Adi-Dravidian, Adi-Andhra, and so forth, and to insist that the census use these terms rather than traditional caste identities. The census became politicised, used by all sides as a legitimator of identities.

Reservations Policy

It was perhaps understandable that the newly independent Indian elite would reject the idea of caste censuses altogether. There was a strong feeling that a new beginning was needed. The idea was being put forward that caste was irrelevant, and that rapid economic development and social welfare programmes were called for. Industrial development was seen as the primary factor, and caste as a backward remnant that was slowly vanishing. Jawaharlal Nehru was a good example of all of this; his *Discovery of India* and other writings showed how he both saw caste as ultimately irrelevant and economically based. At the same time, he romanticised it to some extent (along with the two other "traditional" social structures, family and village) for being based on collective/communitarian values. Similarly, trends in the social sciences that focused the critique on colonial domination and external oppression, or on simply capitalist exploitation, allowed for a neglect of indigenous mechanisms of exploitation.

The simple belief that caste was fading away allowed for new ideological forms of justification of the existing social structure. So it was that the Mandal Commission—which recommended reservation of jobs in the government for backward castes—was opposed by "upper" caste youth who identified themselves as "Youth for Equality", implying that the very effort to redress caste discrimination was itself a sign of casteism. Indeed, reservations have been, if justified at all, seen as "recompense" for past discrimination; they were not looked at as a forward-looking policy of removing the existing vicious systems of discrimination. So the notion grew that there were two types of positions—those that were "reserved" and the ones that were based on "merit". Reservation as recompense was seen as the opposite of merit.

The first commission appointed to deal with the non-Dalit, ex-Shudra "Backward Classes", the Kalelkar Commission, refused to admit that there was a crucial issue. It was only after Karpoori Thakur had introduced reservations for OBCs in Bihar, and the former Shudra castes were beginning to assert themselves politically, that the then in power Janata Party rediscovered the tradition of Jayaprakash Narayan and appointed a new commission, headed by B.P. Mandal, also of Bihar. Now the issue of OBCs had to be taken seriously. Even then, the Mandal Commission was forced to use the term Backward

Classes,[8] and the rather awkward process of proving social and economic backwardness in the absence of really adequate data had to be gone through.

It is thus only gradually, and more recently, with the relentless—and democratic—assertion by subaltern groups, that caste (and in particular efforts to overcome it) has come to be admitted into legitimate political discourse.

Subaltern Assertion

The existence of the census can hardly be blamed for identity-oriented caste assertion. Demand for recognition on a caste basis and use of identities has continued after the censuses stopped using caste as a category. The issue has not been simply about "identity politics"; it has been about the very material benefits that people presumed could be gained from the concessions given to OBCs and to the Scheduled Castes and Tribes. A process of vigorous organising has gone on, with many groups classified as OBCs demanding inclusion in the Scheduled Caste (SC) category, in order to avail of the government benefits that the SCs were eligible for.

The persisting signs of caste are clear: ongoing atrocities against Dalits; vicious discrimination in schools, where children of bhangis are forced to clean up toilets; denial of educational rights to Dalits; use of special cups in tea stalls; and Dalits forbidden to walk through certain caste areas of the village. Within non-Hindu groups as well, discrimination against Dalit converts has continued—among Christians, Sikhs, and Muslims. Backward Muslims have been organising for some time, and the Sachar Committee report has demonstrated the causes behind this. Another case in point are the caste panchayats or "khap panchayats" in much of the Jat areas of north India. Their resurgence has been striking in the last decade. Dozens of young people have been slaughtered and otherwise disciplined for committing the "crime" of marrying within the same gotra; the conservative elders of the community have been asserting themselves.

Political organising has been taking place, of course, in terms of caste. "Vote bank" politics gets blamed, but after all, the democratic arena has been open to such assertion. What was new towards the end of the twentieth century was the rise of caste-based political parties. Some political parties were fairly openly for OBCs or Dalits—the "Liberation Tigers" in Tamil Nadu, the Republican Party factions in Maharashtra. In Tamil Nadu, the PMK, led by Ramdoss, has been clearly a Vanniyar party, though its name gave a "class" focus. In UP and Bihar, the Samajwadi party has been identified with Yadavas. The Bahujan Samaj Party originated as an attempt to unite many of the OBC and Dalit castes under one large "bahujan" banner, but has remained stamped as a Dalit and mainly a Chamar party. Indeed, UP Chamars have formed its loyal vote base, though Mayawati has recently played it in many different ways, first building an alliance with Brahmans that temporarily won great success, then returning to an OBC focus when that failed in the last parliamentary election.

All of this has gone on without any caste-based census. Indeed, the rejection of a caste census has left the country without much data to cope with the problems.

Finally, it has to be admitted that marriages are overwhelmingly still arranged and take place within the caste. The data we have are impressionistic; but aside from a few very visible examples of inter-caste marriage, a look at the matrimonial columns of any newspaper will show the situation. Since marriage and inheritance are the primary carriers of caste, this shows the degree to which it remains.

The Need for Data

In recent years, with sample surveys (such as NSS) showing data that contradicted the Mandal Commission estimates,[9] there has been again a felt need for the census to take up the issue. Now, in the teeth of much opposition from elite sources, this is apparently going to take place.

In fact, without acknowledging social problems, analysing them, and collecting data, it is impossible to have a basis for remedial policy and action. Caste is not simply a thing of the past. It clearly exists today. It exists in changed forms. In most cases, the traditional forms of jajmani service are no longer the basic productive system of the villages. Yet there are some very "feudal" forms of caste that continue—for instance, the fact that manual excrement is removed in wide parts of India by people, mostly women, of a particular ex-untouchable caste.

In this respect, a study of changes in caste since 1991 in an eastern UP village, financed by the University of Pennsylvania and carried out by D. Shyam Babu, Devesh Kapur, and Chandrabhan Prasad, provides some interesting data. The study found that many of the traditional forms of subordination had vanished: Dalits now wore almost the same clothes, ate the same food as caste Hindus and built their houses past the traditional one storey limit. Most significantly, at the economic level, Dalit men no longer worked as ploughmen for the upper caste landlords. Instead, the landlords ploughed their own land with tractors, and even the land of the Dalits—who had some significant share of its possession—was ploughed by them. A social revolution? Yes, but the fact remained that the greatest capital ownership, in the case of this village, were with the landlords: they possessed all the tractors. Again, the question remains: how much is economic position correlated with caste? How much of capital ownership is still in the hands of Banias and Brahmans? A great deal, it would seem, but we simply don't have the data. Undoubtedly, caste has changed in the era of globalisation and capitalist development, but we need to know its specific forms.

This is also true for inter-caste marriages. These do exist, but what is their percentage? In the US, there are accurate data on inter-racial marriages, and interestingly enough, this shows a growing percentage in the last couple of decades. Such information allows us one way to map the lessening incidence of racism in society. In India, again, we simply don't know.

Social Stratification

In sociology, in the United States and Europe, social stratification as a subject of study looks in detail at the various forms of inequality in a society. In Indian universities, for the most part, there are no such courses. Instead, there have traditionally been courses on the "weaker sections" or the "marginalised" groups—Dalits, adivasis, and others. Graduate students were discouraged from writing PhDs on caste (unless to show how it was "constructed" during colonialism), except for students from "lower" castes, who were often encouraged to write on their own particular caste or tribal group.However, the issue is not simply the position and situation of particular groups—it is how the system as a whole works. This means it is not simply a matter of "counting OBCs" in the census: all castes have to be counted. This, of course, includes Brahmans and others of the "twice-born" elite.

When I was a graduate student in the 1960s, the wave of radicalism of those days infused various academic fields: we had "radical political economists", "Marxist Social Scientists" and so on. At the time, the sessions of the major academic bodies were often tumultuous affairs. Young radicals would come to the fancy hotels where they were held, sleep dozens to a room, sell literature, and agitate for their issues. One year, during the business session of the American Sociological Association, one of the organisers, Martin Nicolaus, captured the microphone, and, before the assembled sociologists, gave an impassioned speech. Sociologists, he said, habitually had their eyes down to study the "masses" and their hands held out to grab the money given by the ruling elite. Instead, they should do it the other way around: study the elite for the sake of the working class! After this, studying the "ruling class" became a major theme; young sociologists looked at genealogies and social relationships, where the elite met, how they managed their own interrelations. Many books were produced.

In India, we have been largely in a pre-1960s phase: study the masses. This needs to be changed. In order to map the existing structures of discrimination and the inter-relationship of class, gender, and caste, we need to know about all of the groups—including and perhaps especially what proportion of positions in the power and wealth structures of society continue to be held by Brahmans. This includes, of course, structures involving the production and reproduction of knowledge, which remains a crucial technique of social control. Among other institutions that have remained clearly in upper-caste hands are the universities—something that has affected the very processes of thinking about caste hierarchy and discrimination.

Caste Census: An Approach

Taking a caste-informed census need not be a complicated operation. How many and what types of castes exist in a particular area, the diversities of the structures in different regions of India—all of this need not come under the ambit of a caste census. Caste can simply be a matter of self-identification. Let each person name their own caste, by whatever term she wants to call it. Later, at the State level, a committee can put these various and numerous groups into broad categories. Here again, in determining who the OBCs are, one can look at economic and educational criteria of caste groups.In this process, a person can be completely free to say that she or see has "no caste" or is "mixed" or is "Indian" or whatever. This is a matter of personal preference. As Satish Deshpande has noted, the proportion claiming "no caste" is likely to be small, if not infinitesimal. It will be interesting to know the percentage, and to monitor the growth of people disclaiming a caste identity.

There is no need, in this process, to "classify" or hierarchise within the census itself. Imposing categories of any kind should not be the method. Such classification and analysis will come later, at a minimal level for purposes of publication of census data—though the raw data should always be made available for researchers.

Conclusion

Recording caste in the census will not by itself either increase caste tensions or decrease them. It will not by itself lead to the "annihilation of caste": that requires political will. However, gathering information is a crucial foundation for the process. A caste-based census is thus a progressive step forward, one that will provide useful tools for understanding Indian society and taking policy steps to remedy the centuries-old and still-existing discrimination.

The rejection of a caste-inclusive census after independence left policy makers and social activists, not to mention social scientists, disarmed in their efforts to analyse and act. Now the opportunity to change the system is here. We will have the ability to analyse the complex interactions of caste, class, and gender in India. We also will be able to estimate the number of mixed marriages that are taking place. The hopefully growing incidence of these, and the gradually reducing correlations of caste and economic position, should provide a good basis for really being able to know the degree to which caste and its inherent hierarchy is being overcome.

NOTES

1. Asha Krishnakumar. 2010. "Caste and the Census". *Frontline,* September 2–17, 2011; www.hinduonnet.com/fline/fl1718/17180910.htm.
2. He went on to say: "If you wish, you can record the number of Hindus, Muslims and Christians so that the country will know how many Bangladeshi or Pakistani nationals have infiltrated into our country."

3. Jug Suraiya. "Getting the Maximum Mileage: You're your Vote," in *Times of India*, (http://blogs.timesofindia.indiatimes.com/jugglebandhi/entry/get-maximum-mileage-from-vote
4. In several articles, and a recent book, *Contemporary India: Sociological Issues*, Penguin, 2003.
5. Satish Deshpande. 2010. "Count Caste in this census to annihilate it," *Economic Times*, June 3, 2010.
6. Much of the Indian elite accepted the Aryan theory of caste, while subaltern theorists like Phule and many others who attacked caste used an upside-down version of it.
7. See for instance, a study by Sumit Sarkar, which focuses on Bengal: Sumit Sarkar. 2002. "Identities and Histories: Some Lower-caste Narratives from Early Twentieth-century Bengal," in *Beyond Nationalist Frames*. New Delhi: Permanent Black.
8. The term "classes" indicates economic criteria; but during the colonial period it had been generally used as a category term and also used to refer to castes; for instances Dalits were referred to as the "Depressed Classes".
9. As the Sachar Committee Report has pointed out, the NSS survey relies on self-identification; and the reluctance of some to identify themselves as "backward" may have biased the data. In fact, two NSS surveys show a growing proportion of OBCs, as awareness of some of the benefits of being labeled OBC increases.

10

Challenges of Tribal Development*

Ram Dayal Munda

I remember Dr Durgabai Deshmukh and her husband, Dr Chintamani Deshmukh, as distinguished guests at a high school function organised by my school under a tree half a century ago in 1956 at Khunti, a small sub-divisional town 40 kilometres south of Ranchi. I vaguely remember my then Hindi guruji, Shri Jagdish Trigunayat, introducing the couple as a most extraordinary one. Both the Deshmukhs were then associated with the Planning Commission. I distinctly remember Dr Chintamani Deshmukh, in his speech on the occasion, announcing a gift of two additional rooms for my school to mark the visit. The promise was kept, and the school building got its present E-shaped look.

Moving about in the country, I see so many such projects that stand as reminders of this extraordinary public couple. Over the last 50 years, when I have had occasion to remember the Deshmukhs, I have felt a great sense of reverence towards them. Their commitment to social purpose is a source of inspiration to me, and the present occasion inspires me to rededicate myself to that cause.

India's Tribal People

The tribal people of India, numbering above 10 crores and variously known as aborigines, Scheduled Tribes, adivasis, girijans and, of late, vanvasis, are located mainly in the hill regions of the central belt of the country extending from Gujarat to Arunachal Pradesh. Outside this central India belt, India's tribal people are to be found around the Nilgiris in south India and in the Andaman and Nicobar, and Lakshadweep Islands in the Arabian Sea. The Constitution of India calls them Scheduled Tribes (STs) and Janjati (in Hindi). The United Nations and the ILO have a term—"Indigenous Peoples", but the Government of India is reluctant to equate the Scheduled Tribes with indigenous peoples and has repeatedly been saying in international fora that practically everyone

* Edited transcript of the July 15, 2005, Durgabai Deshmukh Memorial Lecture by Dr Ram Dayal Munda.

in India is indigenous and technically, there are no indigenous people in India, that India is a great melting pot and that indigenous and non-indigenous identities have all disappeared in the process of the evolution of the Indian people. The Constitution, however, clearly distinguishes the tribal segment of the population, terming it the Scheduled Tribes. The tribes have a distinct cultural identity and worldview, determined by their geographical isolation, historical antiquity, and customary laws. This makes them unique, even if all Indians are considered indigenous. The collective/community living of the tribes has contributed to the development of a distinct worldview with the following characteristics.

- A relatively more egalitarian social system.
- An economic life of sharing and caring.
- A polity of consensus-based decision-making,
- Art and aesthetics as a celebration of collective joy.
- Spirituality based on a symbiosis of nature and culture.

Marginalisation and Exclusion

The epic and mythological literature of the dominant Aryan groups in India, expressed through their Sanskrit and Prakrit languages, though not considered history, encapsulate ideas that have shaped the attitudes of the dominant groups who look down on the tribal people. A four level hierarchy can be seen in the characters that are depicted in this ancient Indian literary material: the super human (sura, narayana, deva, yaksha); the human (nara, manava); the sub-human (vanara, kinnara); and the non-human/less than human (asura, rakshasa, danava). The tribal people are relegated to the last two categories in this scheme, accorded an identity that is pejorative; and their physical and cultural attributes are denigrated.

The influence of these people on the development of what came to be known as Indian culture is profound though rarely acknowledged. In the sphere of language, we see that the Sanskrit and the Prakrit languages were gradually Dravidianised and Austricised as these languages traveled to the south and the east respectively.[1] Other evidences of the tribal influence can be found in prominent cultural elements that can be considered as tribal contributions to Indian culture. These include:

- Development of a new set of non-Vedic gods: Lakshmi-Narayana, Shiva-Parvati, and the avatars of Vishnu, particularly in the literature based on the indigenous motifs, and Mother goddesses and Pasupati—which the remains of the Indus civilization bears testimony to.
- The sway of the anti-social Gods, Indra and Brahma, countered.
- Sacred groves, saligrams, phallus worship.
- Role of ancestral spirits.

- Introduction of new cultural elements like rice, turmeric, vermillion, iron-bangles.
- Domestication of animals like the dog, buffalo, and the elephant.
- The great body of stories found in the Puranas—the Kathasaritasagar.
- Village republics, confederated in Asokan and Gupta times, and their continuity even to this day.

These are but a few illustrations of the contribution of these people to Indian culture. The refusal to acknowledge these contributions continues. Indeed, the marginalisation and exclusion of the tribal people has taken on a new dimension, amounting almost to a hidden agenda of the annihilation by the dominant, ruling society through the following methods:

a. *Denial of Identity Rights:* The Government of India and a section of the dominant society avoid the use of the word adivasi ("the earliest inhabitants"), which is acceptable to the tribal people, and instead push for *vanvasis*, a term that suggests wild forest dwellers and includes various animal species or sub-humans. Besides, the tribal people are not recognised as STs—Scheduled Tribes, outside their home States or outside Scheduled Areas.[2] Their languages are not recognised—it took 50 years for India to put Santali and Bodo in the Eighth Schedule. Moreover, the National Policy for Education recommends free and compulsory education through the medium of mother languages at the primary school level, but tribal children are not taught in their own languages, even in the local *ashram* schools.

   Tribal faiths are not recognised as distinct religious systems, but as part of Hinduism and are recorded as such, or are recorded as "Others". Judging from the 1991 census reports, only 54 lakh people are enumerated as adherents of tribal faiths. This means that even if most of the Christians were to be considered converts from the tribal groups, about 7 crore tribal people could be assumed to have been recorded as Hindu. Tribal ritual practices may in many ways look Hindu but looking Hindu and being Hindu are not the same thing. The basic tenet of tribal faith is a symbiosis between nature and culture. That is why formal structures like temples, mosques, churches or mutts are not required. Hills, forests, rocks and rivers are the abodes of the tribal spirits, gods and goddesses. Similarly, the concepts of heaven and hell are alien to the adivasi who believes that the spirit of the deceased returns "home" after the person's death. The idea of ancestors being present in the home and watching one's behaviour has a tremendous impact on one's upbringing. Righteousness becomes a part of one's behaviour. Equally alien is the idea of avatar/incarnations/messiahs, and the notions of sin and merit. Socially approved behaviour is meritorious, and anti-social behaviour, sinful. All these distinctive features of the tribal faiths could be put under what we propose to be called the *adi-dharma* (the primeval faith).

b. *Denial of Political Rights:* States were reorganised during the mid-1950s along linguistic and cultural lines. However, little thought was given to the existence of tribal languages and culture and tribe-majority areas were dissected and distributed over several States, making the tribal groups a minority in whichever State they were in. This happened particularly in the central Indian belt. Thus, the Bhil cultural area was divided into four and distributed over Gujarat, Rajasthan, Madhya Pradesh, and Maharashtra; the Gond area was divided and distributed over Madhya Pradesh, Maharashtra, and Andhra; the Jharkhand tribal area was divided and distributed over Bihar, West Bengal, Orissa, and Madhya Pradesh; the Nilgiri tribal area was distributed over Karnataka, Kerala, and Tamil Nadu; and the Naga area between Nagaland, Manipur, Assam, and Arunachal Pradesh (and there are Naga tribes even in Burma).

In terms of the special funds allocated for tribal areas, the benefits rarely reach the tribal population they are meant for. The tribal sub-plan is used as an area plan and funds meant specifically for tribal areas are diverted elsewhere. There has also been widespread corruption in the use of funds meant for tribal areas. Also, the constitutional provisions for STs have often been misused, for instance, through manipulation of government records, resulting in the increase of fake tribal people. This has happened particularly in Karnataka, Tamil Nadu, and Maharashtra. The same kind of manipulation is involved in reserving seats for Schedule Tribes in ST majority areas in elections to State assemblies and to Parliament.

While Governors are the special caretakers of the Scheduled Areas on behalf of the President of India, no Governor ever uses these special powers to protect tribal interests.

c. *Denial of Human Rights:* The Right to Life is directly impacted by putting tribal persons in confrontational situations in the name of law and order or in the name of controlling Naxalism. Furthermore, the destruction of habitat in the name of national development is the greatest threat to the adivasi's right to live. The so-called large-scale 'national development' projects in mining, hydro-power, and industry have caused disruptions of thousands of communities, and once they have broken up, tribal groups have no chance of survival with a distinctly tribal identity. They are lost like driftwood in the great mahasagar (ocean) that is India!

Dispossession and Displacement

The fundamental issue confronting tribal people globally is dispossession—a separation from the life-supporting resources of land, forest, water, and from their indigenous culture. It so happens that natural resources globally are located mainly in areas where the indigenous/tribal people reside. This is true in India also. Exploitation of mineral and forest resources, which, in pre-Independence India, contributed to the treasury of the British Empire, has accelerated during the post-Independence period to the extent that the very survival of the indigenous/tribal communities is seriously threatened. About one-tenth (one crore) of the tribal population has been displaced by large development projects, as the works of Fernandes and others have shown. Till 2004, there had been no resettlement and rehabilitation policy, and the rehabilitation of displaced people so far has been insignificant. Villages and forests have been submerged by dam-related projects and communities have dispersed, with people moving out to metropolitan cities such as Delhi, Mumbai, Bangalore, Kolkata, and Chennai, where they are not counted as tribal people anymore.

The root cause behind this is the attitude of internal colonialism/neo-colonialism, which results in expropriation of natural and cultural resources without caring for or safeguarding tribal interests. This makes tribal communities poor in a rich area. The people coming in from outside get richer and richer and the local people become poorer and poorer. The land, the water, and the forests in such areas are totally devastated, and these areas are rendered unfit for human habitation. This is what has happened in the mineral rich tribal areas of Jharkhand, Orissa, Chhattisgarh, and Madhya Pradesh. In recent years, this process has extended to Andhra Pradesh, Rajasthan, and the North-East.

One remedy for dispossession is tribal autonomy, as in the case of the Sixth Schedule Areas in the North-East. Free, prior, informed consent, and participation of the people concerned in all development activities is another. This is possible through education/awareness-raising/solidarity building. Also, there is a need for the mobilisation of the masses to draw the attention of the establishment to their plight. Adivasis must negotiate from a position of strength—it was the economic blockades called by the pro-Jharkhand groups that brought the Bihar and central governments to the negotiating table and finally led to the creation of a Jharkhand State.

An Adivasi Panchsheel

Prime Minister Jawaharlal Nehru's introductory remarks in his Foreword to Verrier Elwin's A *Philosophy for NEFA*[3] can be considered the earliest rudiments of a tribal policy. Nehru enunciated the "five fundamental principles"—a *panch sheel,* as a framework within which developmental activities should be pursued in tribal areas:

i. People should develop along the lines of their own genius and we should avoid imposing anything on them. We should try to encourage in every way their own traditional art and culture.
ii. Tribal rights in land and forests should be respected.
iii. We should try to train and build up a team of their own people to do the work of administration and development. Some technical personnel from outside will no doubt be needed in the beginning, but we should avoid introducing too many outsiders into tribal territory.
iv. We should not over-administer the area or overwhelm them with a multiplicity of schemes. We should rather work through, and not in rivalry with their own social and cultural institutions.
v. We should judge results not by statistics or the amount of money spent but by the quality of human character that is evolved.

This philosophy led to the formation of special multi-purpose tribal blocks for community development in tribal areas. As an idea, it was welcome, but in practice, only the requisite infrastructure was created; the communities were not strengthened enough to enable them to develop themselves. Subsequently, in the Fifth Five Year Plan, the concept of the tribal sub-plan was introduced. The emphasis, however, was on area development and focused only marginally on tribal development.

In sum, the seeds of an enlightened policy for tribal development were all there, but they were never elaborated upon and operationalised.

PESA Act

PESA—the *Panchayats (Extension to Scheduled Areas) Act* of 1996 is the best measure Parliament could have taken to safeguard tribal interests in the country. An enactment in the form of a special exemption to the 73rd constitutional amendment, the PESA Act gives the *gram sabha* (GS) or village assembly a legal sanctity and recognises it as the basic unit of administration. It empowers the GS with resources and control at the planning, execution, and evaluation stages. The consent of the GS must be taken in all matters pertaining to development projects that affect the concerned communities, for instance, in matters of land acquisition, compensation, and rehabilitation. The GS can settle land disputes, regulate money lending, restore illegally transferred tribal lands, and issue utilisation certificates for projects undertaken within its jurisdiction.

States with Scheduled Areas were instructed to frame operationalising laws in conformity with the PESA Act within a year, that is, by December 1997, failing which the central act would come into force automatically. Unfortunately, this historic step of Parliament to bring participatory democracy all the way down to the grassroots did not suit the bureaucracy and the common politician. As a result, when States that had Scheduled Areas set out to formulate operationalising laws, they, in varying degrees, watered down the PESA Act (which itself was a watered down version of the Bhuria Committee's recommendations). This led to ineffective implementation and wasteful delays. Moreover, tribal representatives were not consulted by bureaucrats and special interest groups when the State conformity acts were drafted. Due to this, depending on the level of awareness among tribal groups, there has been Public Interest Litigation (PIL) cases filed against various provisions of the acts in all States concerned. This has been more so in a State like Jharkhand where the traditional panchayat system has been in informal operation in some form even to this day. These PILs have given the present administration a pretext to not hold the panchayat elections, already overdue for 25 years.

Challenges of Globalisation

Content wise, there is nothing new in the current development strategy being pursued in the resource rich tribal areas, nothing that has not already been happening under "nationalisation" thus far. What is new is the pace and the intensity of exploitation, and the zeal of the bureaucracy and even certain NGOs in expediting the process. What a national agency would have taken, say, 100 years to achieve, is being accomplished in less than a decade by the processes of globalisation, liberalisation, and privatisation. The extent of devastation in tribal areas and the marginalisation, displacement and pauperisation of the adivasi people that has already taken place has been pointed out by Dr B.D. Sharma,[4] Walter Fernandes,[5] and others. One-fifth of the total adivasi population (about 2 crores) is already displaced and has ended up in the slums of the metropolitan areas of the country. This is not an imagined fear but something that is already happening here and in other parts of the world as well—in South America and South-East Asia, where this process has been given full play. The indigenous peoples of the concerned area, having lost their command over resources, are heading towards total disintegration, some even towards extinction.

Globally, there has been an explosion in the quantum of mining and prospecting for minerals, fossil fuels, and other energy sources in the last 20 years. In India, with the opening up of the mining sector to foreign players, governments of the mineral rich States are vying with each other to woo foreign investment in the extractive industries. The Government of India has also set itself a target of doubling energy production by hydropower within the next decade. These policies, which entail open cast mining on an unprecedented scale and construction of numerous dams in the fragile river valleys and hills of the North-East, will severely impact the last remaining homelands of tribal populations in these states.

As a regular participant in the UN Working Group on Indigenous Populations in Geneva and the UN Permanent Forum on Indigenous Issues at New York, I have witnessed indigenous opinion building on these issues for the last two decades. Listed below are some of the most significant points of advocacy that have emerged, which are of particular relevance in the Indian context:

- In all industrial projects, preference should be given to those projects that do not displace or only minimally displace tribal communities. (This thinking is actually in line with the stated objectives of the National Policy on R&R of the Government of India).
- Restoration of illegally alienated tribal lands, as has been done in Australia (the Mabo case), New Zealand (the Maori case), and Canada (with respect to the Cree nation's claims). The common feature of all these cases is that ancestral lands that were appropriated or taken away in violation of the treaties between native groups and European settlers were returned to the respective tribal groups, with the courts restraining further exploitation and usurpation of tribal lands.
- In any project involving land acquisition or land use changes, the concerned indigenous / adivasi people to be made party to the memorandum of understanding (MOU).
- No tribal lands are to be surrendered forever. Instead, they may be leased out on a short-term basis (10-15 years at most). In the case of Jharkhand, the Chotanagpur Tenancy Act and the Santhal Parganas Tenancy Act prohibits the permanent transfer of such lands.
- Lands to be returned to the original owners after proper post-mining/ excavation with landscaping, filling of the pits, and topsoil restoration.
- The concerned people to be made shareholders in the said project so that some amount of funds is always available for their survival.
- Provision for sufficient lead time during which the concerned indigenous people can be trained to be part of the said project.
- The affected people to be culturally rehabilitated. If communities are being uprooted, communities must be resettled.
- The fund allocations for compensation, rehabilitation, and training to be built into the project itself and the R&R to be subjected to independent monitoring and evaluation.

Some of these demands may seem outrageous at first glance but the principles underlying them have been enunciated in a number of official documents including the Bhuria Committee Report and the Supreme Court's landmark "Samata Judgment" of 1997, which terminated mining leases given to non-tribal private companies in the Scheduled Areas of Andhra Pradesh and encouraged the formation of tribal-owned companies or cooperatives for mineral exploitation in these areas.

Jharkhand: A Case Study

Contrary to expectations, the newly formed Jharkhand State is experiencing great difficulties. The Jharkhand movement for statehood has been seen as a movement of cultural reconstruction. It had a vision of constructing a State modeled after an ideal tribal society—a self-reliant, dignified society based on social equity, economic cooperation, consensual democracy, religious tolerance, cultural coexistence, strong work ethics, and collective joy.

The basic issue, as is the case with all tribal/indigenous areas elsewhere, is economic, social, and cultural dispossession arising from internal colonialism leading to poverty, malnutrition, illiteracy, unemployment, and loss of self-respect among the people of Jharkhand, particularly the adivasi people.

The strength of the area is its abundant natural and cultural resources. If properly utilised, Jharkhand's mineral and forest wealth would give the people of the State year-round employment and a very high standard of living. Its arts, village industries, traditional knowledge systems and diverse cultural traditions could be an important contribution to world heritage.

Yet the achievement of the State in the five years since its formation has been miniscule, basically due to a lack of vision. A vision can only come from the experience of living in this region and through having commitment and loyalty to the area and its people. That, unfortunately, is lacking in the present leadership, adding up to a general lack of will to lead the State to its aspired heights. Dispossession from water, forest, and land—jal, jangal, jamin, continue; there is a general lack of work culture; corruption is at its peak; there is a serious problem of maintenance of law and order and an unprecedented spread of communalism. The State planning effort demonstrates no sense of prioritisation—it is paying more attention to urban development than to rural development and in doing so it has forgotten its tribal agenda.

Therefore, what is needed is a comprehensive review and accordingly, a beginning of effective project formulation and an implementation process where the priority list would be to draw up a well-thought out development blueprint arrived at by consultation and debate among all sections of the population; infusion of will power in the leadership; reawakening of the cultural strength of the people; reversal of the development process from its present top-down mode to a bottom-up approach; rural/tribal development through decentralisation involving participation of the people of every gram sabha as envisaged in the PESA Act; well planned industry and urban development ensuring minimum displacement; and a re-greening of its hills and forest tracts through community based organisations.

The promise of Jharkhand will remain incomplete till this unfinished agenda is fulfilled.

NOTES

1. Anvita Abbi. 1997. *Languages of Tribal and Indigenous People of India: The Ethnic Space.* Delhi: Motilal Banarsidass; T. Burrow. 1969. "Dravidian and the Decipherment of the Indus Script". *Antiquity.* 43:172; T. Burrow and M.B. Emeneau (1998, reprint). *A Dravidian Etymological Dictionary.* New Delhi: Vedam Books; F.B.J. Kuiper. 1948. *Proto-Munda Words in Sanskrit.* Leiden: Orientalia Neerlandica.
2. "Scheduling" was done in such a manner that a Scheduled Tribe would be recognised as such only in the area in which it is scheduled. Thus about 60 lakh Jharkhandi adivasis living in Assam are not considered STs since they are not scheduled as such.
3. Verrier Elwin. 1959. *A Philosophy for NEFA.* Shillong: North-East Frontier Agency.
4. B.D. Sharma. 1995. *Globalisation: the Tribal Encounter.* New Delhi: Vedam Books.
5. Walter Fernandes. 1992. *National Development and Tribal Deprivation.* New Delhi: Indian Social Institute.

11

Deficit Childhood and its Implications for India's Democracy*

Shanta Sinha

Since I hail from Andhra Pradesh, I am naturally proud of Durgabai-*amma*. Her enormous contribution to women's empowerment by bringing the issues of education to the center stage of India's development and democracy is indeed awesome. She courageously participated in the freedom movement even as a young child, and in the process, helped pave the way for millions of women to break the shackles of discrimination and enter public spaces. I cherish her visits to our home with C.D. Deshmukh-ji. We were awed by her devotion, courage, forthrightness, and ability to build sturdy institutions.

It is the stalwarts of that era that gave us the framework for India and its people. In that framework, children and their childhoods were seen as crucial for laying the foundations of India's democracy. Thus Article 39 of the Directive Principles of State Policy stipulates that "children are given opportunities and facilities to develop in a healthy manner and in conditions of freedom and dignity and … childhood and youth are protected against exploitation and against moral and material abandonment." The Directive Principles stipulate also that " … the health and strength of workers, men and women, and the tender age of children are not abused and that citizens are not forced by economic necessity to enter avocations unsuited to their age or strength."

There are other articles that impose more specific responsibilities on the State vis-a-vis the children of the nation, for instance, Article 45, which states: "The State shall endeavour to provide, within a period of ten years from the commencement of the Constitution, for free and compulsory education for all children until they complete the age of fourteen years". Special care was to be taken in the case of children from weaker sections of society. This is implied by Article 46, which states: "The State shall promote with special care the

* Edited transcript of the July 15, 2009, Durgabai Deshmukh Memorial Lecture by Professor Shanta Sinha.

educational and economic interests of the weaker sections of the people, and, in particular, of the Scheduled Castes and the Scheduled Tribes, and shall protect them from social injustice and all forms of exploitation."

The vision was one that emerged in the charged atmosphere of independence from colonial subjugation, in which the liberation of each and every citizen in India, including children, was seen to be within the realm of possibility.

Child Rights

After more than 60 years of Independence, we find that child rights as a claim on the State and the State's obligation to children have yet to become a wholehearted commitment. There is a deficit in childhood in every respect, which is inimical to the development of children's fullest potential, and, in the long run, to their right to citizenship and dignity and to equality and social justice. Deficit childhoods have, over decades, led to deficit citizenship. This has profound consequences for our democracy.

India does have a strong foundation in democracy, in terms of freedom of expression and political participation, and civil and political rights. However, how much our democracy has matured—in terms of equity and social justice, is something we need to reflect upon. How democratic are our institutions in their actual functioning? Do they provide equal access to all citizens? Are they inclusive? Are they fair and sensitive to eliminating all barriers such that people (men and women of all ages, conditions and positions) can enjoy opportunities and benefit from them? India's democracy needs to be nurtured, and we need to take cognisance of our children and their status if we are to be a proud democracy.

It is always good to start with what our achievements have been. India manages the largest network of State-run public institutions for children in the world today. The country has over nine lakh schools and 36 lakh school teachers to cater to 143 million children in the 6–14 years age group. It has the largest noon meal programme, covering 131.69 million children; and the largest immunisation and nutrition programmes, with 10 lakh *anganwadi* centres to cater to over 56 million children. There are programmes for affirmative action on behalf of children from the most vulnerable communities such as the Scheduled Castes and Scheduled Tribes, as mandated by the Constitution of India; and the State provides a range of targeted initiatives and infrastructure such as scholarships, residential schools, hostel facilities, and so on.

In our large and diverse country, however, the quality of services is not consistent and continues to represent a key challenge in ensuring equal access to fundamental rights by children. While there have been significant achievements in some areas in the country, with some States, districts, and blocks doing better than others on the child development indicators of health, nutrition, education, and other entitlements, the showing continues to be abysmally poor in some pockets, for certain classes of children, and in the case of the more disadvantaged communities.

Dangers to Childhood

Contemporary times have intensified the dangers to childhood and have been extraordinarily harsh to many children in our country. Children are now increasingly vulnerable and marginalised. Having no food to eat, and little or no health support, they live in precarious circumstances, are malnourished, experience chronic hunger, and their lives are tragically claimed by infant and child mortality. Older children are trafficked and work as migrant child labourers, usually away from their homes. Networks for trafficking children span the entire country—from Manipur to Chennai; from Bihar to Punjab, Kerala and Rajasthan; and from Orissa to Mumbai and Gujarat. Moreover, it is an undisputed fact that children are subject to abuse, torture, and gross exploitation at work places. Even children who remain in their own communities and are at work are victims of cruel market forces and lack access to State services and protective schemes. Child marriage, child trafficking, and discrimination against girls remain crucial challenges. There are a growing number of children affected by and infected with HIV-AIDS; and there are children who have to endure dislocations on account of displacement arising from natural disasters and civil unrest.

Appalling Statistics

India has the highest proportion of undernourished children in the world, which makes it comparable to countries like Nepal, Ethiopia, and Bangladesh. Forty-six per cent of the children in the country are underweight and 79.2 per cent are anemic. Half a million female foetuses are aborted each year. The infant mortality rate is 57 per 1000, and even more if figures are disaggregated, making the scenario worse than that of sub-Saharan Africa. Twenty-five per cent of girl children born each year do not survive to celebrate their 15th birthday. Fifty per cent drop out even before they complete class 8, and 78 per cent drop out before they complete class 10. 11.2 million girls of primary school age remain out-of-school.

India has the highest number of child labourers in the world, many of them as young as four years. 5,79,841 children in the age group of 0–4 were currently engaged in household activities, according to the Census of 2001. Census data also show that the number of child labourers in the country increased from 11.28 million in 1991 to 12.6 million in 2001. Two third of child workers are engaged in the agricultural sector, where 73 per cent are casual-wage child laborers. Child marriage continues to prevail, with half of India's girls being married of before they are 18 years of age. This is a gross violation of human rights, forcing children to assume responsibilities beyond their capacities and subjecting them to physical, emotional, and sexual abuse. As far as specific laws to protect children are concerned, a large population of children remains excluded, for there is at present no law to protect the rights of children in the 0–6 year age group. When laws do exist, there are serious gaps, which leaves no legal recourse when violations of child rights do occur.

Legal Gaps

One of the important ways to protect children is through legal instruments. There is an eternal argument on efficacy of law, especially regarding stubborn social and cultural practices, since many issues continue to perpetuate inspite of legal proscription. In the Indian context, laws set standards even as they become an indispensable tool for defenders of rights. If there is no law, then an important space for contestation of power is lost for the weak.

- While there are certain legal instruments derived from the labour legislations pertaining to factories, mines, and plantations, construction workers, etc., which mandate that crèches must be provided, the fact is that in reality, they hardly exist. There is a need for legal instruments to set standards for the provision of the physical infrastructure and professional support required to provide children access to health, nutrition, care, and protection.
- It is of utmost importance to have a debate on the basic entitlements of children in the 0–6 years of age, and to explore the need for providing them their fundamental rights. There is indeed a need for a law that guarantees early child care centres, and the setting up of standards for such centres.
- There is need for a law that guarantees protection to children of informal sector and migrant workers.
- There is need for a legal process by which the poor woman in labour can complain about the non-availability of a doctor or even a trained midwife.
- There is a need for a law that mandates the State to provide for all the services and procedures any woman can demand in a primary healthcare centre, sub-centre or a general hospital.
- There is a need for a law on provision of maternal entitlements enabling exclusive breast feeding.
- There is a need for law that would take punitive action if children in a village have not been immunised for months together because of the absence of an auxiliary nurse midwife (ANM) or the required dosages.

On the other hand, when there is a law, it is found to be faulty. For instance, child labour is prohibited in 16 occupations and 57 processes but does not cover children in the 15–18 age groups. Moreover, the Child Labour (Prohibition and Regulation) Act 1986, which seeks to prohibit child labour in certain occupations and processes and to regulate working conditions in other areas of work, excludes agriculture and allied activities and also labour rendered by the child for one's own family. We have insisted on a gradual approach of tackling child labour in "prohibited" lists first, as a practical measure, without taking cognisance of the reality that as long as children are available in the labour pool, it will impossible to abolish child labour. There will always be a set of children to replace those who have been rescued. One wonders if it is practical for the child to be out of school. Whose practicality are we defending?

Another lacuna can be seen in the case of the Prohibition of Child Marriage Act 2006. This act does not make child marriage totally void. It only provides for a child to petition, with the help of a prohibition officer, for nullifying the marriage.

Closed Options

Deficit childhood occurs when there is a lack of reach of the State, its institutions and processes to cover these children. Deficit childhood is a situation of failure of the State to reach to every child and not the incapacity of the child to access her entitlements. Childhood deficits have a profound impact on children. Denied access to basic nutritional and health entitlements, they grow up stunted, wasted, and malnourished, and live precariously. Deprived of education, they lack in confidence and self-esteem. They are trapped in the labour pool of the informal sector, performing jobs that are repetitive and monotonous, with no possibility of mobility, of accessing opportunities that can give them dignity. Their options in the market and in employment are only on a casual basis, as daily workers, migrant labourers, or as bonded labourers. An episode of drought or an illness of even one member of the family, or lack of employment for some length of time, can reduce them to destitution and increase their vulnerability. Children are the worst affected. Many of them are forced into illegal nexuses and even armed conflict. Eventually they are marginalised, having no access or capacities to deal with the system of authority and power. The voices of the poor fail to reach their representatives and the legislature, and are heard mainly through popular movements, community mobilisation, and the sacrifice of thousands who participate in such protests and demonstrations and call for justice, though outside of the framework of formal institutions. Or their voices get heard sometimes through the media.

Childhood, Citizenship, and Democracy

A State supported childhood—for instance, in terms of subsidised school fees, and so on, facilitates enlightened citizenship and radicalises democracy. We all need to take a categorical stand in favour of children's rights—our moral indignation must lead us to action.

We need to join hands to energise the State in implementing long term, rather than *ad hoc* policies to prevent beggary and domestic child labour. We need to adopt a rights based approach, applicable to all. We need to transcend ourselves and put ourselves in the other person's shoes. We need to think beyond family and primordial ties and embrace the human spirit in all its greatness.

12

Trading Our Lives Away: Free Trade, Women, and Ecology*

Vandana Shiva

Trade is not new. It is as old as human economic activity itself. International trade also has an ancient history. Prior to colonialism, international trade was dominated by what today is known as the Third World. Subsequently, especially in the South Asian context, "free-trade" was an important instrument for colonisation. Thus, the East India Company, which made its transition from a trading concern to the ruler of colonial India, first gained a foothold in the Indian subcontinent by means of a free trade treaty of 1717 called the Faruksheer Firman.[1] At the time, "free trade" implied the freedom of the East India Company to have a trade monopoly. In time, colonialism distorted the terms of trade and the Third World was transformed from being an exporter of manufactured commodities to being a supplier of raw materials and a market for British manufacturers. As Radhakamal Mukherjee has noted:

> The year 1800 saw a revolution in India's economy. India was now well-started on the road to transformation from being the industrial workshop of the world to one of its raw material producing regions, the Select Committee of the House of Lords observed in 1830. The Chief manufacturers of India having been supplanted to a great extent by the manufacturers of England, not only in the market of this country, but in that of India itself, it has become an object of the deepest interest to improve the productions of the soil; the committee therefore instituted a full inquiry into the quality of silk and of cotton of India and ... they likewise made inquiries as to sugar, tobacco and other articles of Indian produce. Thus, while the export of such Indian raw materials as cotton, silk, hides, oil seeds, dye stuffs and jute as were essential for the progress of the Industrial Revolution was encouraged by England since the beginning of the 19th century, India entered upon a period of de-industrialisation and increased dependence upon agriculture.

* Edited transcript of the July 16, 1996, Durgabai Deshmukh Memorial Lecture by Dr Vandana Shiva.

Post-Independence, the import substitution policies of free India were in part guided by a need to reverse the de-industrialisation induced by colonial trade regimes. Protectionism was a necessary part of this reversal. Protectionism and free trade are intimately connected. They are the conditions for each other's birth. Thus, removing the structures of post-colonial protectionism is the major justification for the present round of "free trade" launched by the Uruguay Round of GATT (General Agreement on Trade and Tariffs).

Before we turn to these issues in greater detail, let us first undertake a conceptual exploration to facilitate our enquiry.

Metaphors

The word "economy" has its roots in the Greek word *oikos*, which referred originally to the household and its daily operations and maintenance. It was assumed that national economic affairs could be conceived of as merely extensions of the housekeeper's budget. Thus, "household" was originally the metaphor for the economy. Modern economic paradigms however, reconstituted the metaphor of home. "Home" was no longer the model for economic organisation. The home was separated from the economy and made economically invisible. Division of labour between the genders was also mapped homologously, with female and male being projected into the household and the economy respectively. The distancing of "economy" from "household" was also associated with a gendering of both "economy" and "household". Sociologically, this led to what Maria Mies has called the housewifisation of the domestic economy.[2] The domestic economy, associated with production in and for the home and for need, was counted as non-production.

This transformation of value into dis-value, labour into non-labour, knowledge into non-knowledge, is achieved by two very powerful constructs—the production boundary and the creation boundary. The production boundary is a political construct which excludes regenerative production cycles from the domain of production. National accounting systems used for calculating growth through gross national product are based on the assumption that if producers consume what they produce, they do not in fact produce at all—they fall outside the production boundary.[3] Women, who produce for their families; children; and nature—which provides the sustenance base, are thus all treated as non-productive, as economically inactive. The devaluation of women's work, and of work done in subsistence economies in the Third World, is the natural outcome of a production boundary constructed by capitalist patriarchy. The production boundary is closely linked with the "creation boundary", which demarcates the realm of economic value. By restricting economic value to the market, capitalist patriarchy ignores value in two vital economies necessary to ecological and human survival—the domain of nature (nature's economy), and the domain of the sustenance economy. In nature's economy and the sustenance economy, economic value is a measure of the protection of the earth's life and human life. Its currency is life-giving, not cash or market price.

Women play a major role in nature's economy or the subsistence economy by engaging in activities that tap into forest economies, peasant agriculture, craft production, and artisanal fishing. Through this sustenance economy, human beings derive their livelihoods directly from nature.[4] At the level of gender impact, the paradigm of economic value implied by the production boundary and the creation boundary, in one fell swoop, made women's work and all domestic production disappear. The exclusive focus on incomes and cash-flows as measured in GNP has meant that the web of life around women and the environment is excluded from central concern. Sadly, the status of women and children and the state of the environment have never functioned as "indicators" of development. This exclusion is achieved by rendering invisible two kinds of process. First, nature's and women's contribution to the growth to the market economy is neglected and denied, for the dominant economic theories assign no value to tasks carried out at subsistence and domestic levels. Consequently, the world's majority—women and the people in the Third World, are rendered statistically "invisible". Secondly, the negative impact of economic development and growth on women, children and the environment goes largely unrecognised and unrecorded. Both these factors lead to impoverishment.

Among the hidden costs generated by destructive development are the new burdens created by ecological devastation—costs that are invariably heavier for women, in both the North and South. It is hardly surprising, therefore, that rising GNP or global trade figures do not necessarily mean that either wealth or welfare has increased proportionately. I would argue that GNP and growth in international trade is becoming increasingly a measure of how real wealth—the wealth of nature and the life sustaining wealth produced by women—is rapidly decreasing. When trade in commodities is treated as the only economic activity, it destroys the potential of nature and women to produce life, and goods and services for basic needs. More trade and more cash mean less life in nature through ecological destruction and in society through denial of basic needs. Women are devalued, first, because their work co-operates with nature's processes, and second, because work that satisfies needs and ensures sustenance is devalued in general. More growth in what is mal-development has meant less nurturing of life and life support systems.

Three Economies

Nature's economy—through which environmental regeneration takes place—and the people's sustenance economy—within which women draw on nature's economy to produce the sustenance for society through "invisible" unpaid work (called non-work) are being systematically destroyed to create growth in the global market economy. Closely related is the concept of people's economy in Hilka Pietila's categorisation of the free economy in industrialised societies, which consists of the non-monetary core of the economy and society, unpaid work for one's own and family needs, community activities, mutual help and co-operation within the neighbourhood and so on.[5] As Marilyn Waring has documented, national accounts and GNP actually exclude the free economy as lying outside the production boundary. Finally, Pietila describes the "free-trade" economy as the fettered economy which consists of large-scale production for export and to compete with imports. The terms in this economy are dictated by the world market, dependency, vulnerability, compulsive competitiveness and so forth.[6] (In addition, there is the protected sector, which consists of production, protected and guided by official means for domestic markets; food, constructions, services, administration, health, schools and culture and so on).

As the "trade" metaphor replaces the metaphor of "home", economic value itself undergoes a shift. Value, derived from *valere*, which means "worth", was redefined as exchange and trade. Unless something was traded, it had no economic value. "Home" as the root and metaphor for the economy was substituted by "trade" as a metaphor for the economy and as a source of economic value.

The Trade Metaphor

The trade metaphor for the economy has rendered nature's economy valueless. Thus, both the marginalisation of women's work and nature's work are linked to how the metaphor of "home" was reconstituted as the domain where no economic value is produced. This shift in economic value is central to the ecological crisis. It is reflected in the change in the meaning of the term "resource". "Resource" originally implied life. Its root is the Latin verb *surgere*, which evokes the image of a spring continually rising from the ground. Like a spring, a "resource" rises again and again, even if it has repeatedly been used and consumed. The concept thus highlights nature's power of self-regeneration and calls attention to her prodigious creativity. Moreover, it implies an ancient idea about the relationship between humans and nature—that the earth bestows gifts on humans who, in turn, are well advised to show diligence in order not to suffocate her generosity. In early modern times, "resources" therefore suggested reciprocity along with regeneration.

With the advent of industrialism and colonialism, however, a conceptual break occurred. "Natural resources" became those parts of nature which were required as inputs for industrial production and colonial trade. In 1870, John Yeats, in his *Natural History of Commerce*, offered the first definition of the new meaning: "In speaking of the natural resources of any country, we refer to the ore in the mine, the stone unquarried, the timber unfelled (etc.)".[7] In this view, nature has been clearly stripped of her creative power; she has been turned into a container for raw materials, waiting to be transformed into inputs for commodity production. Resources were now merely any material or conditions existing in nature which were capable of "economic exploitation".[8] With the capacity of regeneration gone, the attitude of reciprocity also lost ground. It was human inventiveness and industry that imparted value to nature; natural resources required to be "developed", and only once capital and technology were brought in would nature find her destiny. From then on, it was a matter of common sense that: "Natural resources cannot develop themselves; it is only through the application of human knowledge and skill that anything can be made of them, and most of the necessary work requires skill of a very high order".[9] Nature, whose real propensity it is to rise again, was transformed by this originally Western worldview into dead and manipulable matter. Its capacity to renew and grow was denied.

The trade metaphor is also guiding much of the work of environmental economics that is indifferent to women's sustenance economy and nature's economy. For example, the World Bank policy paper on trade liberalisation for India's agriculture sector recommends the creation of "markets in tradeable water rights". It is argued: "If rights to the delivery of water can be freely bought and sold, farmers with new crops or in new areas will be able to obtain water provided they are willing to pay more than its value to existing users, and established users will take into account its sale value in deciding on what and how much to produce".[10] This institution of tradeable water rights is a guarantee for diverting water from small farmers to large corporate super farms. Tradeable water rights will lead to water monopolies. In the logic of the market, tradeable rights have a tendency to be sold to the highest bidder. This will lead to a water-power linked concentration of wealth. It will also lead to over-exploitation and misuse of water, since those who deplete water resources do not have to suffer the consequences of water scarcity—they can always buy water rights from other farmers and other regions. Besides aggravating the already severe ecological crisis in water resources, tradeable water rights will lead to discord and social disintegration. The social breakdown in Somalia can be traced, in part, to the privatisation of water rights according to the World Bank policy. Tradeable water rights are based on the assumption that no ecological or social limits should be placed on water use. Such use without limits leads to abuse. The World Bank proposals on tradeable water rights are a prescription for social and ecological disaster.

Strangely enough, introducing tradeable land and water rights is often justified on environmental grounds. For example, a World Bank study by Pearce and Warford argues:

> In the absence of rights to sell or transfer land, the land owner may be unable to realise the value of any improvements and thus has little incentive to invest in long term measures such as soil conservation.[11]

This assumption is patently false, since the best examples or soil conservation—the hill terraces of the Himalayas, are in force precisely for the opposite reasons.

Communities, not threatened by alienation of resources, have a long term interest in conserving them.

The marketisation and privatisation of land and water resources is prescribed on the flawed concept of the equivalence of price and value. All movements related to preventing the ecological abuse of land and water and providing justice in land and water rights ask for the opposite—the inalienability of rights, and where the resource is a *common* property resource, like water, the inalienability of *common* rights. Experiments like the *pani panchayat* movement and the *makti sangharsh* movement are showing the direction for the ecological and equitable use of water. Pani Panchayats (water panchayats) were formed to prevent the waste of scarce water resources through inequitable and ecologically destructive, though commercially remunerative cropping patterns. To ensure equity, the Pani Panchayats treat water as a community resource, not as private property. Further, water rights are based on the number of family members, not on the size of land holdings. The experiments of the Pani Panchayat have demonstrated that community management of a scarce common resource is the only way to ensure both justice and sustainability.[12]

Hunger and Food Security

With the Uruguay Round of GATT and the establishment of the WTO (World Trading Organisation), the scope of the trade metaphor has further increased. The two central impacts of the Uruguay Round are the removal of national boundaries in trade flows and bringing into the domain of international trade subject areas that had hitherto been restricted to domestic policy, such as agriculture. The collapse of the border paradigm is linked to the introduction of the "production boundary" at national borders and the reduction of entire domestic economies as non-value generating.

All economic value is therefore reduced not just to market prices, but to global market prices. Not only have the three economies of nature, people and market been reduced to the market alone, the market economy itself has been reduced to the global market dominated by trade in dollars. This dollarisation of the economic value of nature and the products necessary for human survival is an essential part of globalisation. It is a trend in India, evident in recent advertisements, which equate natural resources with dollars and yens. Ecological and social costs and values disappear and are destroyed, and the destruction does not register on the global trade figures.

Thus, the only value of shrimp is its value for American, European and Japanese markets. The increased profits from exports of shrimp show up in national and global economic growth figures. However the destruction of local food consumption, of ground water resources, fisheries, agriculture and livelihoods associated with traditional occupations in each of these sectors does not occur in global economic value—it is only experienced locally. In India, prawns—the most important shrimp species cultivated for exports, are grown in intensive shrimp farms with stocking rates of 100,000 to 300,000 prawns per hectare. The ecological impact of intensive shrimp cultivation has turned the fertile coastal tracts of Nellore (named after *nellu*, that is, rice) and Thanjavur, the rice bowl in the Cauvery delta, into graveyards, destroying both fisheries and agriculture. With drinking water and livelihood options disappearing as a result of intensive shrimp cultivation for exports, it is the women of fishing and farming communities, who have resisted the expansion of shrimp farming, who have suffered the most. As Govindamma of Kurru village puts it: "We were displaced from the sea, we went to agriculture for jobs. Now they are building prawn farm on agricultural lands. Salt farms are also being converted. There too we will lose labour. Where will we earn our living?" In Tamil Nadu and Andhra Pradesh, the social and ecological impact of aquaculture for exports has led women from fishing and farming communities to resisting prawn cultivation through *satyagraha*.[13]

Agricultural exports have adverse consequences for the poor also in terms of its impact on local prices. Indian prices of staple food grains are phenomenally lower than world prices; the price of Indian rice is about 54 per cent lower and the prices of wheat in India are 17 per cent lower than in the world market. However, when rice and wheat get exported, market forces will ensure rising domestic prices, taking these crops beyond the reach of poor people. As a result of increasing domination of market forces in the food sector and reduced public policy intervention for food security, food prices increased by 63 per cent between 1989–90 and 1993–94, leading to a decline in per capita food consumption in the last three years from 510 grams per day in 1991 to 466 grams per day in 1993. In Rajasthan, the quota of wheat available under the Public Distribution Scheme has been reduced from 10 kilograms per unit to 3 kilograms; in Gujarat from 20 kilograms to 10 kilograms; and in Madhya Pradesh, from 12 kilograms to 3.5 kilograms. This is in spite of the fact that the Essential Commodities Act has not yet been dismantled. When, as demanded by trade liberalisation, food will be available only at world market prices, starvation is the only certainty for the majority of the poor who were not getting enough food even prior to the "reforms", and famine the only inevitable future scenario for the country.

Liberalisation of agricultural exports has also led to the exports of cotton and yarn. Export of cotton has led to a doubling and tripling of the cost of yarn and the creation of massive unemployment in the decentralised handloom weaving sector. The handloom sector employs 9 million workers, largely in home-based production. The main reason for the destitution of the weavers is that between 1991 and 1994, the prices of yarn had more than doubled, from Rs 226.30 to Rs 415 per bundle of 20's Count and from Rs 174 to Rs 491 per bundle of 40's Count.[14] The rise of yarn prices was in turn, mainly due to the liberalisation of exports. In 1994, hardly 10 per cent of the looms in Andhra Pradesh were working because of the crisis created by exports. Free exports thus translated into unemployment and starvation.[15] While cotton prices went up by 55 per cent, there was hardly a 5 per cent increase in handloom cloth.

Trade liberalisation is justified in terms of the theory of comparative advantage, which, in its simplest form, states that a nation can enhance efficiency in resource use and hence welfare, by producing and exporting commodities in which it is relatively efficient and importing commodities in which it is relatively not so. However, applying the fallacious logic of comparative advantage to agriculture in poor countries like India can lead to policy prescriptions that increase domestic food prices of cereals like rice and wheat because of exports and destroy the economic base of poor farmers in poor regions because of imports of millets like sorghum, which are largely produced by them. Food security is therefore destroyed by "liberalisation" of both exports and imports. Maximising market efficiency in food production can often be associated with collapse of food entitlements and growth of starvation and famine, as country after country undergoing structural adjustment has shown. Comparative advantage in terms of market forces can lead to total disadvantage in terms of food security and food rights.

Export of agricultural commodities has severe costs for local ecosystems, local communities and local economies. It is, therefore, disturbing to note that Indian agricultural exports have increased by about 71 per cent during the span of the last four years—from Rs 21.98 billion in 88–89 to Rs 37.66 billion in 1992–93. Notably, the agriculture agreement of WTO promotes import and export liberalisation through its market access and export competition clauses.[16] Ignoring the fallaciousness of the comparative advantage logic, the NCAER study on Export Competitiveness for India recommends the export of wheat and rice and the import of sorghum. It does not view coarse grains like sorghum as having export competitiveness. "However, less encouraging export competitiveness of maize and sorghum in itself is not a serious worry because these crops can be import substituted efficiently". [17]

Food security in agriculture is based on a delicate balance between ensuring that food prices are not too high to take food beyond the reach of the already deprived consumers and not too low to push out domestic farmers from production. After all, food is not merely an item of consumption; food production is also the most significant source of livelihood for our people. It is through the *participation* in food production that most people in India have an *entitlement* to food.

As Amartya Sen has so clearly articulated, starvation and deprivation are linked more directly to declining entitlements than to decreased "food supplies".[18] Structural adjustment and trade liberalisation measures can create starvation and famine by removing tariff barriers and allowing the flow of cheap food which displaces peasants and destroys their entitlements. The famines in Somalia, Rwanda and all of sub-Saharan Africa are linked to removal of import barriers and the destruction of the market for domestic producers. Lowering of import barriers and flooding markets with imported food grains sold at low prices because of many levels of hidden subsidies can actually contribute to hunger and starvation in primarily agricultural societies. While lower food prices might be good for societies with hardly any farmers, they are devastating for food security in peasant economies. Therefore, the impact of trade liberalisation on food security is different in different socio-economic contexts. In items whose domestic price is lower than international prices, trade liberalisation leads to exports and thus a rising of the domestic price. In items whose domestic price is higher than international prices, trade liberalisation leads to dumping and a displacement of domestic producers from agriculture. As indicated above, cheap food can be a prescription for famine when it displaces domestic producers and destroys their entitlement.

Further, cheap food does not imply food produced at lower cost. High costs of production can go hand-in-hand with low food prices because agribusiness corporations are the sellers of inputs to farmers, the buyers of agricultural commodities from farmers, and the sellers of processed foods to consumers. Not only are their profits distributed across these different segments of the food production and distribution chain, they are also spread in space across different countries and in time through futures trading. They can bring cheap food to consumers in spite of extremely high costs of production because of their monopoly control on the food chain.

Most national laws related to the production and distribution of food are laws that have been aimed at curbing the monopoly control of trading interests. On the other hand, trade liberalisation is aimed at removing all restrictions for trade and trading interests. Trade-liberalisation therefore results in the removal of food security by removing the legal and policy instruments that protect the entitlements of the poor who have little or no purchasing power and are therefore excluded from the market.

TRIPS

The assumption that industrial activity is true creation because it takes place *ex inhilo* is ecologically false. No technological artefact or industrial commodity is formed out of nothing; no industrial process takes place where nothing was before. Nature and its creativity and other people's social and intellectual labour are consumed at every level of industrial production as "raw material" or "energy". Thus, the biotech seed which is treated as "creation" to be protected by patents could not exist without the farmer's seed.

The assumption that only industrial production is truly creative because it produces from nothing hides the ecological destruction that goes with it. The patriarchal creation boundary allows ecological destruction to be perceived as creation, and ecological regeneration and creation to be perceived as non-creation. This disvaluing of regeneration underlies the breakdown of ecological cycles and the crisis of sustainability. To sustain life means, above all, to regenerate life; but according to the patriarchal view, to regenerate is not to create, it is merely to "repeat"—it is the same as passivity.

Intellectual property rights, especially patents on life, are the ultimate denial of nature's creativity and women's creativity. The Trade Related Intellectual Property rights (TRIPS) agreement of the Uruguay Round of GATT, now institutionalised as the World Trade Organisation (WTO), has, for the first time, brought into global trade the domain of ideas, knowledge and innovation. Of particular interest to us are clauses that refer to IPRs in the area of biodiversity and agriculture, since this subject matter is closely related to women. Women are the original seed keepers and still continue to be custodians of seed diversity.[19] Most women in our region are farmers. Women's rights and knowledge in agriculture and biodiversity are now threatened by the TRIPs agreement of GATT/WTO. The TRIPS treaty is in effect setting up a creation boundary.[20] Such a creation boundary, demarcated in terms of, for instance, the creation of genetically modified seeds by a seed corporation, disregards the genetic resources that these corporations make use of in the first place—genetic resources which have been developed over centuries of selection and innovation by farmers in third world countries.

Seed Monopolies

Under the impact of the TRIPs agreement, Third World farmers will stop being the custodians and owners of seed. The international Convention of the Union for the Protection of New Varieties of Plants (UPOV) had maintained farmers' rights to save seed, but in a March 1991 amendment this clause was removed. The new clause in UPOV (and TRIPs) can be used to enforce royalty payments on farmers if they save seed of their own crop. With the stronger intellectual property rights regime being conceived under WTO, the transfer of extra funds as royalty payments from the poor to the rich countries would exacerbate the current Third World debt crisis ten fold. This is ironical, since most plant diversity originates in the Third World, and seeds and plant materials that today are under the control of the industrialised world were originally taken freely from the farmers to whom they will now be sold back as patented material. As a result, seed companies will reap monopoly profits, while the genius of Third World farmers will go unrewarded and they will be banned from saving and using their own seeds.

IPRs in the area of seeds and plant material are in any case not easy to demarcate, since the genetic resources used by multinational corporations for claiming patents are the product of centuries of innovation and selection by Third World farmers, especially women. The UN Food and Agriculture Organisation (FAO) has recognised these contributions in the form of Farmers' Rights. The Biodiversity Convention signed at the 1992 Earth Summit also recognises them, and accepts the need to make IPRs subservient to the objectives of biodiversity conservation. The TRIPs text, however, biased as it is in favour of acknowledging only the innovation by global patriarchal institutions like Multi-National Corporations (MNCs) goes against these agreements reached on other international platforms. The negative impact on farmers and other Third World citizens will be increased due to the extension of the working and the terms of the patent.

Moreover, article 34 of the text reverses the burden of proof in the area of process patents. In normal law, the accused is innocent unless proven guilty. Under the reversal in the WTO regime, however, it is the accused who must demonstrate their innocence; if they cannot do so, then they are deemed guilty of having infringed upon the right of the patent holder. In the area of agriculture this can have absurd and highly unjust consequences. MNCs are now taking out broad patents on plant varieties, covering ownership of traits and characteristics. With the reversal of the burden of proof clauses, it becomes legally possible for a corporation to accuse the farmers who originally contributed the seeds with a particular trait, of patent infringement. There is no clause in TRIPs to offer protection to farmers in such cases. When this situation is combined with possibilities of cross - retaliation that the WTO will institutionalise, MNCs will have a very powerful tool to subsume all agriculture and all production under their monopoly control. This monopolisation of the entire economy is the main motive for setting up a WTO with a TRIPs council.

Patenting micro-organisms

Article 27.5.3 (b) of TRIPs agreement states: "*Parties may exclude from patentability plants and animals other than micro-organisms...*"

On first reading, it appears that the article is about the exclusion of plants and animals from patentability. This exclusionary phrase also exists in US patent law, but that has not prevented the US from allowing patents for plants and animals. The problem is that the phrase "plants and animals other than microorganisms" does not cover *parts* of animals and plants, nor does it include *altered* plants and animals. It therefore allows the patenting of biological organisms. Further the words "other than microorganisms" *excludes the exclusion of* microorganisms from patentability. Since microorganisms are living organisms, patenting them is the beginning of a journey down what has been called the slippery slope that leads to the patenting of all life. In our culture, and according to our patent laws, life cannot be patented because it cannot be owned and it is not manufactured. GATT will force us to give up our moral values, our economic priorities and our sovereignty. GATT-TRIPs pushes us into making all living organisms the property of a handful of corporations.

The problem with TRIPs text of GATT is that while it appears to be an agreement about *exclusion* of living organisms from patentability, it will in fact put every country on the slippery slope of patenting life forms whose patent applications have already travelled in the US Patent Office or are before the

US Courts. It is in any case a tragedy that an issue directly related to the ecological and ethical fabric of our society, and to the economic options of survival of our people should be left to a ministry of Commerce. Indeed, GATT-TRIPs is not merely about trade. It is also about the ethics of how we relate to other species and what we hold as moral and cultural values of our civilisation. It is about how our biodiversity is used and controlled-by local communities who have protected it, or by corporations which have found new ways to exploit and own it.

The age of globalisation is deepening a special project of a narrow group of men which excludes and denies the recognition of the contributions of all other social groups from the production of intellectual and material wealth, while using the intellectual and productive contributions of others in their wealth and value generation. The categories of economic value guiding globalisation are violent and destructive to nature as a producer and to women as producers and knowers. As the super State system of the World Bank, IMF and WTO and multinational corporations reach for the resources and knowledge Third World women have so far controlled and conserved, conflicts over economic value of nature and knowledge become reflections of globalised gender conflicts. It is the structures of northern patriarchal power that stand in the most extreme opposition to the interests, values, visions and dreams of Third World women. Whether it is the women protecting seeds and fighting IPRs in agriculture through the Seed Satyagraha or it is the coastal communities resisting shrimp farming through their Satyagraha, globalisation has unleashed a new era of gender politics, with the poorest and most marginal women fighting to protect life in its freedom and its diversity.

Trade Related Feminism

January 1, 1995 established a new era in which globalisation would be legislated by the World Trade Organisation (WTO). The WTO is armed with the power to adjudicate in international trade relations and enforce the implementation of the Uruguay Round of GATT, that is, the General Agreement on Trade and Tariffs. The most significant innovation of the Uruguay Round is the creation of the term "trade-related". By adding the prefix "trade related" to any subject, two magical shifts occur. The first has the effect of drawing areas of domestic decision making into the global arena. Thus, intellectual property rights regimes which had so far been subject only to national requirements were made global through the "Trade-Related Intellectual Property Rights" (TRIPs) Agreement of GATT. The second switch achieved by the term "trade related" was to impart reasons for the justification and enlargement of dubious areas of economic activity—areas in which the dark side of free trade was visible. Thus, when environmentalists and labour unions began to criticise GATT because it would destroy jobs and the environment, "trade-related" social clauses and "trade-related" environmental clauses were offered as a panacea. Trade unionists and

environmentalists who had been critical of GATT started, suddenly, to find a Blue GATT with social clauses and a Green GATT with environmental clauses as essential to the protection of workers' rights and environmental rights. What was forgotten was that as mere clauses in free trade-treaties, these fundamental rights no longer exist as rights—they metamorphosed into "standards".

Standards are in the hand of global agencies, rights are in the hands of people. Standards linked to international trade are inadequate instruments for protecting the rights of workers and the rights of nature for a number of reasons.

- They can only be used in areas predominated by international trade and exports and imports, and leave all other areas unprotected.
- Social and environmental clauses can often be a disguised form of trade protectionism engaged in by precisely those countries which have pushed the free-trade treaties and free-trade ideology on the international community.

Movements and governments of the South have resisted social and environmental clauses, though for different reasons. They are against free-trade. They are for a protectionism that is people based, not super power based. They resist "trade-related" conditionalities because they want more local control, local autonomy and local decision making in areas vital to life. Third World governments resist social and environmental clauses because they have fully absorbed the "free trade" ideology of the deregulation of commerce and see in "blue" and "green" clauses a hidden protectionism that violates the free trade logic.

In a seminar on *Global Trading Practices and Poverty Alleviation in South Asia—a Gender Perspective*, organised by UNIFEM, one case study showed that trade-liberalisation has negative impacts on women as producers and consumers, especially in sectors related to essential needs, like those for food, water and clothing. Most women in the South Asian region are engaged in the vital sectors of agriculture, food processing, textiles and garments. These are also the major trade sectors for South Asia. Trends indicate that in these sectors, trade liberalisation leads to women loosing both production options as well as consumption entitlements.

- In the Maldives, when exports in fisheries increased, women's participation in the fisheries sector declined from 62 per cent in 1977 to 20 per cent in 1990.[21]
- In India, an ICSSR study showed that growth in agro processing linked to foreign investment and exports was creating jobless growth. Overall, in the agro-processing sector, employment was going down.[22]
- The growth of aquaculture linked to marine exports has led to salination and destruction of agricultural and fisheries livelihoods by the destruction of coastal ecosystems.[23]
- Exports of agricultural commodities have led to increased food prices

> and declining food entitlements. In India, food prices increased by 63 per cent between 1989–90 and 1993–94, leading to a decline in the per capita food consumption in the last three years from 510 grams per day in 1991 to 466 grams per day in 1993.[24]

In spite of empirical data that shows that trade liberalisation displaces women from production and consumption, there is a new discourse emerging on "integration of women in trade development". The integration of women in trade development and promotion has become a priority concern of the International Trade Centre UNCTAD/GATT which has a five-year work programme in it. If women's critique of mal-development created "Women in Development" (WID), women's critiques of "free trade" are creating "Women in Trade Development"(WITD), in which women's development has been replaced by the development of trade. Instead of women's concern creating a shift in economic paradigms, the dominant economic paradigm aims at using women instrumentally. As the ITC (International Trade Centre) document states: "ITC is convinced that it is essential for women to enter society's mainstream to accelerate the trade development process in individual countries".

Trade promotion is not necessarily the first priority among the roles women can play in development. Nevertheless, it is clearly acknowledged today that women are a major under-utilised resources in the search for increased export earnings.[25]

Instead of women's empowerment being the objective of economic policy, women are thus reduced to being the means. Instead of trade being a means, it has been elevated to being the highest end of all people, societies and countries must strive towards. A new cosmology is being written, with trade at its centre, as the end to which every system must strive, as the source of all meaning. A new "trade-related feminism" is being born, in which it is the freedom of trade, not the freedom of women, that is the primary concern.

An Eco-feminist Agenda

As noted earlier, the Uruguay Round of GATT and the establishment of the World Trade Organisation have created two unprecedented shifts. Firstly, it has drawn issues that are not narrow economic issues into the domain of trade and economics. Secondly, it has drawn all economic and non-economic issues out of domestic decision making and policy into the global arena where ordinary citizens do not have access to instruments of democratically influencing decisions and policies.

International trade has been made the be all and end all of human existence in every society, and the dollar has been made the ultimate measure of value. Limitless destruction of ecosystems and people's economies and livelihoods has been legitimised in order to increase global trade and economic growth as measured in foreign exchange. Large scale ecological disruption, destruction of livelihoods and economic security of millions of people, and the wholesale destruction of biological and cultural diversity is the inevitable consequence.

An ecological and feminist agenda for trade needs to be based on recognising the ecological limits and the social criteria that economic activity should be guided by if it has to respect the environmental principles of sustainability and the ethical principle of justice. This requires that the full ecological and social costs of economic activity and trade be made visible and taken into account. Localisation, based on stronger democratic decision making at local levels, building up to national and global levels is an imperative for conservation as well as democracy.

Localisation and decentralisation do not imply autarky or isolation. It is based on the principle of subsidiarity, and helps discriminate between different aspects of social and economic life and establish the appropriate form of governance for each activity to ensure protection of people and the environment. Aspects of human life necessary for survival need to be governed by a logic deeper and wider than the logic of international free trade. This involves reclaiming areas of ethics, ecology and equity that have been subsumed under trade by the prefix "trade related". We need to redefine issues on the basis of ethical and ecological principles. Thus, while the Uruguay Round transformed patents on life from being an ethical issue to being a merely "trade related" item of GATT, ecological and ethical movements against patenting of life and its products are reclaiming the ethical dimension.[26] Similarly, while food and agriculture were reduced to a trade issue, social and environmental movements are reclaiming these as matters central to human rights and cultural and ecological survival.[27]

As we enter the next millennium, the values emerging from diverse social movements need to locate trade in its ecological and human context. Where necessary, limits need to be put on trade to protect the integrity of the earth and the integrity of society.

NOTES

1. Vandana Shiva. 1994. "The East India Company, Free Trade and GATT". *The Telegraph,* 21 June.
2. Maria Mies.1993. "Feminist research: Science, violence and responsibility", in Vandana Shiva and Maria Mies. *Ecofeminism.* New Delhi: Kali for Women and London: Zed Books
3. Ted Trainer. 1989. *Developed to Death.* London: Green Print.
4. Vandana Shiva. 2006. *Earth Democracy: Justice, Sustainability and Peace.* London : Zed Books. p. 17, http://books.google.co.in/books?id=iQzwwzBYGDkC&pg=PA17&lpg=PA17&dq=Sustenance+economy+Vandana+Shiva&source=bl&ots=rhomC8bpBs&sig=_b2Rx_30vWis7h28MDZ5oypy5jc&hl=en&sa=X&ei=r36yT_2yIs-GrAe82t3nAw&sqi=2&ved=0CFAQ6AEwAQ#v=onepage&q&f=false (last accessed on 15 May 2012).
5. Hikka Pietila. 1985. *Tomorrow Begins Today.* ICON ISIS Workshop, Nairobi.
6. Marilyn Waring. 1998. *If Women Counted.* San Francisco: Harper & Row.
7. *Oxford English Dictionary,* Second Edition.
8. Joseph Meeker. 1987. "Misused Resources". *Resurgence.* 125. December

9. United Nations. 1983. *"Report on the United Nations Conference On the Application of Science and Technology for the Benefit of Less Developed Areas". Volume II: National Resources. Pg. 18.ref. 7. New York: United Nations.*
10. S. Pursell Gulati and A. Gulati. 1993. *Liberalising Indian agriculture: World Bank policy paper No. 1172.*
11. David W. Pearce and Jeremy J. Warford. 1993. *World Without End: Economics, Environment & Sustainable Development.* Washington, DC: World Bank.
12. Vandana Shiva. 1993. *Ecology and the Politics of Survival.* London: United Nations University Press and SAGE.
13. Notably, marine products were the most important agricultural items exported from India in recent years, accounting for Rs1. 7 billion in 1992–93 and Rs 2 billion in 1994. (India's exports of principal agricultural commodities amounted to Rs 6.2 billion during 1990–91, Rs 8.1 billion in 1991–92, Rs 8.9 billion in 1992–93 and Rs12 billion in 1993–94).
14. L.C. Jain. 1995. "The Right Weave". *The Economic Times.* February 3.
15. Asha Krishna Kumar. 1995. "Struggle to Survive". *Frontline,* March 10. pp. 110–112.
16. L.C. Jain. 1995. "The Right Weave". *The Economic Times,* February 3.
17. NCAER. Export Competitiveness of Selected Agricultural Commodities.
18. Amartya Sen. *Poverty and Famines: An Essay on Entitlement and Deprivation.*
19. Vandana Shiva. 1988. "Staying alive: Women, Ecology and Survival in India". New Delhi: *Kali for Women*; Vandana Shiva. 1991. *Most Farmers in India are Women.* FAO, June; Vandana Shiva. 1993. "Women and Biodiversity". *Indigenous Visions.* New Delhi: India International Centre.
20. Vandana Shiva. 1993. "The Seed and the Earth: Biotechnology and the Colonisation of Regeneration", in Vandana Shiva. *Minding Our Lives.* New Delhi: Kali for Women.
21. *Maldives Country Paper.* Presented at the UNIFEM Conference on *Global Trading Practices and Poverty Alleviation in South Asia,* 30th January to 1 February 1995.
22. Devaki Jain. 1995. Keynote address at UNIFEM conference on *Global Trading Practices and Poverty Alleviation in South Asia,* 30th January to 1 February 1995.
23. Vandana Shiva. 1995. Paper presented at UNIFEM Conference on *Global Trading Practices and Poverty Alleviation in South Asia.* 30th January to 1 February 1995.
24. Ibid.
25. The Integration of Women in Trade Development: A proposal for an ITC programme for 1992–1997—*ITCI TM(92)/4*
26. Vandana Shiva. 1994. *Can life be made? Can Life be Owned?* Annual Environment Day Lecture, Parisar, Pune
27. People's Charter on Food Security based on the Policy Dialogue on *"Trade Liberalisation, Natural Resources and Food Security"* held on 4th and 5th Feb 95 in New Delhi. Third World Network, India.
28. See appendix 2 for the stipulations of these articles.

13

Indian Politics in the Age of Globalisation*

Randhir Singh

I did not have the privilege of knowing Dr Durgabai Deshmukh personally, but I belong to a generation which saw and respected her as one of a select group of men and women who not only participated and suffered in India's freedom struggle but also worked, both before and after freedom was won, to put some meaning into this freedom for the long marginalised and excluded sections of our people. It speaks volumes for the kind of "development" or "progress" we have had in the country that even after 60 odd years of freedom, Durgabai Deshmukh's concerns remain unrealised.

While I welcome the opportunity the Council for Social Development has given me to share my thoughts on this vital area of concern, I must confess that I was, and remain, diffident about doing so. This is not only because I lack the scholarship or credentials as an activist that my predecessors in this series could legitimately claim, but also because I have normally addressed myself to a different category of individuals—one comprising young teachers and students in the universities and colleges trying to make sense of what they are doing in the academia, or groups of young radicals struggling to find their bearings in a world now almost universally dominated by capitalism and an India now openly committed to the capitalist path of development.

Marxist Perspective

Before I begin, force of habit, as a teacher, compels me to make a point, which even otherwise, needs to be made. I am reminded of the rebel students of the Paris of the late 1960s, who would ask their interlocutors: 'Where do you speak from?' For every speaker, inescapably speaks from a particular philosophical-political standpoint and owes it to his audience to publicly state it. It is only fair to acknowledge that my viewpoint is that of Marxism, or rather, Marxism as I understand it, for I have no pretensions to scholarship in

* Edited transcript of the July 15, 2008, Durgabai Deshmukh Memorial Lecture by Prof. Randhir Singh.[14]

Marxism. I picked up some along the way and have found it useful not only in my politics, or my profession as a teacher, but in living my life as well. This last is not just a formal statement. Knowing Marx does make a difference to what sense you make of life, how you understand, live, and act in the world. "Indeed, I must confess that Karl Marx made a man of me" is how George Bernard Shaw once put it. Marx, therefore, is important to me and, I believe, he is important to all of us, today more than ever, if for no other reason than this: the world we are living in is a capitalist world, more capitalist than ever before after the Soviet collapse, and Marx more than any other human being, then or now, devoted his life to explaining the reality of this world and his achievement here remains unrivalled.

As a Marxist, I also speak as a socialist. Immediately, I would only suggest that the "Marxism of Karl Marx" with its scientific spirit, critical, and humanist thrust, needs to be distinguished from the scientific, economic, and deterministic "official Marxism" that once flooded in from Moscow and remains recognised as Marxism in most places. As for socialism, one is socialist because of capitalism and not the Soviet Union. Socialism is not what came to be built in its name in the erstwhile Soviet Union, but it is as visualised by its classical tradition: a humane, democratically functioning society providing a superior and advanced form of freedom and self-determination to the people.

I am going to share a basic argument with you, one that is based on my book, *Marxism, Socialism, Indian Politics—A View from the Left*.[1] For me it is important that the *basics* have to be clearly stated and understood to make proper sense of the details. This, however, is not to in any way underestimate the latter's importance, for that is the level at which life is lived and reality has to be ultimately grasped and engaged with. Again, I am not going to burden or bore you with statistics. The evidence for my argument is there, scattered all around us if only we are willing to see—a little reason and ability to interconnect is all that is needed.

Understanding Globalisation

To understand "Indian Politics in the Age of Globalisation", we obviously need to be clear about what globalisation is. A buzzword for 40 odd years now, "globalisation" is far from being an unambiguous or conceptually clear theoretical construct. Peter Marcuse has even called it a "non-concept": "a simple catalogue of everything that seems different since, say, 1970, whether advances in information technology, widespread use of air freight, speculation in currencies, increased capital flows across borders, Disneyfication of culture, mass marketing, global warming, genetic engineering, multinational corporate power, new international division of labour, international mobility of labour, reduced power of nation-states, postmodernism, or post-Fordism".

For its ardent ideologue, Thomas Friedman—a big time columnist of the *New York Times*, globalisation is a new technological-economic system based in the microchip and ruled by an "electronic herd' of financial investors and multinational corporations, sweeping away everything that came before—capitalism and socialism, the nation-state, imperialism, class struggle, everything. And we have even well-meaning mainstream scholars coming up with what can at best be described as deceptively confusing interpretations.

For John Harriss, "globalisation" is a recent phenomenon. He views the use of the term "in the last ten years or so" as "an indication that something has been happening out there", and goes on to describe it in conventional fuzzy terms: "... the world is more interconnected and supposedly more interdependent than it was formerly, as a result of changes in the global economy—notably rapid movements of large volumes of money and the increased volume of trade—as well as of changes in communications and in information technology. These trends are related in turn and more controversially, with a variety of political and cultural changes, including perhaps especially the ideas of "de-territorialisation", of the decline of the nation state ..."

For Amartya Sen, globalisation is almost as old as civilisation itself: "Over thousands of years, globalisation has progressed through travel, trade, migration, spread of cultural influences and dissemination of knowledge (including of science and technology)". Sen recognises "the dual presence of abject misery and unprecedented prosperity in the world in which we live"—"incomparably richer than ever before, ours is also a world of extraordinary deprivation and staggering inequality"—and ends up urging support for globalisation "in the best sense of that idea", and pleading: "what is needed is a fairer distribution of the fruits of globalisation". Globalisation's historically specific reality today is evaded through an appeal to its so-called "idea in the best sense", which only adds to the prevailing fuzziness and confusion in the use of this term or concept.

Globaloney

As a theoretical concept, globalisation came up in the late 1960s and early 1970s to account for a recent complex of developments in the global economy, particularly the major expansion and conquest of markets by multinationals, seeking to present this international capitalist expansion in a favourable light, as an alternative to Marxist vocabulary and its associated concepts of imperialism, capitalism, etc. In its current widely accepted usage, acquiring new credibility with the collapse of "Soviet socialism", the concept is characterised by two distinct emphases. In the first place, this internationalisation of capital has come to be viewed as a tide sweeping over borders in which technology and irresistible market forces transform the global system in ways beyond the power of anyone to do much to change. The view is often buttressed by a kind of technological determinism where the new electronic technologies make globalisation not only possible or necessary, but inevitable. Globalisation is viewed as an entity in itself, an inevitable, irreversible natural process which, independently of any human will or politics, is now taking over and transforming the world.

In its second distinctive emphasis, globalisation is seen as a historical rupture of a qualitative kind from the changes that have been occurring in capitalism since its inception. The changes taking place now represent a distinctive and unique kind of "epochal shift"—a notion which these days runs as a kind of *leitmotif* through a wide spectrum of intellectual currents, where "post" is the presiding buzzword. We are told that we are now, since the early 1970s to be precise, living through an epochal shift, the birth of a new era, a major qualitative leap so different from the earlier changes in the process of capitalist development that the very logic of capitalism stands superseded. In the globalised world of today, there is no capitalism with its exploitation and oppressions, its classes and class struggles, its structural defects and explosive antagonisms, its chronic problems or crises. Imperialism too is now a thing of the past. As such, globalisation is also argued for as a benevolent phenomenon, an almost automatic solution to all the encountered problems and contradictions of our economy, if not our society as a whole—very much like the once similarly hailed and revered notion of the "invisible hand", Adam Smith's assurance that went so grievously sour as soon as the logic of the *capitalist* market asserted itself.

Around this notion of a technology-driven "globalisation" has grown a new orthodoxy, that of "a dematerialised world", which yet again suggests supersession of capitalism as an economic system and therefore obsolescence of the associated categories of analysis. In a recent article, speaking of "the Myth of Weightless Economy", Ursula Huws has written:

> 'The Death of Distance', 'Weightless World', the 'Connected Economy', the 'Digital Economy', the 'Knowledge-Based Economy', the 'Virtual Organisation'. All these phrases were culled from the titles of books published in the six months prior to writing this essay, in spring, 1998. They could have been multiplied many times: 'virtual', 'cyber', 'tele-', 'networked' or even just 'e-' can, it seems, be prefixed interchangeably to an almost infinite range of abstract nouns. Without even straying from the field of economics, you can try 'enterprise', 'work', 'banking', 'trade', 'commerce', or 'business' (although the device works equally well in other areas: for instance 'culture', 'politics', 'sex', 'democracy', 'relationship', 'drama', 'community', 'art', 'society', 'shopping' or 'crime').
>
> A consensus seems to be emerging—in economics as in other fields—that something entirely new is happening: that the world as we know it is becoming quite dematerialised (or, as Marx put it, 'all that is solid melts into air') and that this somehow throws into question all the conceptual models which have been developed to make sense of the old material world.

The ideological-political implications are obvious. In the current conventional conception of "globalisation", capitalism, the historically specific capitalist processes, the capitalist exploitation of human beings and natural resources, simply disappear. The frenetic and feverish manner in which the information revolution is hyped makes it appear that the entire system of organised capitalism dating back to the Industrial Revolution (and even earlier) is being displaced by a new age of "the electronic republic" and "digital futurologies" where information or "knowledge" is the only source of value, and work is something contingent and de-localisable.

As capitalism goes out of sight, "globalisation" as a universal category of analysis displaces the critical socialist concepts of "capitalism" or "imperialism", and, together with its technological determinism, undercuts any notion of radical or systemic transformative politics. Any kind of anti-capitalist project is ruled out. Globalisation is pitched as a natural, inevitable process, and any resistance to it is seen to be futile. There is no alternative but to accept its dictates. "Globalisation" thus disarms any opposition to almighty capital, and becomes an ideological tool instilling a certain fatalism in the working people, nations, and states to induce them to follow policies of adjustment to the demands of global capitalism, at home and abroad.

In fact, the conventional theorising over "globalisation"— "globaloney" it has been called—mystifies the reality of our world. Postulating an utterly fictitious world of superseded capitalism, it makes capitalism safe against criticism and opposition and using the argument of "inevitability", it wants us to believe that in this globalised world, there is no alternative to the meek acceptance of the conditions necessary for its trouble-free functioning, which in effect means trouble-free functioning of the global capitalist system.

It only needs to be added that today quite a few on the left, indeed a painfully large majority, too has succumbed to the in-fashion "globaloney" of the right. This left has presently joined the right in accepting that "There Is No Alternative"—not just no alternative to capitalism but to a more or less (the right goes for more, the left somewhat less) ruthless capitalism.

Globalisation in Past Times

Globalisation, however, is nothing qualitatively new in the history of bourgeois society. It is a process that has gone on for a long time, in fact ever since capitalism came into the world as a viable form of society four or five centuries ago. An ever-changing system, capitalism was born and grew, and grew to maturity only as a world system. In other words, capitalism has always been a global or globalising system, one moving inexorably towards "globalisation" from its very inception. The most significant elements of what is called globalisation have always been part of capitalist development.

That capitalism is, in its innermost essence, an expanding system, both internally and externally, was pointed out by Marx a long time ago. Once rooted, propelled by the law of accumulation of capital, it both grows and spreads. The classic analysis of this double movement is of course Marx's *Capital.* But the *globalising* nature of capitalism was diagnosed and emphasised by him more than 150 years ago in the *Communist Manifesto* (1848) itself. Marx has been proved uncannily right about many things but perhaps nowhere has he been vindicated more completely than in his account of capitalist expansion or globalisation. Here, for example, are a couple of passages from the *Manifesto*: "The bourgeoisie has through its exploitation of the world market given a cosmopolitan character to production and consumption in every country ... All old-established national industries have been destroyed or are being destroyed. They are dislodged by new industries, whose introduction becomes a life and death question for all nations, by industries that no longer work up indigenous raw material, but raw material drawn from the remotest zones; industries whose products are consumed not only at home, but in every quarter of the globe. In place of the old wants, satisfied by the productions of the country, we find new wants, requiring for their satisfaction the products of distant lands and climes... in place of the old local and national seclusion and self-sufficiency, we have intercourse in every direction, universal interdependence of nations...". Again: "The need of a constantly expanding market for its productions chases the bourgeoisie over the whole surface of the globe. It must nestle everywhere, settle everywhere, establish connections everywhere...". Yet again: the bourgeoisie "batters down all Chinese walls" and "compels all nations, on pain of extinction, to adopt the bourgeois mode of production; it compels them to introduce what it calls civilisation into their midst, i.e. to become bourgeois themselves. In one word, it creates a world after its own image."

Of course, these passages from the *Communist Manifesto* (1848) are not a simple description of contemporary reality. A statement of general and long-term processes that have been part of capitalist development from the beginning, they are more an anticipation of the future that is ours today. They represent an analysis which is much truer today than when the *Manifesto* was composed. It is true that Marx underestimated the durability of capitalism and how long it could keep on expanding. But for all today's fashionable talk about "globalisation", it would be hard to find a more effective description of what is happening today than what he wrote 150 odd years ago.

Marx's is analytically the most sophisticated recognition of capitalism as a system that is uniquely expansionary and international, one tangentially "global" since the very beginning. However, a more than working recognition of this dimension of capitalism was common to classical thinkers such as Adam Smith, and later to most mainstream economists before the First World War. Multinational manufacturing firms appeared in the middle of the 19th century and were well established by the beginning of the 20th, so much so that the internationalisation of capital had become a common preoccupation, and not only of Marxist theorists like Luxemburg, Lenin or Bukharin. Analysts have pointed out that foreign trade and overseas income was a greater percentage of GNP in Europe during the late 19th century than at the end of the 20th century—that world financial markets in the late 19th and early 20th centuries were more fully integrated than they were before or have been since. As a commentator for the *Financial Times* of London has recently put it: "Before 1914 the world economy was in many respects as integrated as it is today and in certain respects more so."

Such integration, with capital and commodities freely traversing the globe, had also made for internationalisation of social and economic life. This is how John Maynard Keynes saw it:

> "The inhabitant of London could order by telephone, sipping his morning tea in bed, the various products of the whole earth, in such quantity as he might see fit, and reasonably expect their early delivery upon his doorstep; he could at the same moment and by the same means adventure his wealth in the natural resources and new enterprises in any quarter of the world, and share, without exertion or even trouble, in their prospective fruits and advantages; or he could decide to couple the security of his fortunes with the good faith of the townspeople of any substantial municipality in any continent that fancy or information might recommend. He could secure forthwith, if he wished it, cheap and comfortable means of transit to any country or climate without passport or other formality. But, most important of all, he regarded this state of affairs as normal, certain, and permanent, except in the direction of improvement ... The internationalisation of (social and economic life) was nearly complete ..."

Thus, if "globalisation" is no novelty in the history of capitalist development, the associated notion of "a borderless world" too is no recent invention.

Info-babble

There is an unending hype, "info-babble" really, over information technology which, together with the globalisation it has so remarkably facilitated, is supposed to usher in the epochal shift that takes us into a world beyond and better than capitalism, indeed makes the very notion of capitalism historically irrelevant. Involving two closely linked technological departure points, the computer and instantaneous communication system, a fusion that has developed in an explosive trajectory in recent years, this technological development has been not unjustifiably described as a revolution—an "information revolution", that is. The importance, however ambiguous, of this revolution for our economy and social life is not to be denied. For good or ill, it has enormously significant implications for the present and future of humankind—implications that socialists need to take serious note of. As Reg Whitaker, in a most perceptive essay on the subject, says, "this revolution cannot be ignored by those seeking real alternatives. Cyberspace is a new reality, a spectre haunting the world. As some of the old terrains of struggle shrink, cyberspace expands as a new terrain to be studied, and to be acted upon."

This revolution by itself does not however change the structural logic of capitalism or offer, or make for, any alternatives to the present social order.

New information technology, as with technological innovations in the past, certainly makes people better at doing things they have always done. But even here we do not need to be breathless about it. It is difficult to see how, as claimed, the nature of manufacturing has been "fundamentally altered" by it. The evidence so far shows only a very small impact on productivity from the large investment made in information technology in the United States or for that matter elsewhere. Production has indeed been globalised, but it remains doubtful if the telecommunications revolution has really had a major impact. It has been suggested that "the invention of relatively simple things, like steamship transport, did more for world trade than digitalised data transmission through fibre optic cables." In other words, its truly remarkable technological innovations and the hype over them notwithstanding, in the ultimate analysis, "information revolution" is only another case of incremental change in the way we do things.

"Information revolution" is emphatically *not* itself an answer to the problems we face—problems primarily born of capitalism and its structural logic. These are problems we ourselves have to solve, with or without the aid of technology. "Information is power", or the computer as "empowerment", does have a certain though ambiguous, validity. But "infobabble" over such propositions has little to do with any notion of redistribution of wealth and power in our society. A computer in every office or home will not somehow solve the problem of unemployment or economic crisis or regional economic decline and imbalances. The poor cannot "unload" from the net the food and shelter or equitable economic development they are denied by the capitalist market. Information technology does not and cannot in any way alter capital's drive to accumulate or its quest for higher profits and stock prices. Instead it has only served to make this quest more penetrating and effective. As with other technologies under capitalism, information technology too is today subservient to capitalist imperatives of accumulation and profit maximisation. Command over information and its transmission has already become the key to success in the capitalist marketplace. A wholesale commodification of information by capital is on and the much celebrated "cyberspace" is taking on the appearance of a "vast mysterious collection of data looming like mega-fortresses fiercely guarded by giant corporations—while the "real world" wallows in urban squalor, petty criminality, violence, and tawdry escapism." This is how Reg Whitaker has posed and answered the key question: "Does the Information Revolution offer an alternative? Yes and no. It does offer an *alternative* capitalist future, but it is unlikely, under present circumstances, to offer an alternative to capitalism".

Trajectories of Globalisation

Capitalist development, given the contradiction inherent in capitalism, has always been a crisis-ridden, bumpy, and uneven affair. It is no different with globalisation as a capitalist process. Its progress too has been essentially bumpy and uneven, and shot through with local, regional, and more than regional crises. There have been periods of "high" globalisation and periods in which economic flows have, to a greater or lesser degree, turned inward in response to changed economic and political conditions. Thus, the second half of the 19th century witnessed an escalating thrust of "globalisation" as a part of capitalism's normal existence. It continued in the 20th century and globalisation was really intense until 1914. Two World Wars, the Great Depression, Russian Revolution, and working class struggles somewhat interrupted this trend, creating what Hobsbawn has described as an interlude of national economics between eras of international economics.

That interlude saw the domestic economies turn in on themselves and there was a prolonged shift to a period of "national development", of "largely delinked, managed national economies", as one description has it—the so-called Keynesian era, which was the unique product of a catastrophic period for capitalism in the first half of the 20th century. Once a certain degree of economic and political recovery was achieved, there was an increasing and uneven effort from the 1950s onwards to return to active globalisation. The effort picked up with the onset of the crisis in the 1970s, when, together with a return to its normal functioning at home, capitalism resumed its path towards internationalisation with a vengeance. The erosion and disintegration of Keynesianism (with its regulated capitalism and welfare state) and the onset of so-called "globalisation" not only reflected the depth of the new crisis but also demonstrated capital's inherent, and now increasingly desperate, drive to create a world economy "in its own image".

Viewed in this perspective, the increasing integration of national economies and the globalisation of trade and investment are not new phenomena. They are only a new phase in the normal existence of capitalism as a global system. What has taken place, far from being some new departure, is rather a return, a turning back to trends that marked the "high" globalisation of the 19th century, a resumption of the drive that had temporarily slowed down during the intervening period of "low" globalisation. Thus, the talk about "globalisation" as "a new era" or "an epochal shift" represents more of an ideological-political phenomenon than a serious analysis of a new situation. What is important, therefore, is not to indulge in such talk but to notice the specificities of the current phase of globalisation, each of which can be seen to be directly relevant to what is happening in Indian politics today. All that is needed, as I said earlier, is a little reason and the ability to interconnect.

Underlying Specificities

In the sphere of economy proper, the most important specificity to be noticed about the current phase of globalisation is its radical departure from the way capitalism existed during the previous period of post-war boom, the "golden age" of capitalism. The capitalism of this period was marked by Keynesian strategies of moderate macro-economic regulations and the accompanying limits on capital's unending thirst for more profits, collectively known as the "welfare state", which, incidentally, saved capitalism from its own self-destructive tendencies, for example, in the Great Depression, and also helped it acquire a much-needed "human face" as a counter to the internal and external threat of socialism. The onset of a structural crisis of capitalism that gives every sign of being irreversible, has changed all that.

The 1970s saw the world economy going into a downturn that has worsened through every recession since. The gap between business cycles is getting smaller. Barely does recovery begin before growth falters. "Globalisation", with its neo-liberalism, is essentially a response to this structural crisis of capitalism and signifies a return, as it were, from an atypical to typical capitalism, from the aberration that was the post-war "golden age" with its welfare state to a period of normal, "free-market" capitalism. For capital to remain "competitive" in the global market, Keynesian State interventions in the economy have to go. Nor can capitalism now afford to wear a "human face"; with the threat of socialism having receded, perhaps, it also does not need to wear it any more. The exceptional circumstances that made it possible for the working classes in the West, especially Western Europe, to fight and curb the exploitative logic of capitalism have passed into history. That these working classes are today fighting to defend their hard won gains should not obscure the fact that even in the advanced capitalist West it is no longer capitalism with a human face but back to the laws of the jungle of a normal capitalism. The State must revert to its traditional way of serving capitalism, that is, it must now act as the main agent of globalisation. And this is indeed how the State is now acting.

"Globalisation" abroad has its own specificity in the new phase. If at home "globalisation" is capitalism all over again, albeit now showing itself in its nakedness, abroad it is imperialism all over again, albeit in a new shape or form. The logic of capitalism now becomes more or less universal, and imperialism achieves its ends not so much by the old forms of military expansion but primarily by unleashing and manipulating the exploitative and destructive impulses of the capitalist market. This however is not to deny the continuing importance of wars or the use of military means for imperialist purposes. We have the most obvious contemporary example of America's use of its military power to grab control of the oil resources of the Middle East and Central Asia and to establish pax-Americana in the world, that is, keep the world "free" as a freely exploitable area in which giant American corporations can do business on their own terms.

Beyond these two specific features, globalisation in its current phase has an aspect to it which needs to be specifically noted. Post-Soviet collapse, capitalism's impulse to globalise or universalise has so realised itself that capitalism is today a truly global or universal system, such as it has never been before. This has meant universalisation of its polarisations between rich and poor, exploiters and exploited. Its success, so to speak, has carried its failures with it, which however is nothing new or surprising. This is how it has always been with capitalism—exceptional productivity and most inequitable distribution, production of wealth and poverty at the two poles of society. More significant, however, is the fact of universalisation, and therefore sharpening of its contradictions and self-destructive tendencies, including the inherent tendency to overproduce, to regular crises of overproduction. Historically, capitalism could and was indeed able to resolve or "displace" these contradictions and escape the consequences of its self-destructive tendencies primarily by deeper penetration within and expansion abroad. To the extent it has become universal; the old escape routes are now that much less available. As Ellen Meiksins Wood has written:

> Now, capitalism has no more escape routes, no more safety valves or corrective mechanisms outside its own internal logic. Even when it's not at war, even when it's not involved in the old forms of inter-imperialist rivalry, it's subject to the constant tensions and contradictions of capitalist competition. Now, having more or less reached its geographic limits and ended the spatial expansion that supported its earlier successes, it can only feed on itself; and the more successful it is on its own terms—in other words, the more it maximises profit and so-called growth—the more it devours its own human and natural substance.

The ultimate success of capitalism, its universal ascendancy, has also brought it to the brink of its worst failure. This condition is an important component of the structural crisis—a "depressed continuum", Meszaros has called it—that today grips global capitalism. That some countries are doing well even in the midst of this crisis, or have cyclical upswings, is something that has happened throughout the history of capitalism and does not negate the reality of this crisis, the intractable problems that capitalism as a global system is now faced with.

Of course, capitalism today is not as Marx saw and studied it in the 19th century. It has undergone changes, important changes, since then, and it is necessary to recognise them for understanding, and struggling against, contemporary capitalism. But as Raymond Williams once warned, in taking note of what has changed in capitalism, we must not make the mistake of underestimating everything that has not changed. And this "everything", above all, includes the structural logic of capitalism, the law-like tendencies of its capital-accumulative process which, as Marx explicated, have meant uneven and unequal development within and across countries. The universalisation of capital does not mean the universalisation of capitalist prosperity, success, industrialisation or development, as promised by the globalisers. On the contrary, it can only mean the universalisation of capitalist polarisation, for such is the structural logic of capitalist development. And this is precisely what has been happening. Capitalism's tendency to generate wealth for the relatively few and poverty for the many is as much in evidence today in both the "developed" north and the "developing" south as it was in the 19th century England of "dark satanic mills" that Marx and Engels so perceptively analysed. Now, as then, the poor grow poorer as the rich grow richer. Polarisation abroad has meant the marginalisation and increasing impoverishment of whole regions outside the advanced capitalist countries. The class polarisations of capitalism are as much evident in the North-South divide as in the growing impoverishment of so-called "underclasses" within advanced capitalist countries.

We may here specifically notice a key feature of contemporary globalisation that it retains from its earlier phases: its driving forces are centred in the imperial States and the dominant classes within these States who own or control and run the multinational corporations and banks, duly backed by the international financial institutions. Thus we have, as in the past, "globalising" nations and classes and the "globalised", a hierarchical system of power, exchange, and benefits: there are wealthy creditors and bankrupt debtors, super-rich speculators, and impoverished peasants, and unemployed workers, imperial States that direct international financial institutions and subordinate States that submit to their dictates, and so on. There has been much "globaloney" over "interdependence of nations" and its "globally shared benefits". Surely "imperialism" is a more useful concept to comprehend this aspect of the reality of our globalised world.

Skewed distribution of benefits is however only one issue. "Globalisation" is really the globalisation of capitalism's basic dynamics, including the contradictions inherent in its relentless drive to maximise profit and accumulate. As a consequence, we not only have a ravaging of humanity, mass unemployment, and underemployment and active impoverishment of large populations at the centre and in the periphery of global capitalism and a destruction of natural environment all over the globe but also a global economy characterised by over accumulation, enormous excess capacity and crisis of profitability, an ever-growing structure of debt, speculative volatility, and financial turmoil and, typically, by recurring economic crises and prolonged downturns like the current one. By virtue of its inherent contradictions, though globally dominant, capitalism yet remains fraught with instabilities, beset as it is by economic breakdowns even in its most dynamic centres of investment and trade and by a succession of national and regional crises—in Mexico, East and South-East Asia, Russia, Brazil, Argentina, etc.—produced by the globalist restructuring of recent decades.

US Domination

"Globalisation is only another word for US domination," Henry Kissinger arrogantly claimed. Equally bluntly, Fredric Jameson writes: "... when we talk about the spreading power and influence of globalisation, aren't we really referring to the spreading economic and military might of the US? And in speaking of the weakening of the nation-state, are we not actually describing the subordination of the other nation-states to American power, either through consent and collaboration, or by the use of brute force and economic threat?" He adds: "Looming behind the anxieties expressed here is a new version of what used to be called imperialism, which we can now trace through a whole dynasty of forms. An earlier version was that of the pre-First World War colonialist order, practised by a number of European countries, the US and Japan; this was replaced after the Second World War and the subsequent wave of decolonisation by a Cold War form, less obvious but no less insidious in its use of economic pressure and blackmail ("advisers"; covert putsches such as those in Guatemala and Iran), now led predominantly by the US but still involving a few Western European powers. Now perhaps we have a third stage, in which the United States pursues what Samuel Huntington has defined as a three-pronged strategy: nuclear weapons for the US alone; human rights and American-style electoral democracy; and (less obviously) limits to immigration and the free flow of labour. One might add a fourth crucial policy here: the propagation of the free market across the globe". Jameson sees "the US (and such utterly subordinated satellites as the UK)" as playing "the role of the world's policemen" and enforcing "their rule through selected interventions (mostly bombings, from a great height) in various alleged danger zones".

In its pursuit of global domination, America has, more explicitly than ever before, emerged and self-identified itself as the country with the power and the responsibility to police the world in defence of capitalism. A leading diplomatic historian, Gerald Haines (also a senior historian of the CIA) observed that after the Second World War, the United States "assumed, out of self-interest, responsibility for the welfare of the world capitalist system". President Clinton and his Secretary of State Madeleine Albright saw the US as the world's only indispensable nation, and Anthony Lake, Clinton's National Security Advisor, in line with former National Security Advisor Brezhenski's public defence of the "necessity" of American leadership in the world, even announced a so-called "Clinton Doctrine": "Throughout the Cold War, we contained a global threat to market democracies", now we can "consolidate the victory of democracy and open markets". The formula however is redundant since "open markets" adequately captures what is really meant by "democracy".

More recently (1999), in his much noticed "Manifesto for the Fast World" in the *New York Times Magazine,* the well-known columnist Thomas Friedman has argued that since the United States is the country that benefits most from globalisation, it is also the one that has to take the main responsibility for sustaining it. "Sustaining globalisation is our overarching national interest ... Globalisation-is-US". This, he clarifies, is different from "old-fashioned imperialism, when one country physically occupies another." Now, it's a matter of maintaining "an abstract globalisation system." And this "requires a stable geopolitical power structure, which simply cannot be maintained without the active involvement of the United States." Bush Junior has since, in his own way, made abundantly clear what this means.

US domination today has an interesting ideological dimension in that America has sought a "noble" or "saintly" guise for its policies abroad. It pursues them in the name of "human rights" and "democracy" which only reveals how cynical or hypocritical the sole superpower's global politics can be. Take the UN Declaration of Human Rights. Half of it concerns social and economic rights. The West largely rejects them, the US totally. They limit themselves primarily to what they call civil and political rights. This apart, if the record of the UN on human rights is painfully bad, it is understandably so because it has been, and still is, dominated by the United States, a country with innumerable violations of human rights all over the world, from the Philippines at the turn of the last century to installing Marcos there after the war; from the invasion of Guatemala, the Dominican Republic and Grenada to the Vietnam war; from installing Suharto in Indonesia (more than one million murdered in the course of Suharto's US-backed counter-revolution) to imposing and sustaining dictatorial regimes in Latin America (including that of Pinochet in Chile), in Africa, in the Middle East, and in Greece. Adding to this testimony is the death of one million children in Iraq as a result of sanctions imposed by the United States and rubber stamped by the UN, with the total subservience of its allies. Following this, the US again attacked Iraq in a blatant violation of international law. America's interpretation of human rights, replacing the common interests of humanity with the particular interests and arbitrary actions of the United States, violates any meaningful conception of human rights. Even otherwise America's extremely selective concern with human rights in pursuit of its interests abroad has been justifiably regarded as a new form of imperialism, "Human Rights Imperialism".

It is no different with America's concern for democracy. The essential criterion once again is what best serves American interests. American policy makers have had no hesitation in lining up on their side some of the most corrupt dictatorial regimes, often hailing them as members of their "free world". These have included the apartheid regime of South Africa, Syngman Rhee and the military rulers of South Korea, Ferdinand Marcos of the Philippines, Lon Nol and other dictators of South Vietnam, Ayub Khan and Yahya Khan of Pakistan, the Shah of Iran, the Duvaliers of Haiti, Pinochet of Chile, Suharto of Indonesia, and any number of other tyrants or authoritarian rulers in Africa, Central and South America and the Middle East, including, once upon a time, Saddam Hussein in Iraq. It is to them that American aid and armaments have overwhelmingly gone. "He may be a son of a bitch, but he is *our* son-of-a-bitch". This has been Washington's refreshingly honest view of the Somozas, Batistas, and Duvaliers of the world. Obviously, the absence of democracy is all right so long as a country is supportive of the United States. "Democracy", like "human rights", is only an ideological cover for the pursuit of America's more mundane material, that is, imperialist interests abroad.

Ideological deception has its uses, no doubt, but there is nothing like the exercise of naked military power to secure and sustain particular imperialist interests and overall global hegemony. With the collapse of the Soviet Union, the United States has acquired a global dominance as the one remaining military super power, indeed the dominant imperialist power in the world. Contrary to the notion that globalisation and the establishment of the world market have made military power redundant, the US maintains, by a very wide margin, the world's largest military. Empires throughout human history have relied on foreign military bases to enforce their rule and protect their interests, and in this respect Pax Americana is no different from Pax Romana or Pax Britannica. The United States has military bases in sixty-nine countries, with this number on the increase with the wars against Afghanistan and Iraq. The United States totally dominates NATO—recently redefined as a self-legitimating aggressive force—as well as the Far Eastern military alliances, especially the "US-Japan Security Treaty". Despite the publicly proclaimed end of the Cold War, the US military budget remains very large, accounting for fully a third of world spending on arms. For the US ruling class, in view of what it sees as its responsibilities in the global capitalist order—which one scholar has summarised as: "to keep the system functioning; to control the underlying populations; to safeguard the United States as the centre of the international financial system; to maintain the United States (and, specially, US capitalists/corporations) in the top perch in the imperialist pecking order; and to prevent countries from breaking away from the system of global controls"—it is not enough to have a military bigger than that of any other power; it must be bigger than that of any plausible combination of other powers, and this applies of course not only to the immediate situation but to what the situation might be five or ten years from now, when the potential challenges of today might become real. It is pushing ahead with plans for a capability to fight two major regional conflicts at the same time.

The United States has the world's largest stockpile of weapons of mass destruction, chemical, biological and nuclear, and is the only State ever to have used nuclear weapons. It is an arch votary of the unequal Nuclear Non-Proliferation Treaty and, even as it regularly arm-twists the minor nuclear nations, has refused to ratify the Comprehensive Nuclear Test Ban Treaty (CTBT). It has unilaterally withdrawn from the Anti-Ballistic Missile (ABM) Treaty and is busy developing weapons like the nuclear bunker-busting bombs. According to a classified Pentagon report, the Bush administration has directed the military to prepare contingency plans to use nuclear weapons against countries it sees as America's immediate or potential enemies, and to build new smaller nuclear weapons for use in certain battlefield situations. Despite objections from its European allies that it is unnecessary and will most likely trigger a new arms race, despite the opposition of Russia and China, despite a protest by as many as 50 Nobel Laureates headed by Hans A. Bethe, one of the architects of the atom bomb, who have called it "wasteful" and "dangerous", the National Missile Defence System remains a priority on the agenda of the United States.

The US National Security Strategy, with its policy of military supremacy over the entire earth and the doctrine of pre-emption, is nothing less than the declaration of a new imperial order to be backed up not only by the threat but also the aggressive, pre-emptive employment of overwhelming power against any country not to its liking. Most recently, following upon its yesterday's "Star Wars Project" or the current "Missile Defence System"—argued for as "defensive shields", though nothing of the kind— the United States has gone in for their heavily updated, blatantly offensive successor, codenamed "Falcon" (Force Application and Launch from the Continental US)—its unmanned delivery vehicles carrying a payload of 12,000 pounds and flying at speeds of up to ten times the speed of sound will be able to strike targets 9,000 nautical miles distant in less than two hours. As John Pike, head of the Washington think tank, GlobalSecurity.Org has commented: "It is about blowing people up on the other side of the planet even if no country on earth will allow us to use their territory". The purpose, obviously, is to enable the US to go it alone against whichever country they please, to subdue or destroy in their design to achieve world domination.

The global expansion of military power by the hegemonic world capitalism is an integral part of economic globalisation. (Advanced capitalist countries other than America, tied into the system, are reliant on the US as the main enforcer of the rules of the game). The American ruling class knows that economics is ultimately a matter of politics, that it is relations of power, above all military power, that command the market, that there will be no "global market" without an American military empire. "The hidden hand of the market will never work without the hidden fist—McDonald's cannot flourish without McDonnell Douglas, the designer of the F-15. And the hidden fist that keeps the world safe for Silicon Valley's technologies is called the United States Army, Air Force, Navy and Marine Corps". This is how Thomas Friedman, who incidentally was also an adviser to Madeleine Albright, has put it in an article we have earlier had occasion to take note of. Friedman goes on to quote approvingly from foreign policy historian Robert Kagan: "Good ideas and technologies need a strong power that promotes those ideas by example and protects those ideas by winning on the battlefield. If a lesser power were promoting our ideas and technologies, they would not have the global currency that they have".

Naturally, the hidden fist has to come out of hiding from time to time if it is going to make its point. And here the United States has a long history. From the Monroe doctrine onwards it is a history of armed interventions or wars along with coercive diplomacy, bloody coups and covert actions against other sovereign States to make the world "safe" for American business. In the half century since the Second World War alone, on one pretext or another—"containing communism", "protecting American lives", "punishing "rogue" States", "war on terrorism" or even "promoting democracy", etc.—America has thus aggressed against countries as far afield as Greece and Cuba, Chile and Vietnam, Brazil, Guatemala and the Dominican Republic, Grenada, Nicaragua, El Salvador and Panama, Angola and Mozambique, Iran, Iraq, Libya, and Afghanistan. And the list is far from complete. Here we may also notice that apart from specific economic objectives or military gains, a most significant aspect of America's use of military force since the end of the Second World War, that is, its wars from Korea to the Balkans, the Gulf and Afghanistan, has been its political objectives: the "containment" of external enemies or of internal opposition, diverting attention from tricky domestic problems or even the narrower political objectives of electoral advantage through displays of "toughness" or tough "nationalism".

America's militarism does not generally have territorial ambitions. It does not seek direct physical control or hegemony over specific colonies. It comprises, typically, of massive displays of force to assert the dominance of global capital so that this capital, particularly the American segment of it, can freely navigate the global economy without hindrance. If at times it has the appearance of a naked display of imperial power for its own sake, without any specific or immediate objectives—and an outright military victory is neither an issue nor even a possible outcome—it is just to show who is boss, that is, to make a general point about US domination of the world, and its hegemony over the global economy. As one commentator has it, "such display of imperial power only shows that US imperial hegemony can't now rely, if it ever could, on economic superiority alone, and that it depends on periodic display of sheer force. It hardly matters where or for what ostensible purpose, though it helps if the target is non-European or non-white".

Cultural Imperialism

Beyond these economic, political, and military aspects, a specific feature of the current situation is the ideological and cultural sweep of capitalist ideas and values. Capitalism's technological ingenuity has made it possible for its principles to find their way into social, institutional, and cultural spaces that even a few decades ago were beyond their reach. Commodity relations and moralities of the market are penetrating into every aspect of our lives, producing profit, of course, but also ravaging morals and culture everywhere. A process of culture penetration is on—including what is described as "McDonaldisation", the "American way of life", "homogenisation or leveling down of cultures", or simply as "consumerist culture"—whereby the bourgeoisie today "makes the world in its own image" with an impunity almost unparalleled since Marx wrote these words 150 odd years ago.

This culture penetration is not just an extension but an integral part of globalisation as imperialist domination. Imperialism has never been merely an economic-military system of control and exploitation. Cultural domination, an effort to penetrate and dominate the cultural life of the popular classes in order to reorder the values, behaviour, institutions, and identity of the oppressed peoples in conformity with the interests of the imperial classes, was always an integral part of it. So it is now with globalisation as a new, latest form of imperialism. Besides, there are now direct material benefits to be had, as never before. Recognising American economic and cultural domination in the ongoing globalisation, James Petras has written:

> US cultural imperialism has two goals—one economic and the other political—to capture markets for its cultural commodities and to establish hegemony by shaping popular consciousness. The export of entertainment commodities is one of the most important sources of capital accumulation and global profits displacing manufacturing exports. In the political sphere, cultural imperialism plays a major role in dissociating people from their cultural roots and traditions of solidarity, replacing them with media created "needs", which change with every publicity campaign. The political effect is to alienate people from traditional class and community bonds, atomising and separating individuals from each other.

It may be mentioned that religious fundamentalism (especially the Islamic), so rampant today, is significant, partly at least, for its opposition to "consumerism of the West" or "the American way of life"—the imperialist cultural domination it is resourceless to understand or overcome. But it has acquired this significance primarily because the traditional left alternatives, in particular the great revolutionary traditions of Marxism and Communism seem to have become, for the time being at least, unavailable.

To be particularly noticed is the ideological domination or hegemony that capitalism has come to acquire in the current phase of capitalist globalisation. With capitalism becoming all but universal, it has also become ideologically hegemonic as never before. It is so powerful and pervasive today as to have become invisible, and is all the more powerful for being invisible. You no longer mention or recognise it or even refer to it by its proper name. It is "globalisation", "liberalisation", "structural adjustment", "economic reform", "new economic policy" (and with the new votaries from the left in India joining in) "industrialisation", "development and progress", even "civilisation"—anything but capitalism.

A consensus on behalf of capitalism has emerged that makes it virtually immune against criticism or any discussion of alternatives (which, incidentally also makes nonsense of the much-vaunted pluralism of bourgeois democracy, gaining for it a spurious credibility only by a bizarre blowing up of minor differences among competitors in the politics of "actually existing capitalism"). Given the collapsed Soviet regime's spurious identification with socialism, bourgeois ideologues have gone to town proclaiming the inevitability and virtues of capitalism. It is not only that the world is noisy with the refrain that "there is no alternative", that the "economic reforms" are "irreversible" and that the world must adjust to the so-called rationality and efficiency requirements of "the economy"—today, every human practice, every social relationship, virtually everything under the sun, including the natural environment, is subject to the requirements of profit-maximisation. As Michael Lowy has noted:

> Indeed, never till the end of the 20th century has capital succeeded in exerting such a complete, absolute, undivided, universal, and unlimited sway over the whole world. Never in the past has it had its current ability to impose its rules, its policies, its dogmas, and its interests upon all the nations of the globe. Never have international finance capital and multinational corporations been so out of control by states and peoples. Never before now has there existed such a dense network of international institutions—International Monetary Fund, World Bank, World Trade Organisation—devoted to controlling, governing, and administering human life according to the strict rules of the capitalist free market and unrestricted pursuit of capitalist profitability. Finally, never in any preceding epoch have all spheres of human life—social relationships, culture, art, politics, sexuality, health, education, sports, recreation—been so completely dominated by capital, so deeply submerged in "the icy water of egotistical calculation."

Underpinning this ideological domination are new information and communication technologies which have added immensely to the power of those in command of the mass media, advertisements and entertainment to control popular consciousness, to turn whole people, like individuals glued to their TV sets, into what the German poet Hans Magnus Enzensberger has called "secondary illiterates", those who need neither memory nor any thinking or learning to sustain themselves. These are of little worth to them, the passive subjects in a world where the reigning ideology is consumerism with its exclusive concern for "instant gratification" and "contentment". A market-driven "mass culture" has come up which, on the one hand, aims at developing consumer instincts in the people to the utmost and thereby expanding markets for the greater glory of capitalist profit-making. On the other hand, we see an ideological brainwashing of the people, diverting them from any advanced social ideals and implanting in their minds bland, illusory and often downright false and reactionary views of social and political realities.

A "true idiot culture", Carl Bernstein has called it, where for the "first time in history the weird and the stupid and the vulgar are becoming our cultural norm, even our cultural ideal". Even as a "stupid and vulgar" culture is mass purveyed via television screens, tabloid newspapers, glossy magazines, and similar other means, the tendency is to pitch all messages to the lowest level of mental capacity. Knowledge is reduced to slick, pre-digested, easy to understand capsules, inducing people to want simple answers to difficult problems. People's consciousness is transferred on to philistine, narrow-minded lines and interest in truths that demands hard, complex, and subtle exercise of mind simply recedes into the background. The overall consequence is a dilution and dispersal of people's questioning spirit, their angry or combustible sentiments, an emasculation of their critical consciousness. There is general enervation of civil society, its members rendered incapable of "answering back" as C. Wright Mills once phrased it. According to Jean Baudrillard, the very possibilities of critical examination and reflection are destroyed. In other words, the inundations of consumerism and "mass culture" leave the alienated individuals of contemporary late-capitalist society eminently vulnerable to capitalism's hegemonic control. Though oppressed and exploited, they are now more open to the "colonisation of the mind", that is, the victims' internalisation of the cliche "there is no alternative", their willing suspension of ideals and acceptance of a sub-autonomous existence in the interest of maintaining a secondary or even a tertiary position in the obtaining "reality"—be it the capitalist society or for that matter the global capitalist system. For that is also what the "Third World mentality" is all about.

Indian Scenario

To understand "Indian politics in the age of globalisation", the hard and fateful choices it confronts our people with, it helps to know how we have arrived where we are, with our rulers going in for globalisation as their strategic option. It is not much remembered these days that we were very much a globalised country not so long ago. Before 1947, we were part of a global system, well-integrated into the world market economy. We were globalised, but we did not like it. Our globalisation then also had a name—imperialism—and we struggled against it because it meant—by virtue of its structural logic—accumulation of wealth in England and poverty in India. Like other Third World countries, we wanted to get out of this globalisation. This was a necessary, though not sufficient condition to be able to build a better life for our people. Herein lay the essential meaning of our struggle for freedom. It is significant of our present-day rulers, including those claiming to be successors of Gandhi and Nehru, that they have long forgotten what this struggle was about and would like us all to do the same. But our people need to remember.

The post-Independence (Nehruvian) national project was rooted in an awareness of the exploitative logic of the global capitalist market, of centuries of experience of imperialism that provides little evidence of the beneficial effect of foreign investment in countries of the Third World so far as the common people are concerned. It was, moreover, in its own way, influenced by the interim successes of the Soviet Union. Consequently, it opted for the strategic goal of a State-led self-reliant development, promising economic growth with "equity and distributive justice" to the people. That it did not work out the way it was intended; that there was a significant degree of economic growth but not much equity or distributive justice for the people; that the project ended up building an India-specific government-supported capitalism; that the rhetoric of "a socialistic pattern of society" only deceived the people, legitimising the statist-capitalism that was coming up, and creating confusion as regards "socialism" that persists to this day; that the failure of this capitalism to deliver was, and continues to be, misinterpreted as the failure of socialism in India—all this, its why and how, is not my concern at the moment. The point to be noted is that passing through a series of economic and political crises, the national project, such as it was, finally and definitively collapsed in 1991, foregrounding, once again—now in the context of the changed balances of forces in the world following the collapse of the Soviet Union—the question of strategic options for India's future economic and social development.

Apropos the collapse of the Nehruvian national project, I would like to reproduce here a passage from what I wrote in 1997 on the occasion of the 50th anniversary of India's Independence:

> The evidence of this collapse is there in the disintegration of values and degradation of life all around us, in the continuing poverty of our people and growing consumerism of the elites and a society at once cynical and fearful about the future. It is there in official statistics and pages of the private media ... [It is in evidence in the] so-called "national mainstream" which, bearing the impress of India's corrupt and corrupting, somewhat lumpen capitalist development, is an increasingly dirty affair—corrupt, communal, and criminalised, a repressively homogenising mainstream. The evidence is there in the visionless and so obviously laboured efforts of the powers that be to flog a tired and flabby patriotism into some semblance of life in this fiftieth year of India's independence, including Colgate-sponsored selling of *Vande Matarams* on the television by hordes of India's VIPs and VVIPs. And this evidence is pathetically present in the impotence (or is it hypocrisy?) of the supposedly "stirring" calls being made on the occasion—in Parliament for a "second freedom struggle" and by the Prime Minister to "begin the struggle for economic freedom"! One wonders what these past fifty years have been about. A Finance Minister took India back into globalisation, asking us not to be afraid of the East India Company, opened up India to the multinationals, on the dishonest plea that "the nation has been living beyond its means"—"nation" indeed, when a good majority of our people have simply no means to live and most others none to indulge any "living beyond"! His successor, more honest and ideologically committed, has been publicly pleading with the former globalisers in London to come back to India for another equally long stay (and then gone to town with this pleading in Washington and elsewhere): "You came to India and stayed for 200 years. Now come prepared to invest and stay for another 200 years, and there will be huge rewards". The post-colonial national project is indeed over and done with.

The post-Independence national project having collapsed, 1991 onwards, India's ruling classes, through their different political formations, notably, the Congress and the BJP, have gone in for "globalisation" as their new strategic option—a shift from the State-supported capitalism to a privatised "free market" capitalism and from self-reliance in economic development to reliance on Foreign Direct

Investment and the multinationals, a shift euphemistically described as "economic reforms" which has little to offer to the common Indian people. The much-touted "growth rates" are no indication of general well-being in a capitalist society; instead, as Amit Bhaduri has pointed out, "the unprecedented high economic growth on which privileged India prides itself is a measure of the high speed at which the India of privilege is distancing itself from the India of crushing poverty. ... the higher the rate of economic growth along this pattern becomes, the greater would be underdevelopment of India". The so-called "trickle down", if and when it occurs, is no better than feeding horses with oats so that something passes down to the road for the sparrows, as Galbraith once described it. Over the past decade-and-a-half or so, whatever be the benefits "economic reforms" has brought to a small section at the top, it has further polarised our society, played havoc with the lives of our common people and pushed them still further into a peripheralised existence within the global capitalist system.

This is nothing surprising. "Economic reforms" is only a euphemism for capitalist development whose structural logic a former the President of Brazil once reported to the masters in Washington as: "The economy is doing fine, the people are not". Chary of using the dread word "capitalism", even the advocates of globalisation, Joseph Stiglitz, Amartya Sen, and others, regularly admit and lament that "the fruits of globalisation" are not reaching the people, while Klaus Schwab (of the World Economic Forum) writes: "We are living in an increasingly schizophrenic world, where economies are booming and global signs are promising, but underneath are economic, political and social risks, as well as imbalances and inconsistencies."

A market-governed economic growth simply cannot deliver "inclusive growth", to use another of the proliferating buzzwords of our time. Instead, it is by its very nature exclusionary, and the logic of the market, with its inevitable winners and losers, only makes for "the secession of the successful", as the economist Robert Reich once phrased it. One look at the economic policies or concerns, their lifestyles and values will reveal how far "the successful" of India's marketplace have already "seceded" from the vast majority of their supposedly "unsuccessful" fellow countrymen.

Apropos India's State-supported capitalist development during the Nehru era and later, I had written:

> To borrow from Tom Paine's metaphoric rejoinder to Burke's attack on the French Revolution, admiration for the 'plumage' of India's 'national development' should not prevent us from seeing its failure in 'the dying bird'. The world indeed looks very different from below, when the poor and oppressed of 'our nation' look at it.

This is even more true of the market-led capitalist development during the current era of neo-liberal "economic reforms".

Before proceeding with my argument about what I have elsewhere described as "contemporary India's most important *unraised* political question", the question of a people's strategic option, an alternative path of development distinct from and in opposition to that of India's ruling classes, I would like to touch upon a few aspects or implications of the current shift to globalisation or "economic reforms" which are immediately relevant to several important issues of present-day Indian politics.

To begin with, it is to be noted that State intervention in the economy was deemed necessary by the then economically and legitimacy-wise politically weak Indian bourgeoisie itself (cf. Bombay Plan, 1944). A major beneficiary of "economic growth" during the Nehru era and afterwards, it soon developed substantial strength of its own and grew hopeful of new avenues of profit-making at home and abroad in partnership with global capitalism. The shift to globalisation, therefore, can be viewed as a natural progress for the Indian bourgeoisie, signalling a further consolidation of its position and power in the State.

Again, the shift to "market economy" is usually justified by the bourgeois ideologues as a response to the failure of State intervention in the economy, more commonly the failure of the public sector. Now, apart from the fact that the public sector—which by itself has no socialist implications—has a successful presence in many capitalist economies and was a roaring success in the erstwhile "socialist" countries, the public sector in India has not been the kind of failure bourgeois ideologues make it out to be. There are "the stunning achievements of the National Thermal Power Corporation, Bharat Heavy Electricals, Nalco, the Oil and Natural Gas Commission, the Gas Authority of India or the Indian Oil Corporation", as a knowledgeable scholar has recently pointed out. And even the failure of the public sector in India, such as it has been, is better understood as the failure of Indian democracy, whence alone correctives to its malfunctioning or failure could have come, unlike the case of the private sector where correctives come from the market, though often needing to be backed by the State. Therefore, the answer to this failure is a differently working democracy, an effective exercise of people's power in the State, and not a market-based private sector with its record of now well established failures.

It may be added that even otherwise, Indian democracy is a rather sickly affair and a major, if not the sole achievement of India's "democratic politics" is that it has managed to give politics itself a bad name: it is a dirty business best left to dirty politicians! That Indian democracy's failure to deliver has come to be raised to the status of a theory, indeed a "law" of politics ("anti-incumbency", etc.) is as good an indication of the poor state of health of India's democracy and its "democratic politics" as any other. Yet again: that the shift to globalisation was unaccompanied by any debate or discussion, serious opposition or questioning, points, among other things, to the essential class character of the politics currently dominant in the country.

Marcuse has said somewhere that the success of a system is when it makes alternatives unthinkable. This is the success that capitalism achieved, or seemed to have achieved, in the aftermath of the Soviet collapse. The reality of capitalism catching up, the euphoria over this success is long over in most places. But, while a Sainath may decry "corporate hijack" of media agendas and a Bhikhu Parekh may bemoan the country's lack of "an inspiring moral vision", capitalism's success is resonant in the "silences" of the public discourse in India and in the Indian ruling elite's commitment to "economic reform". Capitalism or "market society" is taken for granted; for them, it is the only possible mode of existence. Even as the reality of a Third-World capitalism is painfully there all around us, not only is socialism forgotten (except for occasional denigration), even a discussion of capitalism is conspicuously absent. In the consensus built around the establishment ideology, to think anti-capitalism remains decreed out of fashion.

The Congress and the BJP share in this consensus and its ideology—a class ideology, it may be noted, is seldom, if ever, all of one piece; generally it is constituted by many ideas, doctrines, systems of dogma, and philosophies which seemingly compete and even contradict each other but are socially supplementary. For the same reason, like the Congress, the BJP represents the interests of India's capitalist class and its allies. The two parties, or their leaderships, are unable to see beyond the limits postulated by the "economic reforms". The only economy they know is the "market economy". The only possible form of development for them is capitalist development. The two are not that different as their leaders think or would have us believe. The differences between the two are important only at the tactical level. Strategically the BJP is as committed to "economic reforms" as the Congress. That is why it is a mistake to see the BJP only as a communal party and that is how, while its opponents, including the Left, impotently locked themselves in a "communalism-secularism" trap, the BJP merrily went on implementing the Congress initiated "economic reforms" without much notice or objection. Radhika Desai, a Canadian scholar, has noted:

> The Indian capitalist class may be senior, practically venerable, among the bourgeoisies of the Third World, and it may have benefited from liberalising economic policies under practically every administration since the late 1970s. But the NDA governments presided over such a massive dose of the most brazen and unapologetic liberalisation as to constitute a virtual rebirth of the capitalist class, sired by the BJP. Indian capitalists' new filial loyalty cannot be underestimated. The NDA oversaw a vast and ungrudging expansion of practically every sector of the urban industrial economy: finance and financial markets, the media, housing and construction, consumer durables and non-durables of every kind. Privatisation was accelerated, giving a great fillip to the stock markets; the foreign exchange regime was further liberalised; FDI and portfolio investments, including by foreign institutional investors, FIIs, flowed in. Consumer credit to finance lifestyles of international standards (indeed, better, thanks to the cheapness

> of domestic labour) for a small but very visible stratum of those in business and professions was expanded and liberalised, as was the import regime. The tax burden on the rich was reduced; innumerable small quotas, and restrictions on economic activity were lifted; the IT sector boomed, employing thousands of young professionals and arousing unprecedented hopes of upward mobility among thousands of others; and, not least, the objective of closer ties between India and its wealthy 'diaspora' in the metropoles was pursued by taking the first steps towards granting dual citizenship. All talk of the poor and of larger social goals was dismissed routinely as the leftover cant of yesterday's 'licence-permit raj'. It was truly a dream government for the possessing classes.

Needless to say, the effect of these measures on the whole economy was less than spectacular and, on the poor majority, positively disastrous. More than ever, the NDA governments created two nations in India, already home to some of the starkest divides between poverty and wealth. Every criticism from the Left had its counterpart in appreciation on the part of the rich, and there is no doubt about a feel-good factor among the propertied elite and foreign interests in India: in fact, an overwhelming pro-BJP sentiment.

This, of course, cost the BJP the 2004 Lok Sabha election. But it was no "rout" as the opponents' wishful thinking tended to view it (the BJP's tally was 136 seats to 145 to the Congress). The corporate world, happy over the BJP's performance in power, are desperately hopeful about its future as a "modern" political party, alternating with the Congress in the much longed-for two-party system in India's parliamentary democracy. The corporates can well do with its *Hindutva* and the accompanying obscurantism. Capitalism needs science and technology, but, as we know from history, capitalist classes have always needed religion and obscurantism too. The BJP's aggressive nationalist posture could well be an advantage in the harsh competitive world of global economy and politics.

It is not surprising that its pursuit of the new strategic option, the so-called "economic reform" had the consequence of the Congress losing its credibility with the people, and its power to the BJP-led NDA. The NDA government in turn pursued the same "economic reform" agenda, necessarily producing, in the words of Radhika Desai, "a feel good factor among the propertied elite and foreign interests in India" and creating "more than ever ... two nations in India, already home of some of the starkest divides between poverty and wealth". It was "India shining", but only for a few at the top, with the many below experiencing its structurally *other* reality. Again, it was not surprising that the BJP lost the 2004 Lok Sabha election and its power at Delhi.

Back in power on the *aam aadmi* plank, compulsions of electoral politics forcing it to take note of the victim of "economic reform"—the so-called *aam aadmi* ("the common man"), the Congress now again speaks the Nehruvian language of economic growth with equity and social justice, etc.—a Manmohan-Sonia farce, as it were, to Nehru's tragedy, to paraphrase Marx's famous observation on the caricatured re-appearance of historical phenomena.

This is how it goes in the opening paragraph of Marx's *The Eighteenth Brumair of Louis Bonaparte*: "Hegel remarks somewhere that all facts and personages of great importance in world history occur, as it were, twice". He forgot to add: the first time as tragedy, the second time as farce.

The Congress now seeks "economic reforms with a human face", but symbolic gestures apart (forced on it by the supporting Left), "economic reform", because of its structural logic, simply cannot deliver. This puts it at odds with democracy in India. In other words, while some muddling along for sometime is always possible, the structural nature of things being what it is, "economic reform" and democracy simply don't go together. I do not have to spell out the negative implications.

It will not be out of place to mention here that the current long-term crisis of global capitalism has compelled it to shed its "human face" even in the advanced capitalist West—dismantling, or struggle over dismantling the welfare State has been a distinct feature of economy and politics in the advanced capitalist countries in recent decades. A return to normal or typical capitalism, as we have already noted, is in fact a major aspect of capital's current phase of globalisation as against the welfarist capitalism of the earlier period which was really a conjunctural aberration in capitalism's long history as an exploitative system.

If economic reform and democracy do not go together, neither does economic reform and another of our cherished values—secularism, which is integral to India's survival as a democratic polity. In its failure to deliver, economic reform regularly generates a basis for anti-secular developments. The shift to the market economy has been accompanied or followed by the rise to prominence of the utterly reactionary, semi-fascist *Hindutva* ideology and politics. Here it needs to be understood that *"Hindutva"* has come up because our society today provides a continuing social-material basis for the production and reproduction, the rise, sustenance and spread of such ideas or ideologies. One does not have to be a Marxist to understand or recognise this. A long time ago, suggesting that ideas do not rise and prosper through some inherent power of their own, Herbert Spencer had said: "Ideas wholly foreign to the social state cannot be evolved, and if introduced from without, cannot get accepted, or if accepted die out." It is the economic, political, and moral wreckage left behind by the failure of the Nehruvian project which has provided the "social state", that is, the necessary social-material basis for the rise and growing acceptance of "*Hindutva*" as religious fundamentalism and a fascistic political ideology.

"Globalisation" or so-called "economic reform", in its economic, political and moral-cultural consequences, is daily piling up more such wreckage, creating more social-material basis for all sorts of fundamentalisms, regressive ideologies and disintegrative politics. That is how the decade of the most vigorous debate over the issue of communalism and equally vigorous advocacy of secularism, the 1990s, was also the decade of the most heinous anti-secular developments and the BJP's rise to power at Delhi. One may well hazard the view that with the globalisation that is on, communalism and its consequences may well be a specific feature of the barbaric situation in India as part of the universal barbarism that capitalism now threatens the world with. That is, if the people do not effectively intervene, and do so in time, with ideology and politics, with a strategic alternative of their own.

Socialistic Development

The ruling classes of India have through their different political formations, decided to "secede" from the people and opted for "globalisation" as their strategic option for the future. The Indian people yet again face the question, whose full implications were somewhat obscured in 1947 due largely to the interim successes of the Soviet Union: what do they do in the current situation of global domination of capitalism? The historical experience in India and elsewhere in the Third World makes it abundantly clear that development which can meet the needs of our people is impossible within the framework of capitalism, national or globalised. Socialism has to be the strategic goal, whatever may be the long or short transitional route to it. As mentioned earlier, it is socialism not as they built it in the erstwhile Soviet Union, rather it is socialism as visualised by its classical tradition: a humane, democratically functioning society providing a superior and advanced form of freedom and self-determination to the people. Historical experience indeed allows no other choice.

This, however, is not posit socialism as achievable today or tomorrow, or even the day after, but to posit it as people's alternative strategic goal, as the principle governing people's politics which links together their immediate, ongoing and emerging struggles in an ultimate project of revolutionary transformation of society, as the goal of a long transitional process whose specifics and speed will depend on the objective material conditions and the nature and balance of class forces involved at each stage of the struggle for the socialist goal. Immediately it means saying "no" to globalisation, a "delinking" from the global capitalist market and opting for a pro-people socialism-oriented autonomous development.

To say "no" to globalisation is not to argue for any kind of "autarky" in economic development. Essentially, it is a question of control over what a country produces and what it buys and sells abroad, the terms on which it does business with foreigners and engages in international exchange. More precisely, saying "no" to globalisation is to pose the issue of development being governed by external imperatives, those issuing from the requirements of the world capitalist market (export-led growth, etc.) and the associated consumerism of the rich, or primarily by internal imperatives, those flowing from an assessment of own resources and the needs of the people. Of course any attempt at saying "no" to globalisation or "delinking" is likely to exact a heavy price in many ways, including an unavoidable trade-off between the requirements of productivity and those of minimising the polarising impact of global capitalism's enormous economic power. But once "productivism" is abandoned and human welfare has the priority, this need not be a deterrent to adopting the strategy that "delinking" involves. Such a strategy, it may be added, is born of historical experience, which shows that the more an economy is part of the international network of capitalist trade and finance, the more it becomes dependent on it, the more its domestic economy must adapt to the world price system, the requirement of international finance (including the discipline imposed by the International Monetary Fund), and the capitalist business cycle, with the result that the constraints of the world market become a dominant influence, and the country so involved increasingly loses control over its own destiny.

The strategy I speak of postulates an effective exercise of people's power in the State, with the State, truly committed to people's welfare, undertaking at the very outset a comprehensive programme of eradication of mass poverty, universal primary education, health care, housing, and provision of basic necessities for all. Initiating steps towards redistribution of incomes and development of backward areas will be a priority for the State's active intervention in the economy. Even as it covers such areas as foreign relations, production and social distribution, research and training, and the like, the State will need to secure an effective transitional combination of planning and market forces without letting the market or its values take over.

The agrarian revolution benefiting the rural proletariat and small farmers, thereby improving the productive capacity in the rural areas, and laying the basis of cooperative effort and voluntary collectivisation of agriculture should be high on its agenda of economic reconstruction, as should be the transformation of the informal sector into a popularly managed transitional economy. A building up or restructuring of industry is obviously necessary. But it can neither be one based on "international competitiveness" (that is promoting exports through low costs of local labour) nor on "import substitution" (promoting production for the consumption of the privileged local classes). Not that all effort in these directions is ruled out; some of it may even be necessary. Only priorities, for years to come, need to lie elsewhere.

The important thing is to develop and organise productive forces in a manner that helps the rural sector leap forward, carries industrialisation to the countryside and in general ensures a pattern of growth which, refusing the wasteful production to satisfy elite consumerism, immediately benefits the popular masses, satisfying their basic needs— needs created and satisfiable by the redistribution of income. It should be obvious that the overall development of our Third World country today cannot support the First World consumption levels of our elites. What is needed is a diversification and development of internal markets for domestic goods and services governed by the overall principle that private needs and wants should be satisfied (and this goes for their increasing satisfaction) only at a level at which they can be satisfied for all. Beyond this all increases in the production of consumer goods should be for collective consumption.

Such a socialism oriented pro-people endogenous development process will draw on its own strengths and domestic resources and capacities, including those of the hardworking poor who yet remain the most creative and productive force in society. It will give the common people—an overwhelming mass of workers and peasants, a positive stake in the economy. It will mobilise them for building a better society as well as for the inevitable struggle against global imperialism and its local allies or partners; an awakened and aroused people are indeed the best defence even against armed aggression. Needless to add, such popular mobilisation and struggle will be all the time necessary to carry through the strategic option that socialism-oriented delinking involves.

What the above strategy in effect demands is that not economics or "the market" but politics, that is people's politics, is put in command of the economy. "Politics in command" means posing such questions as: growth? But which growth? For what purpose? For whose sake, whose benefit or profit? For what kind of society and within which environment? Are social needs the guide, or is it the market and its profit-making that is to hold sway? Is growth to be pursued to get the maximum welfare of all the people, with priority for the needs of the poorest sections and the most backward regions and for the protection of environment? Or is growth to be pursued to satisfy the market-induced, ecologically unsustainable consumerist hunger of the privileged part of the population seeking to maintain or attain the "high" living standards of the West? These are questions which are central to any search for a real alternative to capitalism.

We must ask: is our goal meeting "the needs of the economy", its "anonymous masters" as they have been called—"abstractions such as financial markets, interest rates, exchange rates, commodity prices, indexes, and statistical artefacts of all kinds"—or satisfaction of the needs of the people, allowing citizens the possibility of living as human beings? Is the starting point of our economic exercises to be calculation of deficits in order to cut them at the cost of the people or a determination of resources needed to satisfy people's needs in order to find or raise them? And our language? Do we practise the obscurantism of GDP, fiscal and revenue deficits, balance of payments, growth rates etc., or speak more humanely in terms of such things as food and clean drinking water, health care and sanitation, housing and education, etc. so that the economy becomes a transparent and accountable means of integrating these basic human needs of the people with a planned use of domestic resources, an use which also takes care of questions of equality, social justice including gender justice, employment, ecologically sustainable development, etc.?

Economic and technological backwardness is often pressed as an argument to counter the plea for such autonomous economic development. Getting access to the most modern technology is another usual argument for the need to actively participate in world trade. Here, apart from the fact that in India we are not that lacking in technology or the talent for it, two brief observations are in order. In the first place it is useful to recognise that if, despite economic backwardness, the priority is given to the needs of the poorest and most deprived sections of the people, there is much that can be done at the outset even in absence of growth of productive forces. The redistribution of wealth and the use of idle or under utilised human and material resources, their more productive deployment, can bring quick improvement in health, education, and general living conditions of large masses of people. Early years of post-revolutionary societies in the Soviet Union and elsewhere provide ample evidence of this achievement which could be the basis for further development along socialist lines.

In the second place, we need to overcome the fetishism of science and technology, which, as, for example, with Nehru's "temples of modern India", attributes to them properties or power they do not possess, and at times even expects them to do the job of a social revolution which they simply cannot. As with economic development so with technology, we need to ask the basic question: "technology for what purpose?" Once we realign our thinking along these lines, the argument for getting access to the most modern Western technology via globalisation—even if that was certain, which it most certainly is not—loses much of its force. If the purpose is to satisfy the consumerist hunger of the privileged part of the population and therefore supply it with the most modern gadgets, designs, and goodies of the West, then rushing into globalisation is indeed understandable. But if the purpose or priority is to meet the needs of all the people for decent food, clothing and shelter, clean water, proper sanitation and health protection, education and cultural opportunities and the like, then devoting scarce resources to the most modern technology will only be wasteful because there is little in the latest technology of the West that would make a significant contribution. In fact what is most useful and relevant in technology, Western or otherwise, for improving the way of life of the masses, is widely known. Most of this technology is already available at home and what else is needed is obtainable in the normal course of managed trade.

"Politics in command", that is, a socialism-oriented development, really involves making a fundamental and principled choice, namely, divorcing the criteria of rationality in economic-social life from those that govern the market-based system of capitalism. "Delinking", is making a similar choice in relation to global capitalism. It is reversing the process of peripheral "adjustment" to global capitalism, that is, subordinating external relations to the logic of socialism-directed internal development. Instead of our country adjusting its internal agendas to the world expansion of capitalism, to the imperatives of global capitalism, it is the imperatives of internal socialism-oriented development which must have primacy.

Finally, a few words about this thing called "development", which must not be assumed to be synonymous with capitalist development. That the initial modern economic and industrial development (in the West) occurred in the capitalist form is no reason to believe that this is the only way it can take place. The man who best studied and theorised this development certainly did not think so. Marx was categorical in rejecting the idea that this was the path "every people is fated to tread". He in fact deemed the capitalist path not "worthy of our human nature" .This apart, the concept of "development" is by nature ideological in the sense that it is suggestive of something desirable, involving the overarching question as to what kind of society we, as human beings, want to have. Surely it is people and not "economic growth" or productivity that must come first in such a society. It has to be a humane society that fosters cooperation, solidarity, and respect for universal ethical values, and makes for a non-alienated, "truly rich human life" that Marx spoke of. Of course, such a society is impossible without basic material security and need satisfaction. But to believe that you can assure need satisfaction through greed, private acquisitive drives, universal competition, and strife—the values of capitalism; and this can be done through the capitalist production process which, as Marx said, turns the worker into "an automatic motor of a fractional operation" and "cripples his body and mind"—to believe that this path will lead to a humane society of cooperation and solidarity and social well-being, is utopianism of the worst kind.

Subordinating humanity to economics, to imperatives of the market, capitalism commodifies life and undermines and rots away the relations between the human beings who constitute societies. Its ethos of the market place—competition, egoism, aggression, alienation, universal venality, in short "the rat race, its pseudo-moral principles", as Keynes once put it, "which have hag-ridden us for 200 years (and) by which we have exalted some of the most distasteful of human qualities into the position of the highest virtues", create a moral vacuum in which nothing counts except what the individual wants and can grab, here and now. At the end of it all, even when wants are satisfied, the people are ever more subordinated, ever less free, ever more flattened and made passive by the dictatorship of consumerism that arbitrarily shapes values, imposing on them the heavy burden of uniformity. The values of difference, individualisation (not individualism), all-sided development of man, of human freedom itself, disappear in the market place which is proclaimed to be free. As *human beings,* people simply don't fit into capitalism. A capitalist society is not the society we want to have. However poor or backward today, we need to *move away* from capitalism-oriented development and, however slowly or falteringly, *move towards* building a humane, democratically functioning socialist society that fosters equality, cooperation, solidarity, and respect for universal ethical values.

I had at the outset referred to the hard and fateful choices our people face today. One that encompasses them all (and which I have been discussing) concerns India's path of development. Do we accept the globalisation dictated capitalist path of development our rulers have opted for, which polarises our people and peripheralise them within a global capitalist system? Or do we struggle for a socialism-oriented development with its promise of a humane, democratic and ecologically respectful even if economically less prosperous society, providing a life of security and fulfilment for all?

It is my argument that we choose the latter. This implies, among other things, that we learn from the past experience with economic development, avoid its negative consequences, for example, the damage that capitalist development regularly inflicts upon human beings and the natural environment; that we reject the supposedly Marxist fascination for "the development of production forces" that bedevilled the erstwhile "socialist" economies and the obsession with "economic growth" that plagues a capitalist economy, that we better negotiate the necessary trade-offs between economic development and social justice, between requirement of productivity or efficiency and environmental sustainability or quality life which is not entirely a matter of material progress or economic growth. In other words, we have the opportunity "to do something new", the all important option of a path of development which subordinating economy to humanity, and plans and develops it in a way that is, in Marx's words, "worthy of our human nature."

Given the current balance of forces at the national level, it is likely that the struggle for this option will *initially* come up at the level of India's State politics. Apropos this perspective, I would like to reproduce here a passage from what I wrote recently as a critical comment on the CPM politics in West Bengal:

> It is simply inconceivable that there can ever be a situation where socialist principles do not indicate what can be done and what should not be done in the light of these principles. With politics, that is people's politics, in command, socialism-oriented initiatives are indeed possible at the State and local levels in the Left-ruled states. The need is for the CPM to mobilise all the resources within and without the Left parties to work out an alternative path of development geared to *the strategic goal* of socialism, implement whatever part of it is implementable at the State and local levels in the states where the Left is in power, and mobilise the people elsewhere for it, with primacy given to extra-parliamentary struggles. This will make the Left-ruled states an example for the rest of the country and help the Party and the Left to rally all the radical forces in the country—NAPM, ultra-left formations, militant NGOs, etc.—to emerge as a genuine and effective alternative to the ruling class politics at the Centre, with its own agenda of pro-people, self -reliant socialism-oriented development for the country. Of course, it is going to be a long haul and we don't have to mix up our own mortality with a time-table for the achievement of socialist goals.

I know that this option, the struggle for a socialism-oriented development, means travelling along an uncharted road. It is an option that is liable to be deemed impossible in a situation marked by an extraordinary dominance of capitalist ideology and an equally extraordinary inhibition of social imagination, a state of affairs wherein our people, including those on the Left, seem to have lost the dreams they once had—which is the most terrible thing that can ever happen to a people.

One remembers the admonition of the rebel students of Paris in their May–June uprising of 1968: "Be practical! Do the impossible!"

The situation calls for nothing less. It indeed demands doing "impossible" things.

NOTES

1. Randhir Singh. 2008. *Marxism, Socialism, Indian Politics: A View From the Left*. New Delhi: Akar Books.

14

Demystifying Globalisation's Agenda for India's Education Policy*

Anil Sadgopal

In a brief but scintillating account of Durgabai's life in the first Durgabai Deshmukh Memorial Lecture in July 1992, Dr Suma Chitnis, the speaker on the occasion, cites an anguished comment made by Durgabai in 1964, which is worth quoting again four decades later:

> Two decades of planning have shown that results have not been commensurate with the effort. ... The why of this cries for an answer. Is it the over-emphasis on economic development? Is it the lack of correlation between ends and means? Is it that outmoded administrative techniques are inadequate to the new tasks? The true answer can be found only after prolonged search into several complex factors . ...

As a member of India's first Planning Commission, Durgabai exhibited an unusual sense of honesty in raising this question. Her yearning for the "true answer" constitutes the first of three challenges that I propose, in all humility, to address myself to.

The second challenge emerges from Durgabai's decision to participate in the freedom struggle against colonialism and imperialism, even at the tender age of 11, and eventually, her membership of the Constituent Assembly, which laid the foundation of India's sovereignty, guaranteed Fundamental Rights through Part III of the Constitution, and placed a radical political, economic and social agenda before the nation through the Directive Principles of State Policy. Taking education as a case study, I hope to analyse how the Fundamental Rights have been seriously compromised after the initiation of the so-called economic reforms, the larger Constitutional agenda shelved from our policy discourse, and India's sovereignty threatened by the impact globalisation is making on the nature of knowledge in our education system.

The third challenge, for me, is rooted in the personal struggle of Durgabai

* Edited transcript of the July 15, 2004, Durgabai Deshmukh Memorial Lecture by Prof. Anil Sadgopal.

in rejecting her own child marriage (which took place when she was barely eight years old), her public protest at the age of 12 against the social status of *devadasis*, Muslim women and widows, and her life-long engagement with the issues of women's education and development. I will look at the issue of women's education through the perspective of our education policy and reflect upon how the policy itself has been diluted and distorted under the impact of globalisation and its manifestation—the structural adjustment programme.

Context of Globalisation

To my mind, globalisation represents a crisis of capitalism and it is not exactly a recent phenomenon. In terms of its ruthless pursuit of global markets and control over natural resources and means of livelihood, globalisation has much in common with colonialism of the eighteenth and nineteenth century. Even its methodology and strategies of influencing the State policies through systematic co-option of the Indian corporate houses, politicians, civil servants, and the educated elite, concomitant with increasing lobbying pressure and economic traps on the ruling class, are reminiscent of the early colonial experience of gaining access through traders, upper caste elite and the royal courts. The IMF, the World Bank, WTO, Global Economic Forum, G-8, and a whole spectrum of multi-lateral and trans-national arrangements represent the new structures formed for tightening the stranglehold of global capital on the world economy and extending the market agenda into every sphere of human activity and concern, including education and culture. The NGOs, the so-called civil society organisations and the army of consultants and "experts" of the globalised era, have almost become willing agents for camouflaging the ugly face of globalisation and presenting it in a "humanised" language. Globalisation can, therefore, be viewed as a more evolved, powerful and subtle form of colonialism.

Both colonialism and globalisation have come to be viewed as a response of the then industrialising and now the affluent west to its own internal economic crisis and need for expansion of markets. In recent decades, globalisation has acquired the added dimension of the need for access to new markets for the weapons industry and information and communication technology and control over additional sources of oil, forest, and water. This is now clearly evident in the increasing militarism (combined with shades of fascism) of the western powers led by the superpower USA and non-fulfillment of their international commitments to the developing countries on climate, agriculture, bio-diversity, and sustainable development. The recent US–UK attack on Iraq and the imposition of an alien political dispensation lacking an Iraqi mandate, has totally exposed the imperialist dimension of globalisation and obliterated the thin membrane that seemed to separate the two. What is significant in this experience is the clever manipulation of the language of democracy, humanity, and peace that was used in the Gramscian sense to "win the consent" of the oppressed communities not just in the middle east and within the US or UK but also internationally. The entire exercise fitted what, according to Chomsky amounted to "manufacturing consent" in order to maintain the democratic exterior and seek moral justification for global capital's imperialist quest.

One wonders whether the entire purpose of education in a globalised economy is being perceived in terms of "winning or manufacturing consent" of the future generation. The purpose of "winning or manufacturing consent" is to be pursued even at the cost of objectivity, critical thinking and, of course, the truth.

For teachers, political workers and social activists like us, this understanding is beginning to lay the foundation for demystifying the knowledge agenda of globalisation and, at the same time, redefining the very purpose of education.

Education in India: Policy Frameworks

In order to comprehend how such a knowledge agenda is operating in the Indian elementary education sector, it is necessary to refer to two sets of critical policy-related documents: one national, and the other international.

- A key *national* document is the *National Policy on Education—1986* (henceforth referred to as NPE-1986).[4] NPE 1986 was approved by Parliament in May 1986, and its companion document—*Programme of Action–1986* (henceforth referred to as POA-1986), received parliamentary approval in November of the same year. Both NPE-1986 and POA-1986 were revised by Parliament in 1992 and the amended versions are known as NPE-1986 (as modified in 1992) and POA-1992 respectively.
- The *international* documents are: *World Declaration on Education for All* and its companion document, *Framework for Action to Meet Basic Learning Needs*. These two documents, referred to as the Jomtien Declaration and Jomtien Framework respectively, were adopted by the "*World Conference on Education for All (EFA): Meeting Basic Learning Needs*" at Jomtien, Thailand in March 1990.

The Jomtien Conference was jointly convened by the UNDP, UNESCO, UNICEF, and the World Bank. It was attended by the representatives of 155 national governments (including the Indian government), 20 inter-governmental bodies and 150 NGOs. Follow-up conferences continued to be held at both the regional and global levels during the nineties.[5] The decadal follow-up of the Jomtien Conference was held at Dakar, Senegal in April 2000 wherein the progress made by various nations to achieve the EFA (Education for All) goals as set out by the Jomtien Declaration was reviewed. Just as the Jomtien Declaration guided educational planning throughout the nineties, the Dakar Framework of Action (World Education Forum 2000) has now become the new policy-level international guidepost for the first 15 years of the 21st century. As part of the Dakar Framework of Action, UNESCO now regularly monitors the progress made by each nation in the context of the Dakar Goals and issues an "EFA Global Monitoring Report" annually.[6]

We may recall here that the New Economic Policy, giving primacy to the market forces in national development and "integrating" India into the global economic order was enunciated in July 1991. The political and economic framework for subjugation by the global forces in the education sector emerged when the Indian Government was "persuaded" by the IMF and the World Bank to accept the twin concepts of "Structural Adjustment" and "Social Safety Net" in planning and budgeting for social sectors. There was no choice, the government told the people, justifying its apparent "helplessness" since these were the pre-conditions set by the two Breton Woods institutions for extending further loans. Plainly speaking, these twin concepts implied that the Government will, as part of the Structural Adjustment Programme, incrementally reduce public spending on social sectors such as health, education, and social welfare. Recognising that such a reduction can lead to severe socio-political tensions, the IMF and World Bank "offered" to create a Social Safety Net by extending loans for the social sector on certain terms and conditions.

One would tend to take a position that, in the face of the powerful forces of globalisation, there is no option for the educational system but to accept the larger framework dictated by the global economic order as a *fait accompli*. It is with this mindset that the policy makers in India have unquestioningly accepted the hegemonic role of trans-national corporate forces, the global market system, and the powerful international organisations such as the Breton Woods institutions in directing not just the structure and accessibility but also the very aims and the quality of education (and also health). The Jomtien Conference laid the basic architecture for intervention by the international funding agencies in national educational structures and processes.

Dilution and Distortion

The Jomtien Declaration,[7] which proved to be a turning point in the history of education in India, received a hasty nod of concurrence from the Government of India, which did not even consult Parliament on its major Constitutional and policy implications. This marked the beginning of a gradual but systemic erosion of Parliament in the sphere of educational policy formulation. It also led to an attrition of the Planning Commission and the Ministry of Human Resource Development in formulating the agenda of Indian education and setting priorities.

As provided for in the Jomtien Declaration (Article 10) and the Jomtien Framework (Section 3.3), external aid from a host of international funding agencies operating under the World Bank umbrella was systematically allowed in the primary education sector *as a matter of policy* for the first time in post-

Independence India. Externally aided projects in primary education in Andhra Pradesh (APPEP) and Bihar (BEP) preceded the Jomtien Declaration but these were envisaged as special pilot projects, rather than being a matter of policy. The possibility cannot be denied that the international funding agencies had used the Andhra Pradesh and Bihar pilot projects in the pre-Jomtien phase to gauge the political waters in India, and to test the political will of the ruling elite in respect of its Constitutional obligations and educational policy. Evidently, the Indian political leadership failed the test, for the externally aided projects of the post-Jomtien phase led to major violations of the Constitution and dilutions of the country's educational policy. This policy departure coincided with the beginning of the New Economic Policy in India in July 1991, which required the Government to accept the IMF-World Bank's Structural Adjustment Programme as well as the Jomtien Declaration's policy framework for Education For All (EFA). The launching of the first World Bank-sponsored comprehensive District Primary Education Programme (DPEP) in 1993–4 was part of this requirement as was its attendant Social Safety Net provided under IMF-World Bank design.[8]

The serious implication of the new situation for the independence of the country's educational policy was recognised by the Central Advisory Board of Education (CABE). In its 46th meeting of March 1991, CABE formulated a set of guidelines for externally aided projects. These guidelines, reiterated in CABE's 47th meeting in May 1992, sought to ensure that "external assistance does not lead to a dependency syndrome" and remains "an additionality to the (national) resources for education", while being in "total conformity with the national policies, strategies and programmes"[9]. As my analysis would shortly reveal, each one of these CABE guidelines stand fully breached in both letter and spirit. Yet, Parliament seems entirely unconcerned about this attrition of India's sovereignty.

A series of policy-related documents were issued during the following years, each violating the basic principle of equality enshrined in the Constitution and adversely impacting upon policy in a significant manner.[10] A detailed analysis of the multi-dimensional policy dilution and distortion that took place as a result of this neo-liberal intervention cannot be accommodated here. Only certain aspects of this phenomenon will be highlighted.[11]

An outstanding example of policy dilution was the District Primary Education Programme (DPEP). DPEP eschewed the National Policy's *eight years of integrated elementary education* in favour of the "Basic Education" of the Jomtien and Dakar Frameworks, which is limited to primary education of *five* years only. Elementary education of *eight* years, implied by the Indian Constitution under the original Article 45 as well as the amended Article 21A as the minimum guarantee by the State, is non-existent in these frameworks. Interestingly, the Jomtien Framework concedes that these targets represent a "floor" but not a "ceiling" and parenthetically provides for "primary education or whatever higher level of education is considered as basic" by a particular country (Sections 5 and 8(2) respectively). It is indeed ironic that the Indian policy makers, instead of using these spaces in the framework for persisting with India's Constitutional and policy imperatives, allowed the international funding agencies to dilute *elementary* education to *primary* education as the dominant framework for educational planning and financing in post-Jomtien India. By unquestioningly accepting the Jomtien Declaration's ambiguous notion of *"basic learning needs"* and the amorphous category of *"basic education"* in its haste to attract external assistance, the historical development of the concept of eight years of elementary education, as implied in the Constitution and specified in the 1986 policy, was ignored. Elementary education could be brought back on the agenda, and that too, only nominally, through Sarva Shiksha Abhiyan, after a gap of seven years.[12]

Four aspects of this policy shift may be underlined. *First*, with the initiation of the World Bank-sponsored DPEP, the entire discourse on the socio-economic relevance and pedagogic necessity of elementary education stood arbitrarily substituted by a historical and non-pedagogic discourse around low quality parallel streams of primary or even lower level education.[13] *Second*, the Jomtien Declaration's redefinition of education in terms of "basic learning needs" laid the ground for allowing education to be viewed in terms of mere literacy skills. The serious implications of this shift of emphasis from education to literacy for the majority of the under-privileged children—from the standpoint of educational planning, finance allocation, and the future of Indian society, demand a holistic discussion that would be too complex to be attempted here.

The *third* aspect relates to the manner in which the policy makers meekly allowed Jomtien's undefined notion of "basic education" to replace what India understood by the term "Basic Education" and what was a part of the heritage of our freedom struggle. Jomtien's notion of "Basic Education" must not be confused with the revolutionary pedagogic concept of Basic Education or *Buniyadi Shiksha* evolved by Mahatma Gandhi at the Wardha Education Conference in 1937, as part of the freedom struggle, and further elaborated by a committee under the chairpersonship of Dr Zakir Husain as *Nai Taleem*. The Gandhian pedagogy of Basic Education, of integrating the "world of work" with the "world of knowledge", which evolved into *Nai Taleem* or *Buniyadi Shiksha* under the leadership of Dr Zakir Husain, was soon obliterated from the Indian educational discourse. The almost servile parroting of Jomtien's narrow notion of "Basic Education" by Indian policy makers in the post-Jomtien official discourse amounts to denial of one of the most inspiring features of the heritage of the freedom struggle.

Fourthly, the policy focus changed from the issues of relevance, quality, and equality of education to merely its access. It may be noted that there is no policy document which deliberates upon either the appropriateness or the feasibility of delinking the issue of access from the pedagogic and structural dimensions of education. After a decade of externally aided projects in more than half of India's districts, we are still far from achieving universal access, as perceived and defined by DPEP. Neither the unreliable Gross Enrolment Ratios, nor the Drop-Out Rates have shown any significant change. Worse still, in spite of DPEP's focus on reducing social and gender gaps, the Gender Parity Index, as defined by UNESCO, has remained at a plateau since the mid-nineties and the Drop-Out Rates for the SC and ST communities is so embarrassing that the Government of India has stopped reporting it altogether.

Another dimension of policy dilution concerns the infrastructural commitments made in the 1986 policy. For instance, the commitment to ensure *three teachers per primary school* under Operation Blackboard, with the "number increasing, as early as possible, to one teacher per class", was reduced to one/two teachers per primary school, as evident in DPEP's emphasis on promoting *multi-grade teaching*. Operation Blackboard was also committed to providing each primary school with "three reasonably large rooms that are usable in all weather" and a range of educational aids. This commitment was totally eroded in the Education Guarantee Scheme as it provided for neither any building nor any educational aid. As a result of these policy changes, the minimum norms for school infrastructure and strength of teachers in a primary school, as specified in NPE-1986 (As modified in 1992), stand diluted for Sarva Shiksha Abhiyan and the EFA-National Plan of Action.[14]

The most critical dilution, however, was conceptual (and even moral and ethical), rather than quantitative. The 1986 policy itself was the first official acknowledgement that regular formal schooling would not be provided to all. Instead, almost half (about 10 crores) of India's children in the 6–14 age group, who were deprived of school education at the time of policy formulation, were to be provided low-budget, low-quality and short-duration *non-formal* education. The historical, pedagogic and financial rationale (or rather the lack of it) of this policy shift, promoting both exclusion as well as inequality in education, has been discussed in detail elsewhere.[15] What is significant here is to note that this policy decision to introduce separate and parallel streams of education for different sections of society provided that essential socio-political fault line through which the forces of globalisation could easily introduce their neo-liberal agenda.

The parallel streams institutionalised during the nineties included Alternative Schools, Education Guarantee Scheme (EGS) centres and Multi-Grade Teaching—the so-called "innovations" designed under the canvass of World Bank-sponsored District Primary Education Programme (DPEP). Also, the regular teacher was replaced by a para-teacher—an *under-qualified, untrained and under-paid* local youth appointed on short-term contract.[16] The latest addition in this series was the proposal to introduce correspondence courses for children in the age group 6–14. It also envisaged as part of this scheme of things that the *para-teacher* would be replaced with a *postman*![17] The government was not bothered at all that this policy stance was tantamount to institutionalising discrimination against the poor, the majority of whom were *Dalits*, tribals, and religious or cultural minorities, two-thirds of each segment being girls. Most of the disabled children would also fall in this category earmarked for discrimination.

This policy was ruthlessly pushed forward in spite of wide public criticism, notwithstanding its violation of the principle of equality enshrined in the Constitution. The government's refrain of *"something is better than nothing"* was worse than the policy. It seemed to justify, instead of questioning, the collapse of education policies during the past 57 years. The policy makers have used the concept of multiple track education as a rationale for not focusing political attention on transformation of the mainstream school system in favour of the poor, especially girls and disabled children. Although educational policy in India is clearly committed to establishing a Common School System by promoting neighbourhood schools, as recommended by the Kothari Commission (1964–66), the parallel streams have now become the dominant policy plank. This effectively marginalised the concept of the Common School System as well as the Constitutional principle of equality. It would be no exaggeration to observe that the post-Jomtien policy stance amounts to, for all practical purposes, a *deliberate policy of letting the mainstream school system deteriorate* so that it may be gradually replaced by the market-driven private unaided school system. This has led to quality education rapidly becoming the preserve of the privileged, making education a commodity in the market. With this, the agenda of ensuring *education of equitable quality* has become a non-issue in the national policy discourse, though it continues to be the aspiration of the marginalised masses.

I would now raise the issue of the education of the girl child in the context of neo-liberal policies. Significantly, India's 1986 policy had made a much clearer commitment on "education for women's equality" than the Jomtien–Dakar Framework. It states that "education will be used as an agent of basic change in the status of women" in order to "neutralise the accumulated distortions of the past". It promises that "there will be a well-conceived edge in favour of women" and that education system will "play a positive, interventionist role" in their empowerment, and that "this will be an act of faith and social engineering". The credit for this clarity must entirely go to India's own women's movement.

In this holistic approach to women's education, the issue of girl child's education was not isolated from the question of the low social status of women. The participation of the girl child in school education was envisaged as an inevitable consequence of the change in the status of women. However, the only programme that was designed to reflect this policy insight was *Mahila Samakhya*. Its objective was to enhance the self-esteem and self-confidence of women; build their self image by recognising their contributions to society, to the polity, and to the economy; develop their ability to think critically; enable them to make informed choices in areas like education, employment, and health, especially reproductive health; and ensure equal participation in developmental processes. But it remained marginal throughout the nineties. For every hundred rupees allocated for elementary education in the Union Budget, hardly 25 paise were given to it. In due course of time, even this miniscule programme, operating barely in a few dozen blocks, seems to have lost its basic direction, the notable, and praiseworthy exceptions that continue to be informed by the original vision notwithstanding.

The Jomtien-Dakar Framework does not even refer to patriarchy as an issue and essentially reduces girls' education to merely enrolling them in school registers and imparting literacy skills. This is exactly what happened when the World Bank-sponsored District Primary Education Programme adopted *Mahila Samakhya*. The focus on collective reflection and socio-cultural action by organised women groups was abandoned. It became a mere girl child enrolment programme. Critical issues such as girls' participation in schools, gender sensitisation of learning material, and teacher education and holistic educational aims were ignored. Unfortunately, the notion of gender parity (ratio of enrolment of girls and boys) in UNESCO's EFA Global Monitoring Report 2003–4 also reinforces this confusion. It is a different matter that the findings of UNESCO's report reveal that India will fail to achieve even this diluted objective by 2015. Also, the World Bank diluted the goal of women's education to just raising their literacy levels and productivity (rather than educating or empowering them) and turning them into mere transmitters of fertility control, health or nutritional messages. The Dakar Framework has now added the ambiguous notion of Life Skills that seems to be yet another mechanism for social manipulation and market control of the adolescent mindset, particularly of girls. India unfortunately gave up its progressive policy on women's education in favour of the international framework that was guided more by the considerations of market than by women's socio-cultural and political rights.

Paradigm Shift

Let us recall here the Macauleyan emphasis in the early nineteenth century on controlling and re-orienting higher education in colonial India at the very outset and imposing English as the medium of *instruction* (not education!). The colonial powers knew well (as do the forces of global capital) that it is the higher education sector that generates knowledge for development and change. It is with this understanding that the Ambani-Birla Report, submitted to the Prime Minister's Council on Trade & Industry in April 2000, recommended that the government should allow privatisation of the entire higher education sector.[18] The report further recommended that all those disciplines at the higher education level that have a market value (this includes all sciences and social sciences and even disciplines of humanities such as linguistics) must *not* be supported by the State funds, that such marketable forms of knowledge should instead be supported by market forces. In their scheme of things, only disciplines with no market value, such as oriental languages, archaeology, paleontology, religion, and philosophy, should continue to receive State funding. This implies that the *nature of knowledge* in sciences and social sciences would henceforth be determined by market forces which in turn are controlled by global capital.

Since the knowledge that informs education and its pedagogy from the pre-primary level upwards is also generated in the higher education sector, the Ambani-Birla Report implies that education at all levels will henceforth be determined by the market forces. In this sense, the Ambani-Birla Report extends the agenda put forth by the Jomtien Declaration, though it seemed to be advocating the cause of elementary education by recommending enhanced State support for this sector.

Education is to be no more viewed as a tool of social development but as an investment for developing human resources and global markets.[19] This apparently innocuous statement of the purpose of education amounts to a paradigm shift. The dominant features of education with serious epistemic implications which emerge out of this paradigm shift may be identified as follows:

- Trivialisation of the goals of education.
- Fragmentation of knowledge.
- Alienation of knowledge from its social ethos and material base.
- Determination of the character of knowledge by the global market forces.
- Institutionalisation of economic, technological, and socio-cultural hegemony of the international instruments in the formulation of curriculum.
- Marginalisation of poor children and youth as well as the backward regions through competitive screening and a discriminatory system of institutional assessment and accreditation.
- Introduction of parallel and hierarchical educational streams for different social segments.
- Attrition of the State-supported and democratic structures for educational planning, finance allocation, and management.

Admittedly, however, many of the features enumerated above were also evident either in rudimentary or relatively more pronounced forms in the pre-globalisation phase as well. This is exactly what one would expect in view of the colonial control before Independence, and the hegemony of the ruling classes on the Indian State, with no significant democratic social intervention in educational planning and implementation since Independence. What globalisation has done after 1991 is to heighten and sharpen these pre-existing tendencies.

Negating Critical Pedagogy

The concept of critical pedagogy or critical education, which took shape in the writings of the Brazilian educator Paulo Freire, is rooted in critiquing objective reality and is aimed at transforming it.[20] A further implication of this pedagogy is the dialectical unity between cognition and social reality, thereby calling for engagement of the learning process with social action. This is the praxis also advocated by Paulo Freire. Consider, in this light, the manner in which NCERT's curricular framework (2000)[21] over-emphasises the notion of spiritual values in education. The notion of such values, at least as presented in the curricular framework, is entirely unrelated to the conditions of life or the objective reality around it. In this framework, spiritual values in fact are aimed at enabling you to *escape* from your objective reality instead of *engaging* with it.

The difference between the two theoretical frameworks—critical pedagogy and uncritical education—is of the way you see the very purpose of education. In the former, the purpose is *to engage with and transform* the reality in which you exist whereas in the latter the purpose would be *to simply conserve and reproduce* it. Clearly, globalisation would support and promote uncritical education while de-emphasising critical pedagogy. *Globalisation does not need thinking people, especially those who apply thinking to their objective reality. Such thinking people can pose threat to the neo-liberal agenda. They ask too many uncomfortable questions. They also tend to explore new and divergent paths. Worse are those people who have been educated to do critical thinking!*

The forces of globalisation are determined to suppress all forms and structures of education of the masses that lead to critical thinking and generation of new knowledge linked with humane values and cultural sensitivities, primarily because these would promote equality and social justice, thereby supporting social transformation. Education can be promoted under globalisation only if it is dichotomised from social reality and universal human values. This, too, will be the privilege of the selected few who could be utilised as human resource for advancing the vested interests of global capital. Why else did the Government of Madhya Pradesh order the closure of the 30-year old Hoshangabad Science Teaching Programme (HSTP) in July 2002? Why indeed did the government prevent more than one lakh children from learning science through experiment-based, inquiry-oriented and environment-related pedagogy in 1,000 schools of 14 districts? No other schools in India—not even the expensive and exclusive metropolitan public schools—were practicing this pedagogy. It must also be noted that Madhya Pradesh had until then the largest component of World Bank's District Primary Education Programme (DPEP) in India. Obviously, the World Bank's notion of knowledge for the developing countries was inconsistent with the ways in which HSTP (and also Eklavya's Social Science Programme) viewed knowledge. The government had no choice but to close the programme, lest the World Bank come in conflict with HSTP when, and if at all, it moved to the upper primary levels where the HSTP's pedagogy was being practiced.

Let us also examine another critical aspect of globalisation—one that is related to educational psychology. This has roots in the ideology of behaviourism which was promoted in the United States and Europe in 1930's when the West was undergoing one of its worst economic crises. This ideology views human beings as entities to be regulated, controlled, and directed. It also found expression in the Jomtien Declaration which insisted that all targets of basic education must be "observable and measurable'. It is reflected in NCERT's curriculum framework (2000) too, which lays down long-discarded and irrational parameters such as Intelligence Quotient (IQ), Emotional Quotient (EQ), and Spiritual Quotient (SQ) for measuring, regulating, and screening human behaviour.

Indeed, the basic tenets of the computer-based programmed learning, pre-determined and remote-controlled satellite communication and media packages, fragmentation of knowledge into competencies and tasks (for example, in NCERT's Minimum Levels of Learning, 1991) and trivialisation of human development issues (for example, in NCERT's learning materials on fertility control, AIDS consciousness, anti-pollution drives, anti-terrorist campaign, etc.) flow out of this very ideology of behaviourism that dominates globalisation's knowledge agenda. Any attempt by the people to resist this ideology will necessarily require them to learn to re-construct knowledge that is informed by the behaviourist framework of educational psychology. For this, to begin with, both the child and her learning process will have to be placed in diverse socio-cultural and developmental contexts.

The impact of global market forces, trans-national capital, satellite communication, and digital technologies have become the determining co-ordinates of knowledge inherent in all curricula, from pre-school to universities. This impact is concomitant with the process of privatisation and commercialisation operating at all levels of education, thereby converting education into a marketable commodity. It has led to relegation of the State-supported education to the poor sections of society, institutionalisation of parallel and hierarchical streams of education for different social segments and the phenomenon of increasing abdication by the State of its Constitutional obligation towards *education of equitable quality* of all children.[22] It is no mere coincidence that all of these trends are also supported by the Jomtien Declaration and Dakar Framework as accepted by the Government of India.

State's Abdication

Evidence of the State's tendency to abdicate its Constitutional obligation towards provision of education of equitable quality for all children was already visible in the National Policy on Education 1986 as well as in its modified version of 1992, as these documents accepted the low-quality low-budget non-formal education as a parallel stream for the poor, especially for child labour and girl children.[23] With the market agenda and the Structural Adjustment Programme inherent in the Jomtien Declaration having a significant impact on the State's policies, a further attrition of the State's commitment to its Constitutional obligations occurred during the nineties, in the following concrete ways:

- Education made synonymous with literacy.
- Dilution of *elementary* education of eight years to *primary* education of five or less years.
- Diverting attention from the central issue of transforming the *mainstream* school system with respect to issues such as the lack of social relevance of education, inequity inbuilt in school structure, inflexibility and non-contextuality of the school curriculum, erroneous pedagogic principles on which the teaching-learning process and evaluation parameters are founded, ill-planned curriculum of teacher education, etc.
- Imposing Minimum Levels of Learning (MLLs) as a tool for organising learning material and evaluation, despite the fact that the concept of MLLs is rooted in only a limited and an incomplete view of education, and is aimed at conditioning the child's mind with social biases and market ideology.[24]
- Ignoring the policy commitment to the Common School System.
- Institutionalisation of low-quality low-budget parallel streams of education for the deprived sections of society namely, Alternative Schools, Education Guarantee Scheme, Multi-Grade Teaching, etc.
- Reducing the issue of women empowerment and gender discrimination to the so-called gender parity measured in terms of enrollment ratios.
- Marginalising the issue of social and cultural discrimination against Dalits, tribals, and the minorities, both within and outside the school, and its impact on their capacity to participate in and complete elementary education; again reducing the entire issue to their enrollment ratios.[25]
- Isolating education from its socio-economic context by ignoring issues such as child labour, wage structure, common property resources (for example, fodder, fuel, and water), patriarchy, caste structure, cultural alienation and discrimination, communalisation of the polity, feudal control of Panchayati Raj institutions, etc.[26]
- Reducing the aim of girl child's education to the narrow view wherein women are envisaged as merely "useful products", ready receptors or transmitters of demographic and nutritional messages or proficient wage earners or producers, thereby violating girls child's right to education as a human.[27]
- Violating Operation Blackboard's norms prescribed by the National Policy with respect to the number of teachers and classrooms per

primary school and then legitimising multi-grade teaching for the poor.[28]

- Overlooking the cumulative gap in resource allocation to education that has been building up for the past three decades due to non-investment of the recommended level of 6 per cent of the GDP in education.
- Refusing to re-prioritise the national economy for the purpose of allocating adequate resources for education of the poor and thereby promoting re-distributive social justice; using this reluctance as a rationale for seeking external aid for primary education, promoting privatisation and commercialisation of education at all levels and substituting national concerns with the conditionalities of international aid giving agencies.

The aforesaid trends clearly violate several of the Fundamental Rights and the Directive Principles of State Policy enshrined in the Constitution, apart from diluting and distorting imperatives of the 1986 policy. Yet, there has been almost no debate in Parliament on this critical matter. This is precisely what should concern each one of us, for this "conspiracy of silence" threatens the democratic fabric of Indian society.

Amending the Constitution

The government pushed "The Constitution (Eighty-Sixth Amendment) Bill, 2001" in the Lok Sabha, purportedly to give education the status of fundamental right for children in the 6-14 age group.[29] Approved by the Rajya Sabha in May 2002, it was signed into law by the then President, His Excellency, Dr A.P.J. Abdul Kalam in December of the same year. The Bill was enacted despite widespread public protests, memoranda to the government, and critical speeches by several MPs in both houses of Parliament, among them, the then Leader of Opposition in the Lok Sabha (now Chairperson, UPA). The amendment has the following four major lacunae:

(i) It excludes almost 17 crore children up to six years of age from the provision of Fundamental Right to *free* early childhood care and pre-school education. This is in contravention of NPE 1986 (as modified in 1992), which considers this support during childhood as being crucial for child development and preparation for elementary education (Sections 5.1 to 5.4). The implication is clear: early childhood care and pre-school education will not be guaranteed to at least 40 per cent of the children in this age group, two-thirds of them being girls, whose parents barely manage to earn minimum wages. This will also prevent girls in the 6–14 age group belonging to the same sections of society from receiving elementary education as they will be engaged in sibling care. Moreover, the lack of guarantee of *free* early childhood care and pre-school education will not only result in underdevelopment of the deprived children during childhood but will also adversely affect their learning capacity by the time they are of school going age.

(ii) Even the provision of the fundamental right to education for the 6–14 age group children is made conditional by introducing the phrase "*as the State may, by law, determine*" in the new Article 21A. The implications of this phrase will be discussed below.

(iii) The Constitutional obligation towards "free and compulsory education" stands shifted from the State to the parents or guardians by making it a fundamental duty of the latter under Article 51A(k) to *"provide opportunities for education"* to their children in the 6–14 age group. This purpose is now sought to be achieved by promoting and legitimising "community participation" in raising resources for elementary education in order to substitute public funding,[30] which is yet another measure towards abdication by the State.

(iv) The financial memorandum attached to the Bill provided for only Rs. 9,800 crores per annum (that is, 0.44 per cent of GDP in 2002–3) over a ten-year period for implementing the provisions under the Bill. This commitment was far from being adequate, as it was 30 per cent less than what was estimated by the Tapas Majumdar Committee in 1999 to provide elementary education to all out-of-school children through *regular formal schools*. This lower estimate was made possible by depending on low-quality parallel tracks of education and lowering several other critically important infrastructural and pedagogic norms for the deprived sections of society.[31]

The systematic move towards incremental abdication by the State of its constitutional obligations formed the core of the statement given by the Minister of Human Resource Development while presenting the bill to the Lok Sabha on November 28, 2001. While acknowledging the criticality of early childhood care and pre-school education for the children up to six years of age, the minister was not willing to place this burden on the government. Yet he contradicted himself by assuring the Lok Sabha that this stage of child development shall receive government's full attention. As if to resolve this contradiction, the minister invited "all voluntary organisations and corporate houses" to help the government in this sector. This plea of the minister was tailor-made to fit into the neo-liberal agenda of reducing the role of the State and increasing the role of the market and the private sector, leading eventually to commercialisation. This reading of the Constitutional amendment is also strengthened by the language of the amended Article 45 which carefully avoids giving a guarantee for *free* early childhood care and pre-primary education! The original Article 45 now stands substituted by a modified but diluted Article as a result of the 86th Amendment to the Constitution. Compared to the original Article 45, the dilution is a consequence of (a) de-linking Early Childhood Care and Pre-school Education (ECCE) from elementary education, thereby not viewing education of all children "until they complete the age of fourteen years" as a continuum; (b) withdrawing the Constitutional guarantee for provision of *free* ECCE; and (c) not including a specific time frame for fulfillment of the commitment.

Detailed critiques of the bill contended that the lacunae were deliberate, rather than being a result of oversight.[32] The amendment was being made, these writings sought to establish, not to make elementary education a fundamental right, but to snatch away the educational rights already made available by the Supreme Court's Unnikrishnan Judgment (1993)[33] and to fulfill the dictates of IMF-World Bank's Structural Adjustment Programme that demanded reduction in public expenditure on the social sector. In particular, the above critiques focused upon the implications of the phrase "*as the State may, by law, determine*". No such conditionality existed in the original Article 45. The phrase, it was contended, was meant to legitimise the low-budget, low-quality multiple or parallel tracks of the so-called educational facilities for poor children, as well as to give a stamp of legitimacy to the other policy dilutions and distortions discussed above. The phrase *"as the State may, by law, determine"* also lays the basic framework for the increasing abdication by the State of its constitutional obligation to ensure elementary education of *equitable* quality for all children. Indeed, the draft "Free and Compulsory Education Bill, 2004", finalised by the government for presentation to Parliament became possible only because of the space created by this conditional phrase in the amended Constitution. This is precisely what I had predicted on the day the 86th Amendment Bill was presented to the Parliament more than two years ago,[34] but no one took me seriously.

To the agitated MPs from various political parties who criticised the Bill in both houses of Parliament, an assurance was repeatedly given by the minister that the lacunae in the Bill would be taken care of by enacting a new law. If the government intended to rectify the lacunae later through a law, why was it bent upon introducing these in the Constitution in the first place? The leadership of various political parties neither raised nor pursued such uncomfortable questions in Parliament. The assurance of a law to be enacted later seemed to have led to a curious (or *convenient*?) consensus in Parliament on the constitutional amendment in spite of its unambiguous bias against crores of children (girl children in particular) belonging to various deprived sections of society,[35] and violations of several provisions in the Constitution relating to Parts III and IV. The UPA government has the mandate to take all necessary legislative action to undo the impact of interference in the Constitution by the neo-liberal forces and *restore India's sovereignty*. The nation holds its breath as the UPA government, particularly its Left coalition partners, dither over their future move on the 86th Amendment.

Free and Compulsory Education Bill, 2004

Let me also briefly examine the draft "Free and Compulsory Education Bill, 2004".[36] This is the law that was promised by the previous government in Parliament, presumably to take care of the lacunae in the 86th Amendment Bill. Ironically, a careful scrutiny reveals that, instead of "taking care" of the lacunae in the 86th Amendment, the aforementioned draft bill *increases* the lacunae in several ways. It would suffice to refer to Schedules I & II of the bill which together provide for *three types of centres* for "imparting education", specifying their respective minimum norms. The draft bill thus is an unabashed attempt to legitimise parallel streams of education of differential quality that is, regular schools, existing side by side with EGS Centres and Alternative Schools—an arrangement already institutionalised in the *operating* policy and programmes for the deprived sections of society (for example, in the case of the Sarva Shiksha Abhiyan). This will also legitimise the undesirable sociological principle of "a separate educational stream for each social stratum".

The draft bill is both ambiguous and weak on the inclusion of physically and mentally disabled children in the regular approved schools. Its provisions will encourage as well as facilitate violation of the policy commitment for inclusive education, which is integral to the fulfillment of Constitutional obligation to ensure equality in education and for building up the Common School System.[37] As noted by Jha, the Bill might even promote privatisation and commercialisation of the education of the disabled.[38]

Limited time does not permit me to refer to several other lacunae and contradictions in the draft bill. Some of these will be discussed later in different contexts. A detailed and holistic analysis was presented by me at two consultations organised by MV Foundation and CACL in Hyderabad (January 2004) and in Bhubaneswar (April 2004) respectively. In a sense, the draft bill will carry forward the process of abdication by the State of its Constitutional obligation for which a legitimate space was created by the 86th Amendment by attaching the conditionality "*as the State may, by law, determine*" to the guarantee of the right to free and compulsory education for children in the 6–14 age group.

Assault on Knowledge

As was the case with the Macaulayian approach to education, globalisation also aims at using education as a tool for building up various skills and capacities that are useful to the global economy (recall competency-based approach of MLL). We have already examined the post-Jomtien framework in which educational aims are being trivialised and curricular knowledge is either being reduced to mere literacy skills (for reading product labels and prices) or fragmented into bits of information or competencies (for reading factory instructions, punching keys at the computer keyboard or accepting the dictates of the market *uncritically*). This amounts to rejection of a holistic approach to building up an enlightened and humane society.

As for higher and technical education, commercialisation has been promoted in the post-Jomtien phase under the false argument that *resources need to be shifted from this sector to the primary education sector*, as strongly advocated by the Ambani-Birla Report.[39] It needs to be emphasised that *knowledge is produced and communicated in institutions of higher learning*. This holds true even for knowledge that is essential for improving the curriculum, pedagogy, and the quality of teacher education programmes for school education. If public expenditure in higher education is reduced, it will lead to the following anomalies:

(i) Only those disciplines or sub-disciplines will be allowed to survive that have a marketable value; the rest of the disciplines, irrespective of their socio-cultural or epistemological significance, will gradually wither away.
(ii) The entire higher education system will become oriented to only utilitarian goals, while any knowledge that might lead towards social development or transformation will be marginalised.
(iii) The lower middle-class and the deprived sections of society are likely to be denied access to this knowledge as well as participation in generating and re-constructing it; this will lead to further reinforcement of elitist control over knowledge and its social application.

The Constitutional Review initiated by the previous government but put on the backburner for strategic reasons, was hardly expected to resist the pressure of global market forces when the entire Indian polity had already begun to make major adjustments, if not just succumb. Evidence of this trend (that is, the changing relationship between the State and the market) was also provided by the Supreme Court in its verdict given in October 2002 in what is popularly known as the minorities case (TMA Pai Foundation vs. State of Karnataka). This, by essentially reversing the Supreme Court's Unnikrishnan Judgment (1993), helped "to sustain the ethos in which private interests can boldly advance and the State withdraws".[40]

Globalisation and Homogenisation

The market economy demands that multi-cultural, multi-linguistic or multi-ethnic societies are homogenised so that the marketing of a product is facilitated. The greater the homogenisation (also read, standardisation), the greater will be the size of the market for a specific product. An editorial in a UNESCO Newsletter (October–December 2002) advocated "commoditisation of learning material" for reducing the cost of production. Although, for the corporate world, this immediate economic motivation is an adequate ground for pushing homogenisation, the long-term political gains in terms of dominance of the market forces over global, natural, and human resources also need to be kept in mind.

Indeed, globalisation has the *hidden agenda* of minimising cultural diversity even across national boundaries. A 2000 document released jointly by UNESCO's International Bureau of Education and CBSE[41] notes that globalisation is leading to "*erosion of the power of nation-states*", concomitant with the "*transfer of sovereignty*" from governments to larger geo-political regional entities (for example, ASEAN, CIS, European Union, etc.). The same document further recognises that the development of multi-national corporations has contributed to "*dramatic increase in trans-border exchanges*".[42] With the increasing dominance of Information and Communication Technology in the promotion of "knowledge industry", one can easily see how the process of globalisation is leading towards irreversible homogenisation of plural cultures, ethnicities, and languages, with the objective of increasing the size of the market and enhancing political dominance of corporate powers (McDonalds and Kentucky Chickens are not mere symbols but represent the substantive content of this homogenisation agenda!). The inclusion of these concepts in an educational document shows that the international educational bureaucracy has readily accepted the ideological dominance of globalisation and, that too, with an undercurrent of admiration!

The Breton Woods institutions and the associated international forces promoting globalisation have burnt midnight oil before proposing that the phenomenon of "*erosion of the power of the nation-states*" and "*transfer of sovereignty*" from nations to trans-national corporations are to form the cutting edge of globalisation. However, the phenomenon has to be couched in a language that is politically acceptable. The policy makers have, therefore, discovered that "*interdependence and interrelationships between peoples and cultures*" is the major consequence of globalisation.[43] Further, the International Commission on Education's Report (that is, the Delors Commission's Report, 1996 to UNESCO) states on page 22 that "*learning to live together*" must be one of the pillars of globalised education.

The Communal Assault

My analysis of the impact of globalisation will remain incomplete if I do not refer to the recent assault by the forces of communalism and religious fundamentalism on school curricula. In 1993, seven years before the recent fresh but highly organised wave of communal assault on school curricula, I wrote a detailed analysis of a new textbook prescribed by the first BJP Government of Madhya Pradesh as a compulsory Foundation Course text for the Bachelor Degree programme in all of the seven State universities.[44] In this account, I identified six features of the changes evident in the new text (also in the school textbooks of a comparable period in UP). These changes defined the basic framework for the communalisation of knowledge in subjects such as history, geography, and civics. That was in 1993. In 2000–2003 also we find a similar pattern. Thus, as one examines the nature of the recent changes in the curricular framework,[45] one is struck by the similarity of frameworks that defined the communalisation of texts in 1993 and 2000–3. The following are the chief elements of the communalisation of knowledge.

- To perceive and present all those ethnic or cultural groups that had migrated to the Indian sub-continent from other parts of the world as "aliens", even if the said migration is known to have taken place more than 2,000 years ago. This is precisely why it became necessary for the Sangh Parivar to make an issue out of the origin of Aryans, the presumed "founders" of Hinduism, and to make the controversial claim that their roots can be traced to as far back as the Harappan age. This is also precisely why the Sangh Parivar envisages the history of Indian freedom struggle to be more than 2000 year old, presumably for "liberating" the motherland from the "alien immigrants".
- There is no space for class analysis in *Hindutva* thinking since such an analysis will reveal major socio-economic and cultural contradictions within Indian society through various stages of history, thereby demanding their scientific resolution on the principle of dialectical materialism. It is, therefore, necessary for *Hindutva* to view Indian history in isolation of the productive forces in society and to deny class struggle as a historical phenomenon of social development.
- The traditional Brahmanical, patriarchal and hegemonic culture of India is presumed to be synonymous with the contemporary Indian culture. This incomplete and distorted perception allows *Hindutva* to deny the rich plural cultural heritage of India. In order to sustain this a-historical view, it has become necessary for *Hindutva* to also deny the concept of composite culture and to insist upon its mono-cultural hegemony in contemporary Indian society. There is no space for acknowledging the contribution made by any non-Brahmanical, non-patriarchal or non-hegemonic (that is, an all encompassing, egalitarian and democratic) tradition to Indian history or the making of our present culture. As a corollary of this irrational view, the Sangh Parivar would prefer to ignore the historical contributions made by the tribals, particularly by those of the north-eastern region, to the building up of contemporary India. It also becomes necessary for the *Hindutva* forces to marginalise the role of the *Dalits* and tribals as well as of the other non-Hindu sections of society in the freedom struggle. The freedom struggle is perceived more as a struggle for the defense of Hindu "cultural nationalism" or creation of a "*Hindu Rashtra*" than for liberating India from colonial oppression and resisting imperialism.
- Hindu culture is to be viewed as something "pure" or absolute and the influence of any other culture is essentially to be seen as

> "adulteration". This view implies that culture is a non-changing and inert phenomenon. The protagonists of this view deny that culture has any dynamic relationship with the socio-economic conditions since their claim of the "pure" nature of what they call Hindu culture will become untenable if such a dynamic relationship is granted. This premise allows one to look at values also as being absolute. The de-linking of values from objective reality seems to be central to *Hindutva's* strategy for maintaining the hegemony of upper castes and upper classes over the rest and also to provide an "escape route" to the ruling elite from issues of disparity, oppression, and injustice.[46]

The above framework enables us to both predict and de-construct the nature of the communal assault on the curriculum. In October 2001, on directions from NCERT, the CBSE ordered deletion of certain portions of history texts and directed the affiliated schools neither to teach nor even to discuss these in the classrooms! One of these referred to Emperor Ashoka (273–232 BC) who *"derided superfluous rituals performed by women"* which "*naturally affected the income of the brahmanas*". The text had recorded that the Brahmans "*developed some kind of antipathy to him* (Ashoka).... [They] *really wanted a policy that would favour them and uphold the existing interests and privileges"*. Clearly, the government did not want students to learn how the powerful Brahmins in ancient India exploited women by promoting superstition in the name of culture or how they resisted the progressive State policy of Emperor Ashoka in favour of women.

The Work Education programme in the NCERT syllabus for the secondary stage recommends two sex-stereotyped courses—one for rural girls and the other for urban girls.[47] Worse is NCERT's conception of the pre-vocational activities for the upper primary stage as it includes sex stereo-typed activities such as "maintaining cleanliness at home", "keeping sources of water in the school and the community safe and clean" and, amazingly, "helping parents in looking after younger children and old family members".[48] With a deep-seated gender bias in curriculum framework and lack of any programme for women's empowerment in the *operating* education policy, it is easy to guess as to who would be assigned such sex-stereotyped pre-vocational activities in schools. The syllabi for other subjects also lack a gender perspective. The gender bias can further be seen in the latest NCERT textbooks which only marginally refer to the contribution of women to Indian history and the making of contemporary India.

Also of note, apart from the gender issue, is *Hindutva's* denial of rationality and critical reasoning in education. The allocation of finances by the University Grants Commission in 2001–02 for starting courses in *Jyotirvigyan* (that is, Astrology, not Astronomy) and *Pourohitya* (Brahmanical ceremony and sacrificial rites) is not merely a bizarre, but rather, a preferred manifestation. What is more significant is the de-emphasis, in the NCERT curriculum and texts, of critical thought and scientific temper, which is consonant with the uncritical acceptance of a revivalist worldview.

At this juncture, it may not be out of place to raise the question: What is the linkage between globalisation and communalisation? Religious fundamentalism appears in different forms in different religious or cultural contexts, but the common thread in all kinds of fundamentalist ideologies has been a blind revivalist tendency. This tendency is then used to underline and strengthen a false consciousness of a narrow and exclusivist communal identity. In complex and plural societies like ours, Hindu fundamentalism (read, *Hindutva* of the contemporary Indian polity) can co-exist and flourish alongside with fundamentalist tendencies of other religions. In contrast, some of our neighbouring countries exhibit monolithic fundamentalism. Irrespective of the specific, religious, or cultural context, communal politics and globalisation seem to form an undeclared alliance in spite of their contradictory frameworks and roots.

The two ideologies—globalisation and communalisation—support each other in so far as communalisation and vote bank politics leads to political stability. Similarly, while fundamentalism raises its ugly face, the forces of globalisation would prefer to look the other way, as long as the former is kept within bounds to politically stabilise the market in the long run. Further, as globalisation fails to generate adequate employment, it is expected that there will be a rapid rise in socio-economic tensions, eventually leading to even political unrest. This is exactly what the communalisation of politics averts, by diverting attention of the masses from socio-economic issues to the perceived "dangers" to their religious identity. This should explain why NCERT's new curricular material attempts to simultaneously promote both globalisation and communalisation through education.

External Aid

The externally assisted District Primary Education Programme (DPEP) began in 1993–94. By the year 2000, it had spread to 275 odd districts in 18 States—almost half of the country. The Government of India's Education for All document,[49] while reproducing the Central Advisory Board of Education (CABE) guidelines for externally aided projects, partly stated:

> "It would be fair to say that while external funding would be an interim contribution to meet the resource gap, there is *no alternative other than augmenting domestic resources* to achieve the objective of EFA. Economic liberalisation and the consequent financial restructuring can be *expected to facilitate greater resource flow* to elementary education" [emphasis added].[50]

External aid has had an adverse impact on the political will to mobilise public resources for the universalisation of elementary education. Soon after the 1986 policy, we saw an upswing in the national effort to mobilise public resources for education. By 1989–90, almost 4 per cent of GDP was being spent on

Educational Expenditure as % of GDP

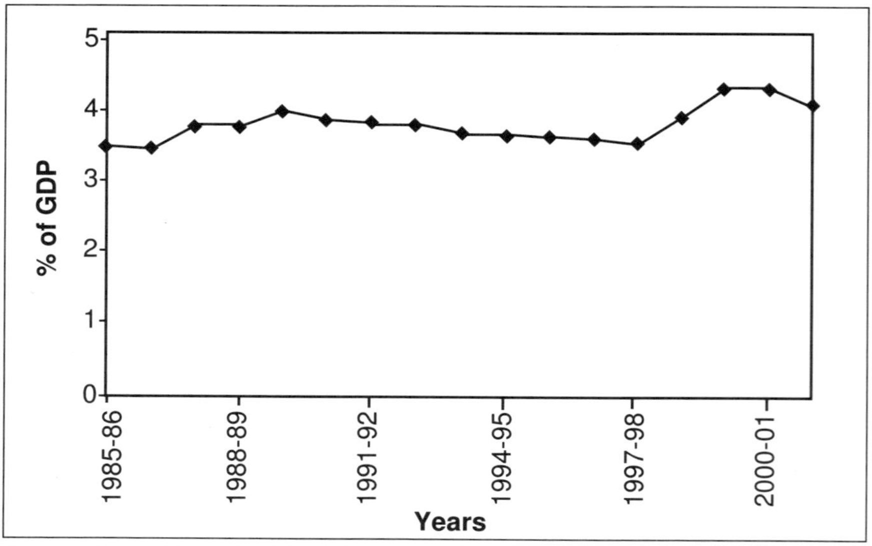

Source: Selected Educational Statistics 2001–02 [Rectified on the basis of 'Analysis of Budgeted Expenditure on Education' (various years) Ministry of HRD]

education, with little less than half on elementary education. Ironically, with the onset of external aid in primary education in the nineties, the investment in education (including in elementary education) started declining steadily and was as low as 3.49 per cent of GDP in 1997–98, the same level as in 1985–86, just before 1986 policy. Clearly, the political will to mobilise resources for elementary education weakened following the entry of external aid. It is only during the last 2–3 years that there has been some improvement, followed by declining trend again in 2001–02, though the level of external aid was twice in this year than that of 1997–98.

In January 2004, the previous government signed yet another agreement with the World Bank for a loan of Rs 4710 crore for Sarva Shiksha Abhiyan for 2004–7 that is, Rs 1,570 crore per year. At the current level of GDP, this loan amounts to merely 0.06 per cent of GDP, that is, merely 6 paise out of every Rs. 100 India will earn in 2004–5 (the level of total external assistance in this sector since 1993–4 has invariably been much lower than this level)! For this pittance, we entered into conditionalities that will never be made public, as has been the case with externally aided projects since 1993–4.

The official stance is in clear violation of the CABE guidelines against the "dependency syndrome" and policy dilutions in relation to external aid.[51] This dependence on external aid in fact implies that *there need not be any change in the priorities of the national economy* since additional funds will keep flowing in, as long as the Government of India is willing to adjust its educational policy to the conditionalities of the international funding agencies. These are matters of great concern for those of us who have been consistently questioning the role of external aid in elementary education. This issue has unfortunately not found any recognition in the Common Minimum Programme of the UPA government and is yet to become a part of the political discourse at the national level.

We need to advance our understanding beyond the Ambani-Birla formulations which gave the false impression that it called for privatisation only in higher education and partly in secondary education—the Report seemed to be saying that elementary education must be entirely a State responsibility. The post-Jomtien policy measures adopted by the Indian policy makers, however, have evidently enabled the State to rapidly withdraw even from the elementary education sector. This is reflected in the ever-reducing financial commitment for this sector, as discussed earlier in the context of the 86th Amendment and elsewhere.

In this context, it may be noted that UPA Government's Common Minimum Programme (CMP) "pledges to raise public spending in education to *at least* 6 per cent of GDP with *at least half this amount* being spent *on primary and secondary sectors.*" This pledge calls for *four* comments.

(i) *One*, Public spending on education to the tune of 6 per cent of GDP was to be initially achieved by 1986. The modified 1986 policy even stated that the outlay will "*uniformly exceed* 6 per cent of the national income" during "the Eighth Five Year Plan and onwards." Since then, practically every major political party has promised to do this in its election manifestos in each General Election. The UPA is, therefore, obliged to produce a clear roadmap for *re-prioritisation of national economy* in order to make its pledge credible.

(ii) *Two*, the UPA needs to be lauded for *at least not diluting* this commitment as the BJP cleverly attempted to do this in its recent manifesto by promising to raise "the *total spending* on education to 6 per cent of GDP by 2010, with *enlarged public-private partnership*." This substitution of policy-level commitment to public spending by private resources was also a part of the NDA manifesto, clearly in deference to the neo-liberal agenda.

(iii) *Three*, the CMP has not acknowledged the urgent need to fill the *cumulative gap* that has been building up for the past three decades due to *under-investment* in education. For elementary education, this was estimated by the Tapas Majumdar Committee (1999) as being equal to Rs 13,700 crores per year for the next ten years which amounts to about 0.6 per cent of the current level of GDP (that is, merely 60 paise out of every Rs 100 of GDP). The UPA is expected to provide for this additionality, apart from reaching the level of 6 per cent of

GDP. A similar estimate of the cumulative gap in secondary and higher education sectors is yet to be made.

(iv) *Four*, India is already spending almost half of its total educational outlay on elementary education. The UPA's pledge to spend at least half the total expenditure "*on primary and secondary sectors*" has *negative implications*. This is because, in 1998–9, 78.7 per cent of the total expenditure was on elementary and secondary sectors taken together. The UPA formulation implies that the priority to be given to both of these sectors will be *reduced to merely 50 per cent* of the total expenditure! Hopefully, this is a result of the usual, but still alarming, *misconception about the category of "primary" education* as referred to in the CMP.

Epilogue

I began by identifying three challenges emerging from the life and thought of of Durgabai. The second and third challenges, I have spoken about at length by attempting to reveal how the impact of globalisation on the character of knowledge influences our education policy, particularly with respect to the attrition of India's sovereignty, violation of Fundamental Rights and Directive Principles of State Policy and finally through dilution and distortion of the national policy with regard to women's education, apart from many other critical aspects as well.

It is the first challenge that calls for a special comment. This is with reference to Durgabai's yearning for an answer as to why India's planning has "not been commensurate with the effort." The answer that I have laboured hard to offer is somewhat off the beaten track. I have tried to establish that it is the policy itself that often has been flawed.

It is, therefore, incorrect to try to find fault invariably with implementation. This misleading pursuit is primarily why the answer Durgabai was seeking four decades ago has eluded us. How can one expect the education system to be any better if flawed policies are being implemented? I would rather contend that the State is normally quite efficient (inefficiency is rather deliberate!). The education system is the disaster that it is due to reasonably *efficient implementation of flawed policies*. A critical lesson here is that we need to sharpen the tools of policy analysis and apply them for deciphering the mindset of the State as well as the global market forces. A preoccupation with implementation must not divert us from this critical task of analysis of the character of the policy itself.

I have further sought to establish that the exclusion and discrimination inherent in the present *operating* education policy, though considerably exacerbated by the impact of globalisation, has its roots in the national policies formulated well before the global market forces gained a dominant position in India. In this we have a significant lesson: as we deepen our analysis to comprehend the nature and full dimension of the adverse impact of globalisation on Indian education, we will find that we cannot exonerate our own policy makers in regard to primary responsibility for the collapse of Indian education policy since independence. Indeed, the weaknesses and internal contradictions in our policy provided the necessary political space for the intervention of the forces of globalisation in Indian education.

Indian education has hardly acknowledged that issues such as disparity, socio-economic stratification and caste hierarchies, patriarchy and gender inequity, conflicts of cultural and ethnic identity, unemployment and disempowerment, regional imbalances, development policy biased against the masses, inappropriate distribution of the economic cake, hegemonic control over natural resources, attrition of values inherited from the freedom struggle and cynical attack on democratic institutions have had a decisive impact on the structure and processes of education. The rise of communalism and the consequent attempts to impose mono-cultural hegemony during the past couple of decades has seriously begun to threaten the multi-ethnic, multi-cultural, and multi-lingual character of Indian nationhood. Policy formulation and any realistic planning of education, therefore, call for reviewing the role of education in social change and re-designing the entire education system to deal with these issues. We must also begin to take note of the rapidly emerging linkages, howsoever tenuous these might seem to be at present, between neo-liberal and communal forces. Neither the Jomtien Declaration nor the Jomtien framework provide the space for a meaningful policy discourse on such critical issues.

Finally, we must learn to recognise the attack of the market forces on education as an assault on the character of knowledge itself and also as a design to control its access, production, and distribution amongst nations and social classes. These forces have decided that it is only by regulating, controlling, and distorting knowledge that they can dictate their neo-liberal agenda on various nations and large sections of the global society. In this sense, the assault of globalisation on education needs to be viewed as an *epistemic challenge*. Only then we will know how to resist and counter it through critical pedagogy, as elaborated upon by Allman.[52] A counter-globalisation and counter-revivalist agenda of educational transformation will aim to empower people to analyse, question, and de-construct the globalised paradigm of knowledge and development and to build an alternative pro-people vision. This can be achieved only by informed and conscious social intervention through a grassroots-based people's movements built on the firm foundation of critical pedagogy.

NOTES

1. National Council of Educational Research. 2003. *Contemporary India: A Social Science Textbook for Class X* (Editor: Nalini Pant), NCERT, March 2003. p. 70.
2. Paula Allman. 2001. "Critical Education Against Global Capitalism: Karl Marx and Revolutionary Critical Education", in Henry A. Giroux, ed. Critical Studies in Education and Culture Series. Connecticut, USA: Bergin & Garvey, pp. 15–16

3. Ibid., p.17.
4. NPE-1986 was preceded by NPE-1968, the first national policy on education, which was in the form of a Cabinet Resolution adopted by parliament.
5. For instance, in 1993, in New Delhi, a follow-up *Education For All Conference* was held for nine countries (collectively referred to as the E-9 countries), namely, Bangladesh, Brazil, China, Egypt, India, Indonesia, Mexico, Nigeria and Pakistan. The group met in Cairo again in December 2003.
6. The EFA Global Monitoring Report 2003-4 focused on the education of the girl child and was issued just before the EFA Conference held at New Delhi on November 10-12, 2003. The report and the preceding one released in 2002 showed that *India was amongst those countries that were unlikely to fulfill any of the six Dakar Goals including the goal of gender parity, by the target year of 2015*. The then Union Minister of Human Resource Development Dr Murli Manohar Joshi took strong exception to this negative assessment in the UNESCO report and claimed that it was based upon outdated data (*Hindustan Times, The Indian Express* & *The Pioneer*, 8th November 2003). However, the Minister's claim was unfounded as shown by this author (Anil Sadgopal. 2003. 'Education For Too Few', *Frontline*, December 5, 2003, pp. 97–100; "Goal Posts Shifted", *Hindustan Times*, November 11, 2003).
7. UNDP, UNESCO, UNICEF, World Bank. 1990. *World Declaration on Education For All* and *Framework For Action To Meet Basic Learning Needs*, World Conference on Education for All: Meeting Basic Learning Needs, Jomtien, Thailand, March 5–9, 1990, New York.
8. Government of India. 1993. *Education for All: The Indian Scene*, Ministry of Human Resource Development (Department of Education), New Delhi, p. 88.
9. Ibid., p. 89.
10. The list and the spheres it impacted include: Government of India 1993. *Education for All: The Indian Scene*. New Delhi: Ministry of Human Resource Development: Department of Education; Government of India. 1995. *DPEP Guidelines*. New Delhi: Ministry of Human Resource Development: Department of Education; Government of India. 1998. *DPEP Moves On*. New Delhi: Ministry of Human Resource Development: Department of Education; Government of Madhya Pradesh. 1998. *The Government of Madhya Pradesh Human Development Report 1998*. Bhopal: Government of Madhya Pradesh, pp. 9-12; Ed Cil. 2000. *Para teachers in Primary Education: A Status Report*. District Primary Education Programme, Ministry of Human Resource Development, Department of Elementary Education and Literacy, New Delhi; Mukesh Ambani and Kumaramangalam Birla. 2000. A Policy Framework for Reforms in Education. New Delhi: Government of India, Prime Minister's Council on Trade and Industry; NCERT. 2000. National Curriculum Framework for School Education. New Delhi; Government of India. 2001. Handbook for Education Guarantee Scheme and Alternative and Innovative Education. Ministry of Human Resource Development, Department of Elementary Education and Literacy.
11. Anil Sadgopal. 2002. "Political Economy of Education in the Age of Globalisation", in Enakshi Ganguly Thukral, ed. *Children in Globalising India: Challenging Our Conscience*. HAQ: Centre for Child Rights, New Delhi; Anil Sadgopal. 2003. "Exclusion and Inequality in Education: The State Policy and Globalisation", *Contemporary India* (Journal of the Nehru Memorial Museum and Library), 2(3), July–September 2003, pp. 1–36; Anil Sadgopal. 2004. Globalisation and Education: Defining the Indian Crisis, XVI Zakir Husain Memorial Lecture, Zakir Husain College, University of Delhi, February 10, 2004.
12. Government of India. 2002. *Sarva Shiksha Abhiyan: Framework for Implementation*. New Delhi: Ministry of Human Resource Development, Department of Elementary Education and Literacy.

13. In the newly declared Sarva Shiksha Abhiyan in Bihar, the Education Guarantee Scheme officially 'guarantees' merely *three years of primary education* (SIEMAT, Bihar, 2000).
14. Government of India. 2002. *Sarva Shiksha Abhiyan: Framework for Implementation*, Ministry of Human Resource Development (Dept. of Elementary Education and Literacy), New Delhi; Government of India. 2003a. *Education For All: National Plan of Action, India*, Ministry of Human Resource Development (Department of Elementary Education and Literacy), New Delhi, June 2003; J.B.G. Tilak. 2003. *A Study on Financing on Education in India with a Focus on Elementary Education*, Ministerial Level Meeting of the South Asia EFA Forum, Islamabad, Pakistan, May 21–23, 2003; Anil Sadgopal. 2003. "Education For Too Few", *Frontline*, 5th December 2003, pp. 97–100; "Goal Posts Shifted", *Hindustan Times*, November 11, 2003;
15. Anil Sadgopal. 2004. Globalisation and Education: Defining the Indian Crisis, XVI Zakir Husain Memorial Lecture, Zakir Husain College, University of Delhi, February 10, 2004.
16. Ed. CIL. 2000. *Para Teachers in Primary Education: A Status Report*. District Primary Education Programme, Ministry of Human Resource Development (Dept. of Elementary Education and Literacy), New Delhi; Government of India. 2001a. *Handbook for Education Guarantee Scheme and Alternative & Innovative Education*, Ministry of Human Resource Development (Dept. of Elementary Education and Literacy), New Delhi.
17. National Council of Educational Research. 2000. *National Curriculum Framework For School Education,* New Delhi, November 2000; Government of India. 2001. *Working Group Report on Elementary and Adult Education: Tenth Five Year Plan 2002-2007*, Ministry of Human Resource Development (Dept. of Elementary Education and Literacy), New Delhi, September 2001; Anil Sadgopal. 2003. 'Education For Too Few', *Frontline*, 5th December 2003, pp. 97–100; 'Goal Posts Shifted', *Hindustan Times*, November 11, 2003.
18. Mukesh Ambani and Kumaramangalam Birla, 2000. *A Policy Framework for Reforms in Education* . New Delhi: Prime Minister's Council on Trade and Industry, Government of India.
19. Ibid.
20. Paulo Freire. 1972. *Pedagogy of the Oppressed*, Harmondsworth, UK: Penguin. Freire's notion of praxis is itself grounded in Marx's theory of consciousness or the theory of the formation of ideas.
21. National Council of Educational Research. 2000. *National Curriculum Framework For School Education,* New Delhi: NCERT.
22. For a detailed analysis, see Anil Sadgopal. 2003. "Education For Too Few", *Frontline*, December 5, 2003, pp. 97-100; "Goal Posts Shifted", *Hindustan Times*, November 11, 2003; Anil Sadgopal. 2004. Globalisation and Education: Defining the Indian Crisis, XVI Zakir Husain Memorial Lecture, Zakir Husain College, University of Delhi, February 10, 2004.
23. Government of India. 1986. *National Policy on Education* and *Programme of Action*. Ministry of Human Resource Development (Dept. of Education), New Delhi; Government of India. 1992. *National Policy on Education-1986 (As modified in 1992)* and *Programme of Action*, Ministry of Human Resource Development (Dept. of Education), New Delhi; Anil Sadgopal. 2000. *Shiksha Mein Badlav Ka Sawal*, Granth Shilpi, Delhi, pp. 175-189; Anil Sadgopal. 2004. Globalisation and Education: Defining the Indian Crisis, XVI Zakir Husain Memorial Lecture, Zakir Husain College, University of Delhi, February 10, 2004.
24. For a detailed commentary, see Rohit Dhankar. 2002. *Seeking Quality Education: In the Arena of Fun and Rhetoric*, in Seeking Quality Education for All: Experiences from the District Primary Education Programme, Occasional Papers, The European Commission, June 2002.

25. Government of India. 1998. *DPEP moves on ...*, Department of Education, Ministry of Human Resource Development, Government of India; Government of India. 1995. *DPEP Guidelines*, Ministry of Human Resource Development (Dept. of Education), New Delhi. Government of India. 2001. *Working Group Report on Elementary and Adult Education: Tenth Five Year Plan 2002–2007*, Ministry of Human Resource Development (Dept. of Elementary Education and Literacy), New Delhi, September 2001.
26. Government of India. 1993. *Education for All: The Indian Scene*, Ministry of Human Resource Development (Dept. of Education), New Delhi, p. 88; Government of India. 1995. *DPEP Guidelines*, Ministry of Human Resource Development (Dept. of Education), New Delhi. Government of India; Government of India. 1998. *DPEP moves on ...*, Department of Education, Ministry of Human Resource Development, Government of India; Government of India. 2001. *Working Group Report on Elementary and Adult Education: Tenth Five Year Plan 2002–2007*, Ministry of Human Resource Development (Dept. of Elementary Education and Literacy), New Delhi, September 2001; Government of India. 2003. "Education for All: National Plan for Action, India". Ministry of Human Resource Development, Department of Elementary Education and Literacy, New Delhi; UNESCO. 2002. "Education for All: Is the World on Track?" Paris: EFA Global Monitoring Report; UNESCO. 2003. *EFA Global Monitoring Report 2003/4: Gender and Education For All—The Leap to Equality*, UNESCO, Paris; Jomtien Declaration 1990; World Education Forum 2000, *The Dakar Framework of Action*, Dakar, Senegal.
27. World Bank. 1997. *Primary Education in India*. Mumbai: Allied Publishers Limited, pp.1, 39.
28. Government of India. 2002. *Sarva Shiksha Abhiyan: Framework for Implementation*, Ministry of Human Resource Development (Dept. of Elementary Education and Literacy), New Delhi; Government of India. 2003a. *Education For All: National Plan of Action, India*, Ministry of Human Resource Development (Department of Elementary Education and Literacy), New Delhi, June 2003.
29. Government of India. 2001. "The Constitution (Eighty-Sixth Amendment) Bill", 2001, Bill No. 106 of 2001 (as introduced in Lok Sabha on 26th November 2001).
30. Government of India. 2004. "The Free and Compulsory Education Bill, 2004". Draft bill dated January 8, 2004 (Draft III) [as circulated by the Secretary, Department of Elementary Education and Literacy, Ministry of Human Resource Development, at a meeting of State/UT Secretaries of the respective Departments of Education, New Delhi. Section 16(5)(iii)
31. J.B.G. Tilak. 2003. *A Study on Financing on Education in India with a Focus on Elementary Education*, Ministerial Level Meeting of the South Asia EFA Forum, Islamabad, Pakistan, May 21–3, 2003; Anil Sadgopal. 2003. 'Education For Too Few', *Frontline*, 5th December 2003, pp. 97-100; 'Goal Posts Shifted', *Hindustan Times*, November 11, 2003; Anil Sadgopal. 2004. Globalisation and Education: Defining the Indian Crisis, XVI Zakir Husain Memorial Lecture, Zakir Husain College, University of Delhi, February 10, 2004.
32. Anil Sadgopal. 2001. "Between the Lines: Writes and Wrongs in Education Bill". *The Times of India*, November 28, 2001; Anil Sadgopal. 2001. "Political Economy of the Ninety-Third Amendment Bill". *Mainstream*, December 22, 2001 (Annual Number), pp. 43–50; Anil Sadgopal. 2002. "A Convenient Consensus". *Frontline*, January 4, 2002, pp. 107–108.
33. A harmonious construction of Part IV with Part III of the Constitution was the basis of the historic Unnikrishnan Judgment, giving education of children "until they complete the age of fourteen years" the status of Fundamental Right (Supreme Court 1993). In this judgment, Article 45 of Part IV was read in conjunction with Article 21 of Part III.
34. Anil Sadgopal. 2001. "Between the Lines: Writes and Wrongs in Education Bill". *The Times of India*, November 28, 2001; Anil Sadgopal. 2001. 'Political Economy of the Ninety-

Third Amendment Bill'. *Mainstream*, 22nd December 2001 (Annual Number), pp. 43–50.

35. Anil Sadgopal. 2001. "Between the Lines: Writes and Wrongs in Education Bill". *The Times of India*, November 28, 2001; Anil Sadgopal. 2001. "Political Economy of the Ninety-Third Amendment Bill". *Mainstream*, 22nd December 2001 (Annual Number), pp. 43-50; Anil Sadgopal. 2002. 'A Convenient Consensus'. *Frontline*, January 4, 2002, pp. 107–108.
36. Government of India. 2004. "The Free and Compulsory Education Bill, 2004". Draft bill dated January 08, 2004 (Draft III) [as circulated by the Secretary, Department of Elementary Education and Literacy, Ministry of Human Resource Development, at a meeting of State / UT Secretaries of the respective Departments of Education, New Delhi. Section 16(5)(iii)
37. Madan Mohan Jha. 2003. *A Note for NIEPA Meeting on Free and Compulsory Education Bill, 2003* (Draft II), December 15, 2003 (Unpublished).
38. Ibid.
39. Mukesh Ambani and Kumaramangalam Birla, 2000. *A Policy Framework for Reforms in Education* . New Delhi: Prime Minister's Council on Trade and Industry, Government of India.
40. Krishna Kumar. 2003. "Judicial Ambivalence and New Politics of Education", *Economic and Political Weekly*, December 6–12, 2003, pp. 5163–5166.
41. P. 10.
42. International Bureau of Education (UNESCO) and Central Board of Secondary Education (India). 2000. *Globalisation and Living Together, The Challenges for Educational Content in Asia*, UNESCO, Paris and CBSE, New Delhi, p. 10.
43. Ibid., p.5.
44. Anil Sadgopal. 2000. *Shiksha* Mein *Badlav Ka Sawal*, Granth Shilpi, Delhi, pp. 124–135.
45. National Council of Educational Research. 2001. *Guidelines and Syllabi for Primary, Upper Primary, Secondary and Higher Secondary Stages*, NCERT, New Delhi, November 2001; National Council of Educational Research. 2003. *Contemporary India: A Social Science Textbook for Class X* (Editor: Nalini Pant), NCERT, March 2003, p. 70
46. Anil Sadgopal. 2000. *Shiksha* Mein *Badlav Ka Sawal*, Granth Shilpi, Delhi, pp. 124–135.
47. National Council for Educational Research and Training. 2000. *National Curriculum Framework for School Education*. New Delhi: NCERT, p. 95
48. National Council of Educational Research. 2001. *Guidelines and Syllabi for Primary, Upper Primary, Secondary and Higher Secondary Stages*, NCERT, New Delhi, November 2001.
49. Government of India. 1993. *Education for All: the Indian Scene*. New Delhi: Department of Education, Ministry of Human Resource Development, Government of India.
50. Ibid.
51. Ibid. p. 89.
52. Paula Allman. *op cit.*

15

Social Development and Social Research*

Leela Dube

It is in a spirit of humility that I seek to pay homage to one who rose above her times to become nothing less than a visionary. Perhaps no other woman in India evinced the capacity and the courage to take crucial decisions about her life at the early age of 12, and then had the conviction and the determination to take upon herself responsibilities that would have frightened even an adult. Both her protests and her constructive activities—in the form of a series of institutions and programmes—demonstrate Durgabai's keen sense of social justice, her vision, her deep sympathy with the disadvantaged, and her faith in purposive action.

The theme I address myself to was inspired by two factors. The first is Durgabai's use of the term "social development" while setting up an institution to acquire the necessary understanding of social reality so that conditions might be improved through well thought-out schemes. The second is my conviction that the social sciences should have both human meaning and social purpose. My major concern here is to bring out the relevance of social research to effective social development.

Social Development

In 1962, with Durgabai at the India International Centre, the need was felt for the integration of social with economic development. This resulted in the formation of a collective of social workers, social scientists, administrators, and planners. It was this study group that grew into the Council for Social Development. In the 1950s and a little after, there were strong misgivings and skepticism about participation in research activities connected with planned change and with the evaluation of the community development programme. Such problem-oriented and time-bound research operations would, it was feared, encourage the rise of indifferent, ill-trained, and self-oriented researchers

* Edited transcript of the July 15, 2000, Durgabai Deshmukh Memorial Lecture by Professor Leela Dube.

and might eventually bring down the quality of the discipline. It was argued that sound sociological research, objectivity, value neutrality, and the development of theory, all would suffer a setback. It is creditable that the Council for Social Development was established when this derisive attitude was in the air.

Social development, which was once used to refer to social evolution with a universal sequence of stages for all mankind, has now acquired a different meaning. More comprehensive than economic development, social development aims at wider objectives and ideals. When critically assessed, economic development, though essential, was seen to be characterised by squalor and poverty amidst gross inequalities, consumerism and wealth. It has therefore to be geared to specific social objectives. Instead of GNP we should think in terms of GNW—Gross National Welfare. At the very least, social development demands an emphasis on larger collectivities and defines social goals in terms of the satisfaction of human needs and of improvement in the quality of human life. It asks for a growth that can be sustained, it questions existing social foundations with a view to restructuring them, it re-examines the objectives of planning, and it ponders over the eradication of social, cultural, and economic inequality. It also looks at possibilities of alternative development in various spheres.

Areas for the assessment of inequality and for needed planning include food, housing, education, health, public order, and the growth of population. An important phenomenon that needs correction is the skewed distribution of power. This is a brief outline of current thinking about social development. It is not exhaustive and it skirts many controversial issues. I would, however, like to emphasise that the subjects for study and evaluation should largely grow from what is happening around. To name a few: exploitation, environmental degradation, communal disharmony, child labour, conflict within the family, the situation of the aged, violence, problems surrounding the question of reservations, gender issues, land alienation, caste conflict. Also salient is the cynical lack of human concern in the mighty hydel and irrigation projects, which wholly ignore the interests of tribes and of other marginal groups. These peoples are uprooted physically, economically, and culturally. This uprooting is real, while resettlement remains a false promise. These are not disparate problems to be looked at in isolation: most are intertwined. For instance, women and children cannot be ignored either as actors or as victims. Quite a few problems are in fact essentially gender problems, although they might need to be understood in wider socio-cultural and historical contexts.

Social development implies a practical commitment to change in the right direction. Which direction is the right one? What are the conditions and limits of possibility? Besides planning, implementation, evaluation, and the search for alternatives, one important aspect of social development is resistance. All these ask for a proper understanding of social reality and from this arises our concern with social research.

Social Research

Let me make a brief digression. The complex, multi faceted field of social development necessarily contains interdisciplinary and cross-disciplinary ventures. But this must not result in the dilution of any one discipline's skills and knowledge. Grounded in one's own discipline, one may learn to make use of other disciplines—borrowing their methods, concepts, and skills, or incorporating the results of work done in them. The human mind has limits, but it also expands under inspiration. We may even say that today we are in an age of multidimensional studies.

In conducting research on social development, issues of what policy relevance our work will have, or our commitment to a path, will not necessarily lead to sacrifice of objectivity in the actual conducting of research. Certainly, committed research does not mean partisan data-gathering or the ignoring of facts that go against our ideas and ideals. This also applies, I should add, to concepts and theoretical models. However, it is important to realise that many seemingly value neutral positions are dangerously value-loaded. It has come to be recognised that the race, nationality, gender, age, training, and personal history of the researcher affect both the collection of material and its interpretation. It becomes necessary, therefore, that our biases be *known* biases. Earlier, personal accounts of fieldwork, when they were given, remained separate from major scholarly writings. Self-awareness and the problem of political responsibility were not prominent. The trend now is to give autobiographical accounts of the contexts of fieldwork or research work and of the researcher's relationship with the people encountered. Perhaps women scholars have shown greater willingness to open up and relate the links between their personal life situations and self-images at particular points of time with the ways they went about their research work, what they observed and absorbed, and how they understood and interpreted the data. Interestingly, some have compared their earlier with their later work among the same peoples in the context of their own changed life situations, altered concerns and intellectual development, and have shown how the same societies looked different to them in many ways.

It cannot be denied that as in actual research, so in writing, there are a series of choices which depend on the selective interest of the researcher, personal biases, and often the stranglehold of one or other school of theory. As a result, monographs presented and read as timeless are in fact selective and historically contingent. Very few scholars have the ethical courage to admit this when it comes to their own work.

During the eighties trend of reflexivity, many a renowned scholar's work was critiqued threadbare, and a skeptical attitude developed towards empirical fieldwork and towards research itself. Since then, fortunately, much soul-searching has taken place, compulsions in academic pursuits have been deciphered, and faith has been reinstated in well- intentioned and consciously planned research and in cautious fieldwork, with an awareness of possible pitfalls. I have brought up this matter here to emphasise that reflexivity and the contextual evaluation of our own research activity and the resultant data have the potential to contribute a great deal to good quality research. At the same time, I do not insist on *open* autobiographical accounts as a necessary condition; every individual has the right to privacy, and researchers can always undertake in their own minds the exercise of self-reflexive activity and of questioning their own procedures, data, and interpretations. Such self-evaluation would bring clarity to the possible need for the retracing of steps, for the making of additions and subtractions and for the devising of new strategies. In the final analysis, all research is interpretation and construction of knowledge, which makes great caution essential.

With the subjects of our research acquiring the skills of reading and writing, and with the extension of the scope of research to literate, even highly educated, populations, the problem of *they read what we write* has become serious. Some western anthropologists have been attacked for faulty substantive data and wrong interpretation by the people of the cultures they studied. This has happened in Africa, Hawaii, and the Mediterranean region. It has also happened in India, though on a modest scale. Ingenious ways of research include interacting, where possible, with the people themselves and discussing with them the findings and interpretations so as to verify the accuracy of translations of culture.

Many programmes of social development have to make use of the survey method, with large-scale samples and mainly with structured instruments. Great caution is required here. There is a tendency to by-pass many steps essential for evolving efficient instruments of data collection which are comprehensible to the people, and which have, logically, consistency and relevance. The stages of observation, informal interviewing, case studies, and use of archival sources must not be ignored. In fact, these have to be used at several stages of research and writing. Nor can we ignore native categories of thought, people's voices, and people's perceptions. Often a combination of micro and macro research gives good results. I say this because it should be our mission to prove that problem—focused sociology need not be second-rate sociology. (I am not by any means implying that research not geared to development issues is by definition research of good quality; but let us not go into that here).

My disciplinary bias does not make me deny the value of demographic surveys, the National Sample Survey and other large-scale surveys. After all, I too use their results. But I believe that depth can be achieved by working in smaller units and by combining quantitative material with qualitative. In large surveys conducted through questionnaires or interview schedules, the issue of where the researcher meets the respondents becomes crucial. Perhaps confining oneself to the workplace and completely neglecting the surroundings—including the households in which the respondents live—may result in partial, even faulty understanding of the issues taken up for study. Much strategising and special efforts are needed in solving such problems. Researchers cannot intrude beyond a point into the private lives of the people they are studying. At the same time, ensuring anonymity and generating confidence can often open people up.

Language is crucial to communicative research, and our people's linguistic skills are limited. Hence there is a special relevance to emphasise the value of involving indigenous researchers and local persons in studies of social and cultural reality. In any culture, subtle aspects of life and contextuality of meaning are difficult to grasp, and so are categories of thought and nuances of behaviour along with their underlying logic. Effective communication in their own language can make people talk openly. Interviews conducted and life histories taken in the local language can be most effective in acquiring reliable material. In this connection I might mention Vina Mazumdar's recent experience of an Action Research Project conducted in Bankura in West Bengal by the Centre for Women's Development Studies. When the plan was made for collecting life histories of women, it was decided to involve a few students of anthropology from Vidyasagar University, which is in the region. These students, of both sexes, easily established communication with women and succeeded in getting excellent life history material through broadly designed but free-flowing interviews. Life histories made the women think about their lives and about those of others, while for the investigators, the whole process was a revelation.

An experiment carried out in Maharashtra in the early nineteen eighties by V.M. Dandekar's colleagues is also worth mentioning. Vidyut Bhagwat was the person in charge. Advertisements were placed in Marathi newspapers asking women for anonymous essays on themes such as "Had I been a woman..."; "The relationship between mother-in- law and daughter-in-law"; "My treatment of sons and of daughters"; and "The balancing of gainful work outside the home with housework". Hundreds of essays were received, written by women of all educational levels, and were analysed. Selected essays were published in a volume. From the letters that the organisers received, it became clear that this was the first time that the writers had seriously thought about the issues that were raised.

Pursuing the issue of language, I am always bothered that large projects involving dams, water management, the environment, tribal peoples, and so on, are mostly conceived and planned in English. Points for investigation and research questions are then translated for use by investigators. The data collected are then translated back into English for analysis and for the final writing-up. Are there people competent to ensure that all this translating is done faithfully? And do the lower-level people who do the translating and the data collection have a voice in conceiving and working out the project, in the forming of conclusions and the taking of decisions? (There is of course also the question of who gets, or takes, the credit for all the work done).

Attending to our own languages—Hindi, Bangla, Marathi, Tamil—is a task that must be taken up. We hierarchise everything: "high" work and "low" work, writing in English, writing in an Indian language. We do not realise that good translation too can be a creative job. Also, should some of us not think of looking at our store of indigenous knowledge from the point of view of social science, traditions and culture? There are many insights in our centuries-old literatures.

In social development research, the literatures in our several languages can be effectively used in order to get ideas for formulating research plans and for obtaining ethnographic information and even cultural insights. Literature can often very usefully depict the life ways and thought ways of people to be studied. It can help in explaining and interpreting the data collected. I recall here S.C. Dube's statement that the kind of sociological understanding about a small town and its social and political life that is contained in, for example, Shrilal Shukla's *Rag Darbari,* cannot easily (or ever) be matched by sociologists' accounts. Development projects should certainly use the depiction in literature of issues relating to women, old age, dalits, familial conflicts, prostitution, children, and a myriad other aspects of social life. Needless to say, while in some ways, literature can match life history material and reveal subtle aspects of social life, his does not mean that literature can be a substitute for methods and techniques developed in the social sciences. Also, in the use of literature, contextualisation and historicisation are essential. As Romila Thapar says in her lecture "Shakuntala: Histories of a Narrative", a narrative can have its own biography, and the changes it manifests can provide us with a view of historical change and historical context.

Dalit literature has described and challenged the oppression and discrimination inflicted by the upper castes. It is well known how Black American literature has exposed the ethnocentrism of the Whites. Black American feminists have taken White feminists to task for holding erroneous views about the former's family life, gender relations, and sexual ways, and have derided the idea that "sisterhood" can come into being in the face of so many racial prejudices. There are several more examples. My point is that both history and sociology/anthropology on the world stage have begun to make more use of literature, folklore, myths, narratives and oral tradition.

To illustrate the use of a variety of sources in exploring the nature of a social phenomenon, let us look briefly at a study of child labour. In India as elsewhere, a series of studies carried out have condemned child labour and have suggested ways to ameliorate this "evil". Poverty is considered the main culprit. In my study, I did look at bonded labour, at child work in small industry and agriculture and in tribal settings, and at domestic labour by children. But I tried also to review the place of children in our society and to look into culturally defined notions of obligations towards them and expectations from them. I found that children were an integral part of the household economy—

thus, work time and school time need to be readjusted, as was done in an experiment by Chitra Naik. I have also looked at the child and at work as these are depicted in Hindu tradition and sacred literature, and have examined cultural notions regarding the stages of human life, placing childhood and the child in a definite perspective. Together these suggest a way of understanding the roots of people's attitudes and views. Children lived at the guru's *ashrama,* were taught there, and worked there. Descriptions of the grazing of cattle clearly indicate that play and work were not antithetical. What was learnt in childhood was retained—even what was learnt in the mother's womb, as the story of Abhimanyu demonstrates. Special value was attached to the training of the muscles, the vocal cords, the movement of fingers. Thus, children were launched at a fairly young age into training for dance, music, weaving, pottery, and many other such skills. This is what happens even today. My argument is that a study of the cultural and historical heritage goes at least some way in helping us to understand child work. It is of course necessary to assess the capabilities of children at different ages so that appropriate work can be added to education and play in such a way as to avoid exploitation.

Resistance as Social Development

Let me end with resistance, which I have said is an integral part of social development. Perhaps, I should not end a talk with resistance, but I have a streak of non-conformism in me. Whether it is a study of forms of everyday resistance or one of an actual resistance movement, an understanding of ground realities, of people's beliefs and of their ways of life, is essential. The logic of people's behaviour cannot be understood through one's own perceptions. For example, the efforts of those who seek to launch an agitation can go off at a tangent—or can have unexpected or even opposite results—because issues are approached in the wrong way. The commotions over sati, over child marriage and over the Shah Bano case, all needed sound bases of understanding for the devising of effective strategies. Anyone who seeks to *study* these commotions similarly needs an understanding of the lives, thinking and feelings of the people involved.

I have emphasised resistance because I believe that new constructions have always to face some destruction and must accept resistance and appreciate subversion. These things, often termed "negative", definitely are part of social development.

Contributors

Anil Sadgopal, a PhD in biochemistry and molecular biology from the California Institute of Technology (1968), resigned from the Tata Institute of Fundamental Research, Mumbai, to organise a rural development and education programme through *Kishor Bharati* in Hoshangabad district, Madhya Pradesh (1972–92). In 1972, collaborating with the Friends Rural Centre, Rasulia, he initiated the Hoshangabad Science Teaching Programme (HSTP), which initiated teaching science to school children through an inquiry-oriented, experiment-based, and environment-related approach. In 1982, he helped found *Eklavya*, which subsequently extended HSTP to almost 1000 schools in 15 districts of Madhya Pradesh.

Dr Sadgopal joined the People's Science Movement and the Movement for Civil Liberties and Democratic Rights in the early eighties. As an activist, he was also engaged in the struggle of the Bhopal gas tragedy victims to get medical treatment and rehabilitation from the government and from Union Carbide.

Since 1994, Dr Sadgopal has been a professor of education in the University of Delhi. From 1998–2001, he served as the Head, Department of Education and Dean, Faculty of Education. In 2001, he undertook to study education policy as a Senior Fellow of the Nehru Memorial Museum and Library.

Aruna Roy is a social and political activist. She was born in Chennai in 1946, and joined the IAS in 1968. She resigned from the IAS in 1975 to devote her time to social work and social reform.

In 1990, along with Shanker Singh, Nikhil Dey, and many others, she helped form the Mazdoor Kisan Shakti Sangathan, a grassroots people's organisation that engages with the concerns of peasants and workers, and also with wider issues of participatory democracy and democratic struggle.

In 2000, she was awarded the Ramon Magsaysay Award for Community Leadership. In 2010, she received the Lal Bahadur Shastri National Award for Excellence in Public Administration, Academia and Management. She was a member of the Central government's National Advisory Council from 2004–6, where she played a key role in incorporating strong citizens entitlements in the recently enacted Right To Information and National Rural Employment Guarantee Acts. She is a member of the National Employment Guarantee Council and has been a member of the National Campaign for People's Right to Information.

Gail Omvedt is a PhD in sociology from the University of California, Berkeley. She is, at present, a professor, Dr B.R. Ambedkar Chair of Social Change and Development, in Indira Gandhi National Open University, New Delhi, India.

Professor Omvedt was born in Minneapolis, USA, and has been an Indian citizen since 1983. She has actively participated in social movements in India, including *Dalit* and anti-caste, environmental, and farmers movements. She has worked especially with rural women, actively engaging with the *Stri Mukti Sangharsh Chalval*, which works on issues of abandoned women in Sangli and Satara districts of northern Maharashtra, and the *Shetkari Mahila Aghadi*, which works on issues of woman's land rights and political power.

She has been a consultant to various UN agencies and NGOs, and has served as Dr Ambedkar Chair Professor at NISWASS, Orissa. She has also held many academic positions in various academic institutions across the country.

Professor Omvedt's numerous books include *Seeking Begumpura: The Social Vision of Anti-Caste Intellectuals*; *Ambedkar: Towards an Enlightened India*; and *Dalits and the Democratic Revolution*.

Leela Dubey, an anthropologist, has studied Gond tribals in Madhya Pradesh, and carried out anthropological studies in Uttar Pradesh, Maharashtra, Kerala, and the coral islands of the Lakshadweep in the Arabian Sea.

She has been a Senior Fellow of the Nehru Memorial Museum and Library, Shree Krishnaraj Wodeyar Professor of Anthropology, University of Mysore; National Fellow, Indian Council for Social Science Research; Distinguished Fellow, Centre for Women's Development Studies; and Head of the Department of Anthropology and Sociology, University of Saugar. She has served on many professional bodies, including International Women's Anthropology Conference (as Vice President) and Indian Association for Women's Studies (as Vice President). She has authored books and contributed several papers in reputed journals.

Leila Seth, the first woman Chief Justice of a High Court in India (the Himachal Pradesh High Court), was also the first woman to top the Bar examinations in London.

She became an IAS officer in 1958, and became the Chief Justice of Himachal Pradesh in 1991. She was the Chair of the Commonwealth Human Rights Institute for several years. Her autobiography, *On Balance*, was published by Penguin India in 2003.

MAHASWETA DEVI is an activist and a novelist. Born in 1926 in Dacca (now in Bangladesh), Mahasweta Devi was educated in Santiniketan where Rabindranath Tagore had established a school which later formed part of the Viswa Bharati University. Subsequently, she graduated from the University of Calcutta. Her family shifted to India during Partition, and she later earned a Masters in English from the Viswa Bharati University. In 1964, she began teaching at Calcutta University's Bijoygarh College, which was then an institution for working class women students. In those days, she also worked as a journalist and creative writer.

In her Bengali fiction, she depicts the brutal oppression of tribal people and the untouchables by powerful, authoritarian upper caste landlords, money lenders, and venal government officials. She is known for her studies of women, *Dalits*, and the rural communities of West Bengal. In her role as an activist, she is dedicated to the cause of the tribal people in Bihar, Madhya Pradesh, and Chhattisgarh.

In 2006, Maheswata Devi was appointed a National Professor for five years by the Government of India. In 2011, her term as National Professor was extended by another five years.

N. H. ANTIA (1922–2007), MBBS, FRCS (the UK), FACS (honorary, the USA), was Director and Trustee of the Foundation for Medical Research and Foundation for Research in Community Health, and served on several committees and panels, including those of the Indian Council of Medical Research (ICMR), Indian Council of Social Science Research (ICSSR), Ministry of Health and Family Planning, the Planning Commission and the Planning Board of Kerala. His major areas of interest were: plastic and reconstructive surgery, biomedical research, and community health, Panchayati Raj and rural development. He was the Member-Secretary of the path-breaking ICSSR–ICMR report, *Health for All: An Alternative Strategy*.

He was the recipient of numerous awards and honours including the Hunterian Professorship of the Royal College of Surgeons of England in 1962; Honorary Fellow of the American College of Surgeons in 1979; the Padma Shri in 1990 and the G.D. Birla International Award for Humanism in 1994.

He had over 300 publications on various subjects and had delivered several national and international lectures and orations based on his pioneering work in the field of leprosy, burns, plastic surgery, biomedical research, and community health.

PUSHPA M. BHARGAVA is a scientist, writer, thinker, institution builder, and administrator. The founder of the Centre for Cellular and Molecular Biology (CCMB), Hyderabad, he is widely regarded as the architect of modern biology and biotechnology in India. He studied at the Varanasi and Lucknow universities, and obtained his PhD at the age of 21. He has worked in the USA, the UK, France, and Germany, and has travelled in over 50 countries.

Professor Bhargava is one of the most highly cited Indian scientists, and has over 125 major scientific publications to his credit. He is the author of four books, including a 500-page monograph on *Proteins of Seminal Plasma* (John Wiley, New York). He has served as President of major institutions in the country including the Society of Biological Chemists of India and the Indian Academy of Social Sciences.

He is the recipient of over 70 major national and international honours and awards, including the Padma Bhushan (1986); the Gandhi Prize, Navdanya, New Delhi; the Wattumal Memorial Prize for Biochemistry; Fellowship of the World Academy of Art and Science; the Legion d'Honneur (from the President of France); Visiting Professorship, College de France; and Life Fellowship, Clare Hall, Cambridge.

RAJIV BALAKRISHNAN holds a PhD in Population Studies and a Masters in Sociology from the Jawaharlal Nehru University, New Delhi; and a Bachelors degree in Economics from the University of Madras. In his professional career, he was on the faculties of prestigious research institutes in India. He served on the faculty of the Council for Social Development (CSD), New Delhi, for fifteen years, during which time he engaged in teaching and research, organised two seminars, and, for a period of three years, stewarded the Council's journal, Social Change, as its Joint Editor. After he left the CSD, he was re-engaged as a Senior Consultant on an assignment to bring out this book. He is the principal author of four previous edited tomes (Details on his website: https://sites.google.com/site/rajivb3504). Currently, he is a Senior Consultant to the Schumacher Centre in New Delhi.

RAM DAYAL MUNDA (1939–2011), an anthropological linguist by training, was educated at the universities of Ranchi and Chicago, and taught at the University of Minnesota and the Australian National University at Canberra, before joining Ranchi University in 1981 as the founder-head of the Department of Tribal and Regional Languages.

As an intellectual-activist, Dr Munda was an ideologue of the Jharkhand movement for autonomy, which, in 2000, culminated in the formation of the new State of Jharkhand.

In 1983, he was the Visiting Professor at the Australian National University. He was the Vice Chancellor of Ranchi University (1985–88). In 2001, he was Visiting Professor, Tokyo University, Japan. He was President of the Jharkhand Sanskriti Morcha and the Jharkhand Buddhijivi Morcha. He had been on the National Committee for Promotion of Social and Economic Welfare and the Expert Committee, Sahitya Akademi. Dr Munda had been a regular participant at the meetings of the UN Working Group on Indigenous Peoples and the UN Permanent Forum on Indigenous Issue at Geneva and New York respectively. In 2010, he was awarded the Padma Shri for this contributions to the field of art.

RANDHIR SINGH is a leading Indian political philosopher who has made a significant contribution to the understanding of theory and practice of socialism in the modern world.

After studying in Foreman Christian College, Lahore, he moved to Delhi where he taught first in the Camp College and then at Delhi College (later renamed Zakir Husain College). Subsequently, he joined the Department of Political Science at the University of Delhi in 1973. He had a legendary reputation as a teacher of political theory, and he retired in 1987.

As a concerned scholar and social activist, he has stood for democratic rights of struggling people throughout his life, courageously defending the cause of oppressed groups.

Some of his well-known works such as *Reason, Revolution and Political Theory*, *Of Marxism and Indian Politics* and *Five Lectures in Marxist Mode* have gone into many editions.

SHANTA SINHA, a child-rights activist, is a Professor in the Department of Political Science in Hyderabad Central University. She was appointed the Chairperson of the National Commission for the Protection of Child Rights in 2007 and was reappointed for a second term in 2010.

She is the founder of Mamidipudi Venkatarangaiya Foundation, popularly known as M.V. Foundation, which partners with government teachers, women's groups, youth associations, local bodies and non-governmental organisations. Named in memory of her grandfather Mamidipudi Venkatarangaiah, the foundation has been involved in programmes for elimination of child labour through universalisation of elementary education in Andhra Pradesh. Shanta Sinha and the M.V. Foundation volunteers and activists have been working to bring to the poor children in Rangareddy district unconditional access to mainstream education, with a special focus on the girl child and children working as bonded labourers.

Ms Sinha won the Magsaysay Award in 2003. She was awarded the Padma Shri in 1999, and in the same year, received the Albert Shanker International Award.

Suma Chitnis is an eminent sociologist. She served as a professor and Head, Unit for Research in the Sociology of Education, Tata Institute of Social Sciences, Mumbai; as Vice Chancellor of SNDT University, Mumbai; and as executive director of the Tata Endowment for the Education of Indians. In December 2010, the Indian Sociological Society conferred the Lifetime Achievement Award on her, for her contribution to the discipline and profession.

Swami Agnivesh, a leading proponent of the Arya Samaj, has relentlessly waged struggles on behalf of India's poor, weak, and defenseless. His campaigns have led him to fight alcoholism, female foeticide, bonded labour and child labour, and lead the struggle for the emancipation of women. His current mission includes fighting the consumer culture and the Western model of development in India, opposing Western cultural imperialism, and battling casteism, obscurantism, and communalism.

He was a member of the Haryana Legislative Assembly (1977–82) and was appointed the Minister of Education in Haryana in 1979. He has also actively participated in international peace movements and has been a part of international bodies such as the International Niwano Peace Prize Committee, Tokyo (Vice President; 2003–05) and International Peace Council (member; 2003–present).

He is the recipient of the Anti-Slavery International Award (London, 1990); the Freedom and Human Rights Award (Bern, Switzerland, 1994); the Rajiv Gandhi National Sadbhavana Award (New Delhi, 2004); and the Right to Livelihood Award (Sweden, 2004).

Vandana Shiva obtained a PhD in Physics from the University of Western Ontario, Canada, and later shifted to inter-disciplinary research in science, technology and environmental policy at the Indian Institute of Science and the Indian Institute of Management, Bangalore.

In 1982, she set up the Research Foundation for Science, Technology, and Natural Resource Policy in Dehradun, her hometown. In 1991, she founded *Navdanya*, a national movement to protect the diversity and integrity of living resources, especially native seed; the promotion of organic farming; and fair trade.

She is the recipient of the Right Livelihood Award (1993); the Sydney Peace Prize (2010); the Order of the Golden Ark; Global 500 Award of the United Nations; Earth Day International Award; and the Lennon Ono Grant for Peace.

Vina Mazumdar is a national research professor at the Centre for Women's Development Studies (CWDS), New Delhi. She was founder-director of the CWDS from 1980 to 1991. Subsequently, she served the CWDS as a Senior Fellow, and as then as the Chairperson. She was secretary of the first Committee on the Status of Women in India, which brought out the first ever report on condition of women in the country, *Towards Equality*, in 1974.

In addition to the CWDS, Professor Mazumdar also founded the Indian Association of Women's Studies. She was Director, Programme of Women's Studies, at the Indian Council for Social Science Research (1975–80). She also serves as Member-Secretary of the Standing Committee on Women's Studies of the Government of India.

Her memoirs, *Memories of a Rolling Stone*, were published in 2010.